Bloom's Modern Critical Interpretations

J.R.R. Tolkien's
The Lord of the Rings
New Edition

Edited and with an introduction by
Harold Bloom
Sterling Professor of the Humanities
Yale University

BLOOM'S
LITERARY CRITICISM
An imprint of Infobase Publishing

Bloom's Modern Critical Interpretations: The Lord of the Rings—New Edition

Copyright © 2008 Infobase Publishing

Introduction © 2008 by Harold Bloom

Bloom's Literary Criticism
An imprint of Infobase Publishing
132 West 31st Street
New York NY 10001

Library of Congress Cataloging-in-Publication Data
J.R.R. Tolkien's The lord of the rings / edited and with an introduction by Harold Bloom. — New ed.
    p. cm. — (Bloom's modern critical interpretations)
  Includes bibliographical references and index.
  ISBN 978-1-60413-145-1 (hardcover : acid-free paper) 1. Tolkien, J. R. R. (John Ronald Reuel), 1892–1973. Lord of the rings. 2. Fantasy fiction, English—History and criticism. I. Bloom, Harold. II. Title: Lord of the rings. III. Series.

  PR6039.O32L63457 2008
  823'.912—dc22

                              2008007062

Contributing Editor: Pamela Loos
Cover designed by Takeshi Takahashi
Printed in the United States of America
Bang EJB 10 9 8 7 6 5 4 3 2 1

800
TOLKIEN
368-6113

Contents

Editor's Note

My introduction, much at variance with most of the essayists who follow, sadly asks whether Tolkien's trilogy is not a large period piece? Its style is quaint, pseudobiblical, overly melodramatic, and its personages are so much cardboard. But then, I am aware that my standards are literary-critical, and many now find them archaic in our age of pop culture.

Michael Moorcock sensibly indicts *The Lord of the Rings* for infantilism, after which Jane Chance seriously meditates upon "difference" in Tolkien.

Utterly under Tolkien's sway, Michael N. Stanton finds the *Lord* trilogy to be replete with Christian emotion, while Mark T. Hooker examines Sam in his role of "batman" or soldier-servant to Frodo.

Jared Lobdell praises the Englishness of Tolkien's *Lord* series, after which Marjorie Burns broods on the darker aspects of Gandalf and Galadriel.

Victorian medievalism is invoked as the proper context for Tolkien by Andrew Lynch, while Sue Zlosnick studies gothic motifs in the *Lord* trilogy.

Verlyn Flieger discusses Tolkien's unfinished "Book," after which Mary R. Bowman employs narrative theory better to understand the *Lord* series.

In this book's final essay, Nancy Enright defends Tolkien from those feminist critics who fail to apprehend the Christlike renunciations of his most virtuous female characters.

HAROLD BLOOM

Introduction

I will attempt, rather briefly, to define my aesthetic doubts about Tolkien's trilogy by contrasting them to the shrewd defence by Roger Sale, Tolkien's best critic, of what he regards as Tolkien's and the protagonist Frodo Baggins's heroism.

Tolkien, at twenty-three, went off to the Western Front, was wounded, and lost to the war nearly all his friends in his own generation. For Sale, the trilogy is Tolkien's delayed, ultimate reaction to the Great War, which decimated Great Britain's young men. Tolkien dated his lifelong love of fairy stories to his turning away from the war, and *The Lord of the Rings* is a vast fairy story.

Sale accurately observes that the trilogy purports to be a quest but actually is a descent into hell. Whether a visionary descent into hell can be rendered persuasively in language that is acutely self-conscious, even arch, seems to me the hard question. I am fond of *The Hobbit*, which is rarely pretentious, but *The Lord of the Rings* seems to be inflated, overwritten, tendentious, and moralistic in the extreme. Is it not a giant Period Piece?

Sale nevertheless makes quite a strong case for the trilogy, and a vast readership implicitly agrees with him. I don't know whether Frodo Baggins breaks free and away from Tolkien's moralism to anything like the extent Sale suggests. Frodo, and Tolkien's deep creation of fairy lore, are the strengths of the trilogy, in Sale's account.

But there is still the burden of Tolkien's style: stiff, false archaic, overwrought, and finally a real hindrance in Volume III, *The Return of the King*, which I have had trouble rereading. At seventy-seven, I may just be too old, but here is *The Return of the King*, opened pretty much at random:

> At the doors of the Houses many were already gathered to see Aragorn, and they followed after him; and when at last he had supped, men came and prayed that he would heal their kinsmen or their friends whose lives were in peril through hurt or wound, or who lay under the Black Shadow. And Aragorn arose and went out, and he sent for the sons of Elrond, and together they labored far into the night. And word went through the city: 'The King is come again indeed.' And they named him Elfstone, because of the green stone that he wore, and so the name which it was foretold at his birth that he should bear was chosen for him by his own people.

I am not able to understand how a skilled and mature reader can absorb about fifteen hundred pages of this quaint stuff. Why "hurt or wound"; are they not the same? What justifies the heavy King James Bible influence upon this style? Sometimes, reading Tolkien, I am reminded of the Book of Mormon. Tolkien met a need, particularly in the early days of the counterculture in the later 1960s. Whether he is an author for the duration of the twenty-first century seems to me open to some doubt.

MICHAEL MOORCOCK

Epic Pooh

Why is the *Rings* being widely read today? At a time when perhaps the world was never more in need of authentic experience, this story seems to provide a pattern of it. A businessman in Oxford told me that when tired or out of sorts he went to the *Rings* for restoration. Lewis and various other critics believe that no book is more relevant to the human situation. W. H. Auden says that it "holds up the mirror to the only nature we know, our own." As for myself I was rereading the *Rings* at the time of Winston Churchill's funeral and I felt a distinct parallel between the two. For a few short hours the trivia which normally absorbs us was suspended and people experienced in common the meaning of leadership, greatness, valor, time redolent of timelessness, and common traits. Men became temporarily human and felt the life within them and about. Their corporate life lived for a little and made possible the sign of renewal alter a realisation such as occurs only once or twice in a lifetime.

For a century at least the world has been increasingly demythologized. But such a condition is apparently alien to the

From *Wizardry and Wild Romance: A Study of Epic Fantasy*, pp. 121–139. London: Victor Gollancz. © 1987 by Michael Moorcock.

real nature of men. Now comes a writer such as John Ronald
Reuel Tolkien and, as remythologizer, strangely warms our souls.
Clyde S. Kilby: "Meaning in the Lord of the Rings",
Shadows of Imagination, 1969

I have sometimes wondered how much the advent of steam influenced
Victorian ballad poetry and romantic prose. Reading Dunsany, for instance,
it often occurs to me that his early stories were all written during train
journeys:

> Up from the platform and onto the train
> Got Welleran, Rollory and young Iraine.
> Forgetful of sex and income tax
> Were Sooranard, Mammolek, Akanax:
> And in their dreams Dunsany's lord
> Mislaid the communication cord.

The sort of prose most often identified with "high" fantasy is the prose
of the nursery-room. It is a lullaby; it is meant to soothe and console. It is
mouth-music. It is frequently enjoyed not for its tensions but for its lack of
tensions. It coddles; it makes friends with you; it tells you comforting lies.
It is soft:

> One day when the sun had come back over the forest, bringing
> with it the scent of May, and all the streams of the Forest were
> tinkling happily to find themselves their own pretty shape
> again, and the little pools lay dreaming of the life they had
> seen and the big things they had done, and in the warmth
> and quiet of the Forest the cuckoo was trying over his voice
> carefully and listening to see if he liked it, and wood-pigeons
> were complaining gently to themselves in their lazy comfortable
> way that it was the other fellow's fault, but it didn't matter very
> much; on such a day as this Christopher Robin whistled in a
> special way he had, and Owl came flying out of the Hundred
> Acre Wood to see what was wanted.
> *Winnie-the-Pooh*, 1926

It is the predominant tone of *The Lord of the Rings* and *Watership Down*
and it is the main reason why these books, like many similar ones in the
past, are successful. It is the tone of many forgotten British and American
bestsellers, well-remembered children's books, like *The Wind in the Willows*,
you often hear it in regional fiction addressed to a local audience, or, in a

more sophisticated form, James Barrie (*Dear Brutus, Mary Rose* and, of course, *Peter Pan*). Unlike the tone of E. Nesbit (*Five Children and It* etc.), Richmal Crompton (the 'William' books) Terry Pratchett or the redoubtable J.K. Rowling, it is sentimental, slightly distanced, often wistful, a trifle retrospective; it contains little wit and much whimsy. The humour is often unconscious because, as with Tolkien, the authors take words seriously but without pleasure:

> One summer's evening an astonishing piece of news reached the *Ivy Bush* and *Green Dragon*. Giants and other portents on the borders of the Shire were forgotten for more important matters; Mr. Frodo was selling Bag End, indeed he had already sold it—to the Sackville-Bagginses!
>
> "For a nice bit, too," said some. "At a bargain price," said others, "and that's more likely when Mistress Lobelia's the buyer." (Otho had died some years before, at the ripe but disappointed age of 102.)
>
> Just why Mr. Frodo was selling his beautiful hole was even more debatable than the price ...
>
> *The Fellowship of the Ring*, 1954

I have been told it is not fair to quote from the earlier parts of *The Lord of the Rings*, that I should look elsewhere to find much better stuff so, opening it entirely at random, I find some improvement in substance and writing, but that tone is still there:

> Pippin became drowsy again and paid little attention to Gandalf telling him of the customs of Gondor, and how the Lord of the City had beacons built on the tops of outlying hills along both borders of the great range, and maintained posts at these points where fresh horses were always in readiness to bear his errand-riders to Rohan in the North, or to Belfalas in the South. "It is long since the beacons of the North were lit," he said; "and in the ancient days of Gondor they were not needed, for they had the Seven Stones."
>
> Pippin stirred uneasily.
>
> *The Return of the King*, 1955

Tolkien does, admittedly, rise above this sort of thing on occasions, in some key scenes, but often such a scene will be ruined by ghastly verse and it is remarkable how frequently he will draw back from the implications of the subject matter. Like Chesterton, and other orthodox Christian writers who substituted faith for artistic rigour he sees the petit bourgeoisie, the honest artisans and peasants, as the bulwark against Chaos. These people are always sentimentalized in such fiction because, traditionally, they are always the last to complain about any deficiencies in the social status quo. They are a type familiar to anyone who ever watched an English film of the thirties and forties, particularly a war-film, where they represented solid good sense opposed to a perverted intellectualism. In many ways *The Lord of the Rings* is, if not exactly anti-romantic, an anti-romance. Tolkien, and his fellow "Inklings" (the dons who met in Lewis's Oxford rooms to read their work in progress to one another), had extraordinarily ambiguous attitudes towards Romance (and just about everything else), which is doubtless why his trilogy has so many confused moments when the tension flags completely. But he could, at his best, produce prose much better than that of his Oxford contemporaries who perhaps lacked his respect for middle-English poetry. He claimed that his work was primarily linguistic in its original conception, that there were no symbols or allegories to be found in it, but his beliefs permeate the book as thoroughly as they do the books of Charles Williams and C. S. Lewis, who, consciously or unconsciously, promoted their orthodox Toryism in everything they wrote. While there is an argument for the reactionary nature of the books, they are certainly deeply conservative and strongly anti-urban, which is what leads some to associate them with a kind of Wagnerish Hitlerism. I don't think these books are "fascist", but they certainly don't exactly argue with the 18th century enlightened Toryism with which the English comfort themselves so frequently in these upsetting times. They don't ask any questions of white men in grey clothing who somehow have a handle on what's best for us.

I suppose I respond so antipathetically to Lewis and Tolkien because I find this sort of consolatory orthodoxy as distasteful as any other self-serving misanthropic doctrine. One should perhaps feel some sympathy for the nervousness occasionally revealed beneath their thick layers of stuffy self-satisfaction, typical of the second-rate schoolmaster so cheerfully mocked by Peake and Rowling, but sympathy is hard to sustain in the teeth of their hidden aggression which is so often accompanied by a deep-rooted hypocrisy. Their theories dignify the mood of a disenchanted and thoroughly discredited section of the repressed English middle-class too afraid, even as it falls, to make any sort of direct complaint ("They kicked us out of Rhodesia, you know"), least of all to the Higher Authority, their Tory God who has evidently failed them.

It was best-selling novelists, like Warwick Deeping (*Sorrell and Son*), who, after the First World War, adapted the sentimental myths (particularly the myth of Sacrifice) which had made war bearable (and helped ensure that we should be able to bear further wars), providing us with the wretched ethic of passive "decency" and self-sacrifice, by means of which we British were able to console ourselves in our moral apathy (even Buchan paused in his anti-Semitic diatribes to provide a few of these). Moderation was the rule and it is moderation which ruins Tolkien's fantasy and causes it to fail as a genuine romance, let alone an epic. The little hills and woods of that Surrey of the mind, the Shire, are "safe", but the wild landscapes everywhere beyond the Shire are "dangerous". Experience of life itself is dangerous. *The Lord of the Rings* is a pernicious confirmation of the values of a declining nation with a morally bankrupt class whose cowardly self-protection is primarily responsible for the problems England answered with the ruthless logic of Thatcherism. Humanity was derided and marginalised. Sentimentality became the acceptable substitute. So few people seem to be able to tell the difference.

The Lord of the Rings is much more deep-rooted in its infantilism than a good many of the more obviously juvenile books it influenced. It is *Winnie-the-Pooh* posing as an epic. If the Shire is a suburban garden, Sauron and his henchmen are that old bourgeois bugaboo, the Mob—mindless football supporters throwing their beer-bottles over the fence the worst aspects of modern urban society represented as the whole by a fearful, backward-yearning class for whom "good taste" is synonymous with "restraint" (pastel colours, murmured protest) and "civilized" behaviour means "conventional behaviour in all circumstances". This is not to deny that courageous characters are found in *The Lord of the Rings*, or a willingness to fight Evil (never really defined), but somehow those courageous characters take on the aspect of retired colonels at last driven to write a letter to *The Times* and we are not sure—because Tolkien cannot really bring himself to get close to his proles and their satanic leaders—if Sauron and Co. are quite as evil as we're told. After all, anyone who hates hobbits can't be all bad.

The appeal of the Shire has certain similarities with the appeal of the "Greenwood" which is, unquestionably, rooted in most of us:

> In summer when the sheves be shene
> And leaves be large and long,
> It is full merry in fair forest
> To hear the fowle's song;

> To see the deer draw to the dale,
> And leave the hilles hee,
> And shadow them in levès green,
> Under the greenwood tree.

A Tale of Robin Hood
(quoted in *Ancient Metrical Tales*, 1829)

There is no happy ending to the Romance of Robin Hood, however, whereas Tolkien, going against the grain of his subject matter, forces one on us—as a matter of policy:

> And lastly there is the oldest and deepest desire, the Great Escape: the Escape from Death. Fairy stories provide many examples and modes of this—which might be called the genuine escapist, or (I would say) fugitive spirit. But so do other stories (notably those of scientific inspiration), and so do other studies ... But the "consolation" of fairy-tales has another aspect than the imaginative satisfaction of ancient desires. For more important is the Consolation of the Happy Ending.
>
> J. R. R. Tolkien, "On Fairy Stories"

The great epics dignified death, but they did not ignore it, and it is one of the reasons why they are superior to the artificial romances of which *Lord of the Rings* is merely one of the most recent.

Since the beginnings of the Industrial Revolution, at least, people have been yearning for an ideal rural world they believe to have vanished—yearning for a mythical state of innocence (as Morris did) as heartily as the Israelites yearned for the Garden of Eden. This refusal to face or derive any pleasure from the realities of urban industrial life, this longing to possess, again, the infant's eye view of the countryside, is a fundamental theme in popular English literature. Novels set in the countryside probably always outsell novels set in the city, perhaps because most people now live in cities.

If I find this nostalgia for a "vanished" landscape a bit strange it is probably because as I write I can look from my window over twenty miles of superb countryside to the sea and a sparsely populated coast. This county, like many others, has seemingly limitless landscapes of great beauty and variety, unspoiled by excessive tourism or the uglier forms of industry. Elsewhere big cities have certainly destroyed the surrounding countryside but rapid transport now makes it possible for a Londoner to spend the time they would have needed to get to Box Hill forty years ago in getting to Northumberland. I think it is simple neophobia which makes people hate the modern world and its changing society; it is xenophobia which makes them unable to imagine what rural beauty might lie beyond the boundaries of their particular Shire. They would rather read Miss Read and *The Horse Whisperer* and share a miserable complaint or two on the commuter train while planning to take their holidays in Bournemouth, as usual, because they can't afford to go to Spain this year. They don't want rural beauty anyway; they want a sunny day, a pretty view.

Writers like Tolkien take you to the edge of the Abyss and point out the excellent tea-garden at the bottom, showing you the steps carved into the cliff and reminding you to be a bit careful because the hand-rails are a trifle shaky as you go down; they haven't got the approval yet to put a new one in.

I never liked A. A. Milne, even when I was *very* young. There is an element of conspiratorial persuasion in his tone that a suspicious child can detect early in life. Let's all be cosy, it seems to say (children's books are, after all, often written by conservative adults anxious to maintain an unreal attitude to childhood); let's forget about our troubles and go to sleep. At which I would find myself stirring to a sitting position in my little bed and responding with uncivilized bad taste.

According to C. S. Lewis his fantasies for children—his Narnia series of seven books beginning with *The Lion, the Witch and the Wardrobe* and ending with *The Last Battle*—were deliberate works of Christian propaganda. The books are a kind of Religious Tract Society version of the Oz books as written by E. Nesbit; but E. Nesbit would rarely have allowed herself Lewis's awful syntax, full of tacked-on clauses, lame qualifications, vague adjectives and unconscious repetitions; neither would she have written down to children as thoroughly as this childless don who remained a devoutly committed bachelor most of his life. Both Baum and Nesbit wrote more vigorously and more carefully:

> Old Mombi had thought herself very wise to choose the form of a Griffin, for its legs were exceedingly fleet and its strength more enduring than that of other animals. But she had not reckoned on the untiring energy of the Saw-Horse, whose wooden limbs could run for days without slacking their speed. Therefore, after an hour's hard running, the Griffin's breath began to fail, and it panted and gasped painfully, and moved more slowly than before. Then it reached the edge of the desert and began racing across the deep sands. But its tired feet sank far into the sand, and in a few minutes the Griffin fell forward, completely exhausted, and lay still upon the desert waste.
>
> Glinda came up a moment later, riding the still vigorous Saw-Horse; and having unwound a slender golden thread from her girdle the Sorceress threw it over the head of the panting and helpless Griffin, and so destroyed the magical power of Mombi's transformation.
>
> For the animal, with one fierce shudder, disappeared from view, while in its place was discovered the form of the old Witch, glaring savagely at the serene and beautiful face of the Sorceress.
>
> L. Frank Baum, *The Land of Oz*, 1904

> Elfrida fired away, and the next moment it was plain that Elfrida's poetry was more potent than Edred's; also that a little bad grammar is a trifle to a mighty Mouldiwarp.

For the walls of Edred's room receded further and further till the children found themselves in a great white hall with avenues of tall pillars stretching in every direction as far as you could see. The hall was crowded with people dressed in costumes of all countries and all ages—Chinamen, Indians, Crusaders in armour, powdered ladies, doubleted gentlemen, Cavaliers in curls, Turks in turbans, Arabs, monks, abbesses, jesters, grandees with ruffs round their necks, and savages with kilts of thatch. Every kind of dress you can think of was there. Only all the dresses were white. It was like a *redoute*, which is a fancy-dress ball where the guests may wear any dress they choose, only the dresses must be of one colour.

The people round the children pushed them gently forward. And then they saw that in the middle of the hall was a throne of silver, spread with a fringed cloth of chequered silver and green, and on it, with the Mouldiwarp standing on one side and the Mouldierwarp on the other, the Mouldiestwarp was seated in state and splendour. He was much larger than either of the other moles, and his fur was as silvery as the feathers of a swan.

E. Nesbit, *Harding's Luck*, 1909

Here is a typical extract from Lewis's first Narnia book, which was superior to some which followed it and is a better than average example of Lewis's prose fiction for children or for adults:

It was nearly midday when they found themselves looking down a steep hillside at a castle—a little toy castle it looked from where they stood which seemed to be all pointed towers. But the Lion was rushing down at such a speed that it grew larger every moment and before they had time even to ask themselves what it was they were already on a level with it. And now it no longer looked like a toy castle but rose frowning in front of them. No face looked over the battlements and the gates were fast shut. And Aslan, not at all slacking his pace, rushed straight as a bullet towards it.

"The Witch's home!" he cried. "Now, children, hold tight."

Next moment the whole world seemed to turn upside down and the children felt as if they had left their insides behind them; for the Lion had gathered himself together for a greater leap than any he had yet made and jumped—or you may call it flying rather than jumping—right over the castle wall. The two girls, breathless but unhurt, found themselves tumbling off his back in the middle of a wide stone courtyard full of statues.

The Lion, the Witch and the Wardrobe, 1950

As a child, I found that these books did not show me the respect I was used to from Nesbit or Baum, who also gave me denser, better writing and a wider vocabulary. The Cowardly Lion was a far more attractive character than Aslan and Crompton's William books were notably free from moral lessons. I think I would have enjoyed the work of Alan Garner, Susan Cooper and Ursula Le Guin much more. They display a greater respect for children and considerably more talent as writers. Here is Garner:

> But as his head cleared, Cohn heard another sound, so beautiful that he never found rest again; the sound of a horn, like the moon on snow, and another answered it from the limits of the sky; and through the Brollachan ran silver lightnings, and he heard hoofs, and voices calling, "We ride! We ride!" and the whole cloud was silver, so that he could not look.
>
> The hoof-beats drew near, and the earth throbbed. Cohn opened his eyes. Now the cloud raced over the ground, breaking into separate glories that wisped and sharpened the skeins of starlight, and were horsemen, and at their head was majesty, crowned with antlers, like the sun.
>
> But as they crossed the valley, one of the riders dropped behind, and Colin saw that it was Susan. She lost ground though her speed was no less, and the light that formed her died, and in its place was a smaller, solid figure that halted, forlorn, in the white wake of the riding.
>
> The horsemen climbed from the hillside to the air, growing vast in the sky, and to meet them came nine women, their hair like wind. And away they rode together across the night, over the waves, and beyond the isles, and the Old Magic was free forever, and the moon was new.
>
> *The Moon of Gomrath*, 1963

Evidently, Garner is a better writer than Lewis or Tolkien. In the three fantasy novels *The Weirdstone of Brisingamen* (1961), *The Moon of Gomrath* (1963) and *Elidor* (1965) his weakness, in common with similar writers, is his plot structure. In a later, better-structured book, *The Owl Service* (1970), he improved considerably.

This deficiency of structure is by no means evident in Ursula K. Le Guin, Gillian Bradshaw or Susan Cooper. For my taste Susan Cooper has produced one of the very best sequences of novels of their type (modern children involved in ancient mystical conflicts). They have much of Masefield's *Box of Delights* magic. Her sequence, *The Dark is Rising*, has some fine moments. The strongest books are the title volume and the final volume *Silver in the Tree* (1977), while some of the best writing can he found in *The Grey King* (1975):

> They were no longer where they had been. They stood somewhere in another time, on the roof of the world. All around them was the open night sky, like a huge black inverted bowl, and in it blazed the stars, thousand upon thousand brilliant prickles of fire. Will heard Bran draw in a quick breath. They stood, looking up. The stars blazed round them. There was no sound anywhere, in all the immensity of space. Will felt a wave of giddiness; it was as if they stood on the last edge of the universe, and if they fell, they would fall out of Time ... As he gazed about him, gradually he recognised the strange inversion of reality in which they were held. He and Bran were not standing in a timeless dark night observing the stars in the heavens. It was the other way around. They themselves were observed. Every blazing point in that great depthless hemisphere of stars and suns was focussed upon them, contemplating, considering, judging. For by following the quest for the golden harp, he and Bran were challenging the boundless might of the High Magic of the Universe. They must stand unprotected before it, on their way, and they would be allowed to pass only if they had the right by birth. Under that merciless starlight of infinity any unrightful challenger would be brushed into nothingness as effortlessly as a man might brush an ant from his sleeve.

Ursula K. Le Guin in her trilogy *A Wizard of Earthsea* (1968), *The Tombs of Atuan* (1971) and *The Farthest Shore* (1972) is the only one of these three to set her stories entirely in a wholly invented world. She writes her books for children as conscientiously as she writes for adults (she is a leading and much admired sf author whose work has won many awards). Here is a passage from near the beginning, again with its echoes of Frazer's *Golden Bough*:

> On the day the boy was thirteen years old, a day in the early splendour of autumn while still the bright leaves are on the trees, Ogion returned to the village from his rovings over Gont Mountain, and the ceremony of Passage was held. The witch took from the boy his name Duny, the name his mother had given him as a baby. Nameless and naked he walked into the cold springs of the Ar where it rises among the rocks under the high cliffs. As he entered the water clouds crossed the sun's face and great shadows slid and mingled over the water of the pool about him. He crossed

to the far bank, shuddering with cold but walking slow and erect as he should through that icy, living water. As he came to the bank Ogion, waiting, reached out his hand and clasping the boy's arm whispered to him his true name: Ged.

Thus was he given his name by one very wise in the use of power.

A Wizard of Earthsea

Lloyd Alexander is another American writer who has had considerable success with his books set in an invented and decidedly Celtic fantasy world, but for my taste he never quite succeeds in matching the three I have mentioned. He uses more clichés and writes a trifle flaccidly:

The Horned King stood motionless, his arm upraised. Lightning played about his sword. The giant flamed like a burning tree. The stag horns turned to crimson streaks, the skull mask ran like molten iron. A roar of pain and rage rose from the Antlered King's throat.

With a cry, Taran flung an arm across his face. The ground rumbled and seemed to open beneath him. Then there was nothing.

The Book of Three, 1964

One does become a little tired, too, of Hern the Hunter turning up here. Another legacy from Frazer. Sometimes he appears in books of this kind almost as an embarrassment, as if convention demands his presence: an aging and rather vague bishop doing his bit at official services.

There are a good many more such fantasies now being written for children and on the whole they are considerably better than the imitations written ostensibly for adults. Perhaps the authors feel more at ease when writing about and for children—as if they are forced to tell fewer lies (or at least answer fewer fundamental questions) to themselves or their audience.

Among these newer writers, Gillian Bradshaw has produced yet another Arthurian trilogy. This one, however, is written from the point of view of Gwalchmai, the son of the King of Orkney and Queen Morgawse (who might be a sorceress). He encounters the Sidhe, some of whom help him as he journeys to be with King Arthur who is fighting a desperate battle against the Saxon invaders. Bradshaw's writing is clear and vibrant, her story-telling has pace and verve.

She lifted her arms and the Darkness leapt. But she was distant again, and I stood at Camlann. I looked up and saw Lugh standing in the west, opposite Morgawse, holding his arm above the island so that the Queen could not touch it. Behind was light too brilliant, too glorious to be seen. For a moment I saw these two confronting one another, and then my field of vision narrowed. I saw the island and the figures of armies. I saw the Family and myself in it. The armies began to move, and the sounds of battle arose. I realized that I saw things that were yet to come, and was terrified. I covered my face with my arms and cried, "No more!"

And abruptly there was silence.

Hawk of May, 1981

The subsequent hooks in this sequence are *Kingdom of Summer* (1982) and *In Winter's Shadow* (1983).

Several of the emerging children's novelists actually display more original gifts and greater talent than the majority of those ostensibly for adults. In my view Robin McKinley is one of the very best of these. Her *The Blue Sword* (1982) won the John Newbery Medal in 1984 and she is building an excellent reputation. *The Blue Sword* is the first of her Chronicles of Damar. She has a fresh and interesting approach to the genre which immediately makes it into something of her own. Her style is robust, elegant and considered, qualities which are a great relief after so many clunking archaicisms and cuticisms which inhabit the great majority of present-day fantasies. Angharad Crewe, the young woman who is her central character, is far more likeable than the tribe of leggy, slightly awkward, pony-loving teenagers appearing all too frequently in recent fantasies. Again McKinley's writing makes me wish I had been able to read them when I was young. They would have been a wonderful antidote to the bland fare which generally became acceptable on all the myriad planes and demi-planes of the English middle-class when I was young.

The power that washed over that face, that rolled down the arms and into the sword and shield, was that of demonkind, and Harry knew she was no match for this one, and in spite of the heat of Gonturan in her hand her heart was cold with fear. The two stallions reared again and reached out to tear each other; the white stallion's neck was now ribboned with blood, like the real ribbons he wore in his mane. Harry raised her sword arm and felt the shock of the answer, the hilts of the swords ring together, and sparks flew from the crash, and it seemed that the smoke rose from them and blinded her. The other rider's hot breath was in her face. His lips parted and she saw his tongue: it was scarlet, and looked more like fire than living flesh.

The Blue Sword

After reading a good many of these contemporary fantasy stories I remained impressed by the number of authors of adult books who described their characters as children and the number of children's writers who produce perfectly mature and sensible characters who think and act intelligently. I found myself wishing that the likes of McKinley would choose to do more work for grown-ups. Perhaps the reason they don't is that they find they can, writing for teenagers, preserve a greater respect for their audience. Another variety of book has begun to appear, a sort of Pooh-fights-back fiction of the kind produced by Richard Adams, which substitutes animals for human protagonists, contains a familiar set of middle-class Anglican Tory undertones (all these books seem to be written with a slight lisp) and is certainly already more corrupt than Tolkien. Adams is a worse writer but he must appeal enormously to all those many readers who have never quite lost their yearning for the frisson first felt when Peter Rabbit was expelled from Mr. Macgregor's garden:

> As Dandelion ended, Acorn, who was on the windward side of the little group, suddenly started and sat back, with ears up and nostrils twitching. The strange, rank smell was stronger than ever and after a few moments they all heard a heavy movement close by. Suddenly, on the other side of the path, the fern parted and there looked out a long, dog-like head, striped black and white. It was pointed downward, the jaws grinning, the muzzle close to the ground. Behind, they could just discern great, powerful paws and a shaggy black body. The eyes were peering at them, full of savage cunning. The head moved slowly, taking in the dusky lengths of the wood ride in both directions, and then fixed them once more with its fierce, terrible stare. The jaws opened wider and they could see the teeth, glimmering white as the stripes along the head. For long moments it gazed and the rabbits remained motionless, staring back without a sound. Then Bigwig, who was nearest to the path, turned and slipped back among the others.
>
> "A lendri," he muttered as he passed through them. "It may be dangerous and it may not, but I'm taking no chances with it. Let's get away."
>
> *Watership Down*, 1972

Adams's follow-up to this was *Shardik* (1974), better written, apparently for adults, and quite as silly. It was about a big bear who died for our sins: *Martyred Pooh*. Later, *The Plague Dogs* (1977) displayed an almost paranoid conservative misanthropism.

I sometimes think that as Britain declines, dreaming of a sweeter past, entertaining few hopes for a finer future, her middle-classes turn increasingly to the fantasy of rural life and talking animals, the safety of the woods that are the pattern of the paper on the nursery room wall. Old hippies, housewives, civil servants, share in this wistful trance; eating nothing as dangerous or exotic as the lotus, but chewing instead on a form of mildly anaesthetic British cabbage. If the bulk of American sf could be said to be written by robots, about robots, for robots, then the bulk of English fantasy seems to be written by rabbits, about rabbits and for rabbits.

How much further can it go?

Of the children's writers only Lewis and Adams are guilty, in my opinion, of producing thoroughly corrupted romanticism—sentimentalized pleas for moderation of aspiration which are at the root of their kind of conservatism. In Lewis's case this consolatory, anxiety-stilling "Why try to play Mozart when it's easier to play Rodgers and Hammerstein?" attitude extended to his non-fiction, particularly the dreadful but influential *Experiment in Criticism*. But these are, anyway, minor figures. It is Tolkien who is most widely read and worshipped. And it was Tolkien who most betrayed the romantic discipline, more so than ever Tennyson could in *Idylls of the King*, which enjoyed a similar vogue in Victorian England.

Corrupted romanticism is as unwholesome as the corrupted realism of, say, Ayn Rand. Cabell's somewhat obvious irony is easier to take than Tolkien's less obvious sentimentality, largely because Cabell's writing is wittier, more inventive and better disciplined. I find William Morris naïve and silly but essentially good-hearted (and a better utopianist than a fantasist); Dunsany I find slight but inoffensive. Lewis speaks for the middle-class status quo, as, more subtly, does Charles Williams. Lewis uses the stuff of fantasy to preach sermons quite as nasty as any to be found in Victorian sentimental fiction, and he writes badly. A group of self-congratulatory friends can often ensure that any writing emerging from it remains hasty and unpolished.

Ideally fiction should offer us escape and force us, at least, to ask questions; it should provide a release from anxiety but give us some insight into the causes of anxiety. Lin Carter, in his *Imaginary Worlds*—the only book I have been able to find on the general subject of epic fantasy—uses an argument familiar to those who are used to reading apologies from that kind of sf or thriller buff who feels compelled to justify his philistinism: "The charge of 'escapist reading,'" says Carter, "is most often levelled against fantasy and science fiction by those who have forgotten or overlooked the simple fact that virtually all reading—all music and poetry and art and drama and philosophy for that matter—is a temporary escape from what is around us." Like so many of his colleagues in the professional sf world, Carter expresses distaste for fiction which is not predominantly escapist by charging it with being "depressing" or "negative" if it does not provide him with the moral and psychological comforts he seems to need.

An unorthodox view, such as that of Tolkien's contemporary David Lindsay (*Voyage to Arcturus*), is regarded as a negative view. This, of course, is the response of those deeply and often unconsciously wedded to their cultural presumptions, who regard examination of them as an attack.

Carter dismisses Spenser as "dull" and Joyce as "a titanic bore" and writes in clichés, euphemisms and wretchedly distorted syntax, telling us that the Pre-Raphaelites were "lisping exquisites" and that Ford Madox Brown (1821–93) was a young man attracted to the movement by Morris's (1834–96) fiery Welsh (born Walthamstow, near London) dynamism and that because Tolkien got a CBE (not a knighthood) we must now call him "Sir John"— but Carter, at least, is not the snob some American adherents are (and there is nobody more risible than the provincial American literary snob—Gore Vidal being the most developed example). In a recent anthology compiled by Robert H. Boyer and Kenneth J. Zahorski, *The Fantastic Imagination*, we find the following: "In addition to their all being high fantasy, the stories selected here are good literature." Amongst the writers to be found in the volume are C. S. Lewis, John Buchan, Frank R. Stockton and Lloyd Alexander, not one of whom can match the literary talents of, say, Fritz Leiber, whose work has primarily been published in commercial magazines and genre paperback series. For years American thriller buffs with pretensions ignored Hammett and Chandler in favour of inferior English writers like D. L. Sayers and here we see the same thing occurring with American fantasy writers. Those who produce the closest approximation to an English style are most praised. Those who use more vigorous American models are regarded as less literary! The crux of the thing remains: the writers admired are not "literary" or "literate". As often as not they flatter middle-brow sensibilities and reinforce middle-class sentimentality and therefore do not threaten a carefully maintained set of social and intellectual assumptions.

Yet Tennyson, who had his moments, inspired better poets who followed him, who sought the origin of his inspiration and made nobler use of it. Both Swinburne and Morris could, for instance, employ the old ballad metres more effectively than Tennyson himself, refusing, unlike him, to modify their toughness. Doubtless Tolkien will also inspire writers who will take his raw materials and put them to nobler uses. I would love to believe that the day of the rural romance is done at last.

The commercial genre which has developed from Tolkien is probably the most dismaying effect of all. I grew up in a world where Joyce was considered to be the best Anglophone writer of the 20th century. I happen to believe that Faulkner is better, while others would pick Conrad, say. Thomas Mann is an exemplary giant of moral, mythic fiction. But to introduce Tolkien's fantasy into such a debate is a sad comment on our standards and our ambitions. Is it a sign of our dumber times that *Lord of the Rings* can replace *Ulysses* as the exemplary book of its century? Some of the writers who most slavishly imitate him seem to be using English as a rather inexpertly-learned second language. So many of them are unbelievably bad that they defy description and are scarcely worth listing individually. Terry Pratchett once remarked that all his readers were called Kevin. He is lucky in that he appears to be the only Terry in fantasy land who is able to write a decent complex sentence. That such writers also depend upon recycling the plots of their literary superiors and are rewarded for this bland repetition isn't surprising in a world of sensation movies and manufactured pop bands. That they are rewarded with the lavish lifestyles of the most successful whores is also unsurprising. To pretend that this addictive cabbage is anything more than the worst sort of pulp historical romance or western is, however, a depressing sign of our intellectual decline and our free-falling academic standards.

JANE CHANCE

"Queer" Hobbits: The Problem of Difference in the Shire

From the very beginning of *LotR*, the issue of social and cultural difference marks the speech and behavior of the Hobbits in their home environment, creating a miniature war among its inhabitants. The reader does not at first notice this difference because the Shire exudes a pastoral innocence that masks the seeds of its potential destruction. And Gandalf, the norm for correct perspective throughout, both for the Fellowship and for us as readers, worries that the "charming, absurd, helpless hobbits" (1:79) in the Shire might become enslaved by Sauron. These Hobbits Gandalf identifies as the "kind, jolly, stupid Bolgers, Hornblowers, Boffins, Bracegirdles ... not to mention the ridiculous Bagginses" (1:79). We are told that for the moment they are protected because Sauron has "more useful" servants, but that the Dark Lord is always a threat because of his "malice and revenge." And yet the difference between the isolated, safe, jolly Shire and the distant, evil Dark Power is not as marked as it might seem, for power struggles exist among the different Hobbit families in the Shire region, absurd in some cases and significant in others. Indeed, sensitivity to this politics of difference in the Shire, a faculty born of nurture and nature, marks the special ability of Bilbo and Frodo— their power—that will facilitate Frodo's mission and attract followers.

The political problems in the Shire grow out of its deceptively "safe" isolation from the rest of Middle-earth. Its inhabitants distrust those who come

From *The Lord of the Rings: The Mythology of Power*, pp. 26–37. © 2001 by the University Press of Kentucky.

from outside be cause they differ from them in ways they do not understand. A stranger such as a Brandybuck arouses mistrust, and the inhabitants band closer together; later and more ominously a Dark Rider will arouse that same mistrust. Sandyman the Miller, through his suspicious notice of the queerness of the visitors to Bag End (among whom are the strange Dwarves and the magical Gandalf), from the beginning creates a problem for Frodo. This queerness therefore extends also to Bag End itself and ultimately, by association, to its owners, Bilbo and then Frodo (1:47). Sameness, in contrast, implies the familiar and secure, and sameness means Hobbitlike. The Hobbits relish what is natural for them, which involves physical activities, living close to nature—dwelling in holes, eating, smoking tobacco. To do otherwise is un-Hobbitlike. "Hobbits," Tolkien once acknowledged, "have what you might call universal morals. I should say they are examples of natural philosophy and natural religion." Marks of distinction—wealth, education, even leadership—can set a Hobbit apart, make him different. The major political problem for any potential leader, then, is to maintain the trust of those led—to make leadership seem "natural" and to diminish his own "queerness."

Bilbo is "very rich and very peculiar," largely because of his perpetual youth (1:43), both of which make him seem different, "queer": "It isn't natural, and trouble will come of it!" (1:43). Part of this "trouble" results from social inequities that his wealth and good physical fortune exacerbate. In addition, however, Bilbo is "queer" to the other inhabitants of the Shire (1:77) because he has been changed by his travels—his knowledge of the world—and by his possession of the Ring, which has stretched him thin. (In other words, his awareness of moral issues—his knowledge of good and evil—has been expanded by his having carried the Ring for so long, while his very awareness has debilitated him.) The tug between the desire of the self for the Ring (for the "Precious," or for what the self wishes to incorporate into the self) and the Hobbit's desire to think of others beyond himself (to protect the Shire and the world by keeping the Ring hidden from Sauron's eye) has made him thin. It is no accident that the natural wearing of the Ring on the finger renders its wearer invisible, for when the Ring masters its wearer, it totally erases the *identity* of the wearer, and he becomes without a self. Unfortunately, Bilbo never connects any change in the Ring with the Ring itself, instead taking "credit for that to himself, and he was very proud of it. Though he was getting restless and uneasy. *Thin and stretched* he said. A sign that the ring was getting control" (1:77). Ironically, the Ring appeals to the desires of the self for gold, power, and love, as a means of mastering that individual.

The anticipated "trouble" is, however, averted in part by Baggins's generosity. He shares his money with his friends and relatives: "He had many devoted admirers among the hobbits of poor and unimportant families" (1:43). Again, generously sharing his fortune allays the fears of difference among the less fortunate Hobbits. He is considered "well-spoken," polite, and gentle, largely because, as well-off as he is, he treats his servant the Gaffer (Sam Gamgee's father) with great deference for his knowledge—reversing the usual master-servant relationship: "Bilbo was very polite to him, calling him 'Master Hamfast,' and consulting him constantly upon the growing of vegetables—in the matter of 'roots,' especially potatoes, the Gaffer was recognized as the leading authority by all in the neighbourhood (including himself)" (1:44–45). Bilbo's sensitivity to the lower social class of his servant allows him to balance out their relationship through a genteel deference to the authority his servant does demonstrate, in particular, knowledge of vegetable growing. Bilbo has also taught the gardener's son Sam to read (1:47)—a Middle-earth reflection of the Victorian ideal of educating the poor. The mutual respect of the Hobbit aristocrat and the gardening servant-authority underscores Bilbo's gifts as an astute politician.

Two major social problems engage the political skills of Bilbo. First is the arrival of Frodo, an orphan and his heir, which causes the Sackville-Bagginses (Bilbo's other close heirs) consternation because their expected inheritance will presumably be reduced. Second is the necessary inheritance of Bag End (and its "treasure") by Frodo, predicated on the disappearance of Bilbo at the advanced age of 111 after a magnificent (and long-expected, according to the chapter title) birthday party. Because of the continued enmity of the detested Sackville-Bagginses after the disappearance, Frodo will inherit these same familial problems requiring *his* political skills.

The birthday party, in the Shire, represents a symbolic paradigm for the ideal relationship between master and servant, wealthy aristocrat and members of the populace. As a site for potential self-aggrandizement and indulgence—which would not have been tolerated by the inhabitants within had they been either not invited or invited but expected to bring gifts—its signification for the political Hobbit Bilbo is to mark the abundance of self-confidence, largess of the self, by *giving* gifts to all who attend and by offering them the splendor of fireworks, songs, dances, music, games, and fine and abundant food. It is, then, the perfect symbolic and political moment for Bilbo to disappear—that is, his largess signifies the disappearance of *selfishness* and masks his literal individual disappearance. At this party no one is not invited, and every guest is *given* presents, in the Hobbit fashion (1:50). Indeed, the liberality of Bilbo in inviting everyone to his birthday party is, as the Gaffer reminds the suspicious and manipulative Sandyman, another, more positive aspect of Bilbo's "queerness." The party thus also symbolizes Bilbo's enduring political concern for others—he is noble, a true gentleman, *because* he thinks only of others. And Hobbits, who have the custom of giving presents to others on their own birthdays, are in general the least acquisitive of beings. The Sackville-Bagginses—Otho and his wife, Lobelia—attend even though they "disliked Bilbo and detested Frodo" (1:57), largely because of the magnificence of the invitation.

Politic Bilbo in his speech to the Hobbits expresses his fondness for them all and praises them as "excellent and admirable" (1:54). This speech is important, for the occasion also honors his heir-nephew's birthday, which means Frodo will come of age and therefore Bilbo must make his disappearance. But even generous Bilbo, as a natural aristocrat, has difficulty in ridding himself entirely of the Ring: Hobbit that he is, he is still related to the Sackville-Bagginses and thus shares in their excessive (even for Hobbits) greed. Desire is a part of what the Ring represents.

The Ring of course works its power—illustrating the nature of the novel as a work about power—because more than anything it wishes to return to its maker-master and therefore wants to be put on (to make the wearer *naturally* invisible but supernaturally visible to the Eye of Sauron). In relation to the individual, then, possessing the Ring means that the individual loses sense of who he is and what he truly wants.

The specialness of the Ring—and therefore the specialness it confers on its owner—enhances the self, fills the individual with the illusion of power. And perhaps that specialness is what has made him "queer" to others. Bilbo initially has difficulty giving up the Ring to Gandalf—he wants to keep it, or the Ring wants him to—and he loses sight of that facility of the Ring, which makes him mistrust others as different and therefore (as with Sandyman) not with-me, not for-me: "'Now it comes to it, I don't like parting with it at all, I may say. And I don't really see why I should. Why do you want me to?' he asked, and a curious change came over his voice. It was sharp with suspicion and annoyance. 'You are always badgering me about my ring: but you have never bothered me about the other things that I got on my journey'" (1:59). Bilbo wants to keep the Ring because it is his—he found it: "It is my own. I found it. It came to me" (1:59). It is the last gift, the one he most has to give away—first to Gandalf and then to his heir Frodo. As with Frodo on Mount Doom, however, fighting first with himself and then with Gollum, Bilbo resists Gandalf as an adversary, using the same language as Gollum: "It is mine, I tell you. My own. My precious. Yes, my precious" (1:59).

To free himself Bilbo has to let it go—which he finds difficult. Gandalf's demand for the Ring (as it lies on the mantel) arouses Bilbo's suspicions that the wizard is a thief. Gandalf wins him over by saying, "I am not trying to rob you, but to help you. I wish you would trust me as you used" (1:60). Bilbo apologizes: "But I felt so *queer*.... And I don't seem able to make up my mind" (1:60–61). What does the queerness represent, if not Bilbo's power in the Shire, which he regrets giving up—his power as "lord"? His specialness as an individual, the reason he is young perpetually, wealthy, generous? It is an enabler. For this reason it is difficult for Bilbo to give up the Ring, and yet death—which Bilbo's "disappearance" ultimately signifies—is what all humans must pass through, to give up themselves. Renunciation is the final gift: to allow the self to grow and mature, the individual must learn to be selfless. Thus, the "presents" given to Bilbo's relatives are all "corrective," intended to change menial sins in the relatives (a pen and ink bottle to a relative who never answers letters, for example). Despite this admonitory and educational function of the gifts, "The poorer hobbits, and especially those of Bagshot Row, did very well" (1:65).

The gift that Bilbo gives to his nephew Frodo is similar in function—the Ring. With this possession comes the necessity for the quest—no "gift" at all but an unequaled opportunity for individual and even heroic maturation. Frodo at age fifty (when Gandalf pronounces the need for the quest to return the Ring) indeed "comes of age," becomes himself, an individual. But in this narrative, unlike the normal bildungsroman (novel of education or maturation) on which this work is modeled, Frodo must return his "gift" to its maker, Mount Doom. With such a "return" of the gift to its maker—to its "mother" source rather than its "father" creator, Sauron—the Ring is the ultimate Hobbit birthday gift. Instead of going on a quest to obtain some significant knowledge or item of value, Frodo goes to divest himself (and the world) of this power. In life, if maturity means the loss of the child to adulthood, then this quest reverses that idea: the adult Frodo must attempt to recuperate the child, as the Ring returns to its origin.

What does this quest signify? We have established that the political Hobbit Bilbo "rules" his Shire through self-abnegation and generosity; however, the rule implied by the dominating Ring is entirely different. As the inscription testifies, it allows for differences—Elves, Dwarves, Men—but only because there is "One Ring" intended to align their differences:

> One Ring to rule them all, One Ring to find them.
> One Ring to bring them all and in the darkness bind them,
> In the Land of Mordor where the Shadows lie. (1:81)

Returning the Ring to its origin means refusal of power as domination by the One—by sameness, homogeneity—and therefore acceptance of respect for difference and diversity. It is Frodo, more different even from other Hobbits than his unnatural cousin Bilbo, who is better suited to this quest.

Different from Bilbo because of his mother's dark familial roots in the Old Forest, Frodo may be acceptable to the Shire only because of his cousin Bilbo's wealth and favor. Yet, like Bilbo, Frodo is "queer." Most interestingly of all, Frodo Baggins begins his fictive life (as his creator Tolkien does his maturity) an orphan and (also like Tolkien) an orphan from "across the river" (given his birth in South Africa). Frodo is a Baggins from Hobbiton, but his mother was a Brandybuck from Buckland, "where folks are so queer," says Old Noakes (1:45). Their "queerness" is caused by living on the wrong side of the Brandywine River, next to the Old Forest, and also by the fact that they use boats on the big river, which "isn't natural," says the Gaffer, at least for Hobbits (1:45). Indeed, Frodo's father, Drogo Baggins, was a "decent respectable hobbit" until he drowned in an uncustomary river outing. Drogo and Miss Primula Brandybuck (Bilbo's first cousin on his mother's side) took out a boat one night after a grand dinner at the home of his father-in-law, Old Gorbadoc, and either Drogo's weight sank the boat or Primula pushed him in (1:46).

After Bilbo's disappearance—that is, upon his successful self-renunciation—Frodo's first test as Lord of the Manor comes of course from the Sackville-Bagginses, who offer him low prices for other things not given away and spread rumors that Gandalf and Frodo conspired to get Bilbo's wealth. That Frodo can tolerate difference is symbolically clear to the reader (if not to Lobelia Sackville-Baggins) because he is accompanied by his cousin Merry Brandybuck, who, like Frodo's mother, hales from Buckville near the Old Forest. But Frodo mistakenly assumes at first that Bag End is his "inheritance"—his for keeping. As time passes, Frodo perpetuates Bilbo's reputation for "oddity" (1:70) by continuing to give birthday parties for his cousin. His closest friends are Merry Brandybuck (one of the "queer" Brandybucks), Peregrin Took, and other younger Hobbits who are descended from the Old Took and were fond of Bilbo (1:71). (Bilbo's mother was Belladonna Took.) Like Bilbo, Frodo preserves his youth, so much so that at fifty he is considered "queer" by the Shire inhabitants.

This tension between the "normal" and the "queer" Hobbit will blossom in later chapters and books into the ethical drama of *LotR*. The question Tolkien addresses is this: How can individuals (and nations) so different from one another coexist in harmony? The danger is clear: the Brandybucks will be forever stigmatized by the Shire inhabitants because they choose to live beyond the river in un-Hobbitlike fashion. And what is to prevent a Dark Hobbit Lord from then using this Shire fear of difference to separate the Brandybucks from the Bagginses? To divide one family branch from another? To insist that all must be the same and live within the Shire? To act and to think and to dress like the Shire inhabitants?

Difference, for Tolkien, leads to recklessness (the unusually youthful Frodo stealing mushrooms and venturing into others' lands), adventure (Bilbo and Frodo going off on their respective journeys), and ultimately wisdom and understanding. Difference can also be social—the difference between a Baggins and a Gamgee, which is artificial and serves no valid purpose if used as a means to separate the two. The validity of lower-class occupations involving manual labor (for example, gardening, domestic service) is ultimately certified by Sam's heroism in literally carrying Frodo up Mount Doom, just as Gollum's moral deficiency is validated by his final contribution to civilization and cosmic good when he disobeys his "Master," Frodo, and steals the Ring. The servant—Sam or Gollum—ultimately contributes as much or more to Middle-earth than the Master Frodo. For Tolkien it is the generosity of the Master but also his obverse chief weaknesses—pride and avarice—that depend on and demand the unflagging support and dedicated valor of the humble servant, whose chief strength is his humility but whose chief weakness is his lack of self-assertion. Tolkien's point is that each serves the other; where the difference of one ends, the complementary difference of the other begins. The relationship is circular and yet based on both need and desire, necessity and obligation, the dance of Self and Other, until the music ends.

Despite seeming initially different, Gollum remains a much diminished Hobbit, descended from the wandering, matriarchal Stoor branch of the Gladden Fields rather than a typical Harfoot Hobbit from the Shire or Bree, or a fair adventuresome Fallohide from the upper Anduin or Eriador (the branch from which leaders often come, and the line from which the Tooks, Brandybucks, and Bolgars descended). In this sense Gollum represents an alter ego for Bilbo-Frodo (just as the Cain-and-Abel parable of Déagol-Sméagol emphasizes family murder and cousin hate). And so Gollum, like Frodo, regards the Ring as his "Birthday Present" because he has acquired it on that special day. For Frodo, Gollum is the Shire equivalent of a Brandybuck living across the river, so that the Ringbearer initially reacts to Gollum's strangeness, his "queerness," as Sandyman did to his—with suspicion and indignation. Therefore at first Frodo wishes Gollum had been killed long ago (1:92), not understanding the mercy or pity that stayed Bilbo's hand, that same merry or pity that will grow in him and eventually save him as he teeters precipitously on the lip of Mount Doom. Even more ironically it is Gollum's disobedience toward his "Master" Frodo at Mount Doom—only in a greater and providential sense to be construed as mercy or pity—that saves Frodo. And it is not that Gollum's (or Frodo's) hand is stayed—again ironically it is his finger that is bitten off, with the Ring still attached—that saves Frodo and also Middle-earth.

If we look more closely at the role of minor characters, the tension of difference between Self and Other, familiar and unlike, becomes more clear-cut. Tolkien's joy in creating characters is to reverse suspicious expectation in his "heroes" and in his readers. For example, it is not clear to Frodo whether Farmer Maggot is friend or foe (1:132), in that his name suggests a disgusting creature associated with the eggs of flies and decaying organic matter, death; the earth. And to adult Frodo, whose youthful memories recall the anger of Maggot and his dogs over the theft of mushrooms, Farmer Maggot looms as an adversary. Maggot, however, provides a different point of view for Frodo when he recalls Frodo as "reckless," one of the "worst young rascals" (1:136). The truth is that a protective Maggot has shielded the Hobbits from the inquiries of a hooded Black Rider and also that the recklessness of youthful Frodo foreshadows his present heroics and venture into Mordor. Nevertheless, Farmer Maggot remains a Hobbit whose advice to Frodo now reflects the typical suspiciousness of the Shire: "You should never have gone mixing yourself up with Hobbiton Folk, Mr. Frodo. Folk are *queer* up there" (1:136; my italics).

Furthermore, Frodo's fellow Hobbits Merry and Pippin and his servant Sam have "conspired" (Tolkien's word) behind Frodo's back to accompany him on his journey. This normally pejorative "conspiracy" occurs despite Frodo's protective attempts to keep the purpose of his mission (and the existence of the Ring) a secret from them. His misguided attempts to shield them from danger seriously underestimate their own "queerness" (for Brandybucks and Tooks live beyond the river next to the Old Forest) and thus their own potential for heroism and adventure (to say nothing of their common Hobbit desire to serve, epitomized in the gardener Sam Gamgee, the most modest, socially and personally, of them all). In *The Lord of the Rings* difference, fueled by the power of words, polarizes the forces of good and evil, social class, and political group.

MICHAEL N. STANTON

Mind, Spirit, and Dream in
The Lord of the Rings

This chapter attempts to deal with matters that run all through Tolkien's story, both on and below the surface, and which therefore cannot be assigned to a discussion of any specific episode in the narrative, or the development of any characters, or to the culture of Middle-earth itself. Yet these matters enrich and color and give tone and feeling to all else. The poems Tolkien wrote for his book, the spiritual perceptions of its characters (and, it may be diffidently stated, of its creator), and the vivid and useful dreams of those characters all provide texture and meaning to the world of Middle-earth.

POEMS AND SONGS

Tolkien said that the poems and songs in *The Lord of the Rings* were not there for their own sake, nor because of any intrinsic poetic merit, but for dramatic or narrative effect at the particular point of their appearance.[1] It would therefore seem that form and style should not matter much in the verse. Nonetheless, there is a wide variety of forms, types, and styles of poetry in the tale. Depending on how you count repetitions, reprises, and variants, there are between fifty and sixty examples of verse in *The Lord of the Rings*. They can be classified in several ways.

From *Hobbits, Elves, and Wizards: Exploring the Wonders and Worlds of J. R. R. Tolkien's* The Lord of the Rings, pp. 159–170. © 2001 by Michael N. Stanton.

27

The most frequent verse form is the rhymed couplet, appearing in a number of different meters, with twenty-two examples. There are six examples of tetrameter quatrains (three of them variants of "The Road goes ever on and on"), six examples of Old English prosody (discussed below), four of ballad stanza, and seventeen or so of various nonce-forms of stanza, rhythm, or rhyme scheme.

The important thing to remember about these poems is that most aspire to the condition of song. Most of these verses are not in fact poems per se but song lyrics. Of the fifty and more sets of words which one could call verses, thirty-one are expressly said to be sung; a couple are chanted; several are recited (as by Sam, in his schoolroom manner, hands behind his back); and one exists, so to speak, only in writing (Snowmane's epitaph, which the text gives us, but which is not spoken by anyone).[2]

As for authorship, as might be expected in a book as hobbitocentric as this one, nineteen poems are by Hobbits, varying from Gollum's riddle of the fish (II, 288; 269) to Bilbo's poem of Eärendil (I, 308–11; 282–5, at 124 lines almost twice as long as any other poem in the book), from bath songs to road songs, to Frodo's lament for Gandalf (I, 465–6; 424–5). Ten are Elvish in origin, some traditional ("A Elbereth Gilthoniel"), some composed by Galadriel, some by Legolas; two given in the original Elvish (in the Elvish language, Tolkien was indisputably the world's greatest poet). Six are from Ents, a couple from Tom Bombadil, one by Gimli, and one rather grisly piece is chanted by a Barrow-wight. The rest, including eight in the measure of Rohan (Old English verse) are contributed by Men, counting Gandalf in Man-form for this purpose. He speaks, if not originates, several (some of which he calls Rhymes of Lore); and Aragorn speaks, and apparently originates, several others.

Several modern poets, including writers like Richard Wilbur, have attempted to re-create or emulate Old English poetry, but none has been as successful as Tolkien in capturing both the prosody and the spirit of that verse. (Tolkien might indeed give praise to Seamus Heaney's new translation of *Beowulf*.) This poetry is characterized by a strong medial pause or caesura such that a line is in effect two half-lines, with four beats to a line, and heavy alliteration on each side of the pause:

Doom drove them on. Darkness took them,
horse and horseman; hoofbeats afar
sank into silence: so the songs tell us. (III, 92; 83)

Here the pause is marked by actual punctuation in all three lines. The alliterating elements are the "d's," the "h's," and the "s's," and the stresses or beats can be variously read. One possible pattern is:

DOOM drove them ON. DARKness TOOK them,
HORSE and HORSEman; HOOFbeats aFAR
SANK into SIlence: SO the songs TELL us.

Plainly this is poetry meant to be recited aloud from memory, whether on
a festal or a funereal occasion; it is poetry that is also record-keeping, a way
of preserving history and lore. And indeed the Anglo-Saxon or Old English
poetic tradition was an oral one, with bards, or *scops* (pronounced "shops")
reciting in a meadhall like Meduseld or Heorot, probably for generations
before a line of poetry was ever written down.

As conveyed by Tolkien, Old English is a poetry of somber celebration
with a strongly fatalistic cast. It celebrates the deeds of Men (literally—it
is the poetry of a warrior society), whether of martial ardor and impetus
toward victory ("Arise, arise . . . ," see III, 137; 123), or of loss ("Mourn
not . . . ," see III, 145; 130). Unlike Hobbit verse it is never light; unlike
Elvish poetry it is often grim.

Excepting the unique properties of Old English verse, belonging mostly
to Rohan, there seems to be little correlation between the origins of a poem
and its form. That is, for instance, Elves as well as Hobbits can compose in
ballad stanza, as a comparison of Bilbo's "I sit beside the fire . . ." (I, 364–5;
333–4) with Legolas's "An Elvin-maid . . ." (I, 440–2; 401–3) shows.

Most of the poems are occasional—they are written to celebrate or
commemorate some specific occasion, whether it is a hot bath and its pleasures,
or the bittersweetness of leaving Lothlórien, or the fateful ride of Théoden and
the Rohirrim. They reflect or heighten the emotion of the occasion whatever
it may be. In the case of Rohan they also record the historical impact of
events. Other poems are occasional in a different way: they are helpful on
a particular occasion, as is old Ioreth's rhyme about the usefulness of *athelas*
for the Black Breath, lines which the herb-master of the Houses of Healing
wrongly dismisses as doggerel.

Still other poems verge on being riddles, or are highly cryptic, such as
the words spoken by the voice in the dream that Faramir and Boromir had:
"Seek for the Sword that was broken" (I, 323; 296), or the words of Malbeth
the Seer, which Elrond bid Aragorn remember at a particular moment; the
passage is about the Paths of the Dead and the need to take that route. After
Aragorn recites the lines, Gimli comments that the Paths themselves are no
darker than the meaning of Malbeth's words (see III, 64; 58–9).

And at least one poem serves as a kind of signal, when Sam is seeking
Frodo in the Tower of Cirith Ungol and sings "In western lands . . ." and
thinks he hears "a faint voice answering him" (III, 226; 204–5).

In *The Lord of the Rings*, as in many other works of literature, music
and poetry are the expressions of memory (looking back) and desire (looking

forward). They are, that is, expressions of spirit. Much less obvious but equally valid as an expression of spirit is religion. Tolkien's faith or belief, and how it is rendered in *The Lord of the Rings*, has been the subject of much discussion.[3]

TOLKIEN'S BELIEFS AND HIS BOOKS

There are no religious institutions in Middle-earth. With one possible exception there are no religious observances.[4] Yet, like his friend C. S. Lewis, Tolkien was a deeply religious man. He was raised in the Roman Catholic faith (his guardian for a time after his mother's death was a priest, Father Francis Morgan). He surely did not check his faith and belief at the door when he sat down to write. We must, however, look beneath the surface of the story to find its religious coloration, and to see if that coloration is specifically Christian.

At the root of Tolkien's conception of literary art is the belief that imagination is the gift of God. As God is Creator, Humankind is sub-creator, or secondary creator of imagined worlds. As Tolkien says in "On Fairy-stories," we have the power to "make . . . because we are made . . . in the image . . . of a Maker."[5]

Such theology as *The Lord of the Rings* embodies is conventional or traditional enough, at least as it concerns the nature of evil. Evil is a falling away from good, a negation of good, an absence, rather than a positive and original force in itself. "'For nothing is evil in the beginning,'" Elrond tells his council (I, 351; 321). Because evil is a negativity, it cannot create. It can only mock living forms, as Treebeard tells Merry and Pippin: trolls and Orcs mock or parody Ents and Elves, respectively (see II, 113; 105), and Frodo affirms that view of the Dark Lord's limitation much later in Mordor. Whether crude imitation or mockery, the products of that uncreating word, such as Orcs, demonstrate the profoundly anti-creative nature of evil.

Evil hates life. It especially hates free life, and its hatred takes minor forms like chopping down trees, and major forms like blighting whole regions so that they can no longer support life. The supreme evil in the Third Age of Middle-earth is Sauron, and we have seen how he swallows up other life, so that ancient kings are now wraiths, and the Mouth of Sauron has no name.

But for all his enormous ego and hunger, Sauron is essentially a negation. When Frodo sees the Eye in the Mirror of Galadriel, it is "a window into nothing" (I, 471; 430). Because it is so absorbed in self, evil cannot imagine the other (imagination is a gift from God after all): Gandalf has counted all along on Sauron's inability to consider that, having the Ring, the West would not use it; that the Free Peoples would actually seek to destroy it Sauron cannot even begin to conceive (see II, 127; 119).

This is all traditional enough; Sauron in these qualities has considerable resemblance to Milton's portrayal of Satan in the early books of *Paradise Lost*. At the same time, Tolkien takes care to eschew traditional Christian symbolism, especially figurations of Christ. If Christ is thought of as world-redeemer, his analogue might be Frodo, and Tolkien is careful to emphasize that Frodo failed. If Christ is thought of as resurrected deity, his analogue might be Gandalf, and Tolkien is careful to point out how impious the comparison would be.[6]

My own estimate, after some thinking, is that the book's essential religious nature and even its specifically Christian cast lie not in theology nor in symbolism but in emotion. And the emotions in which these matters are embodied are hope and despair.

Despair is briefly dealt with, especially since Gandalf forbade it. To despair is to commit an enormous act of pride or hubris, for it means seeing the end beyond all doubt, that is, being omniscient. To be disheartened and discouraged is a rather frequent state in the story, but only twice, I think, do we see actual despair; both instances are, as might be expected, rather late in the tale. Sam at the Black Gate of Mordor is in despair; Denethor during the Siege of Gondor likewise despairs (the two events, on opposite sides of the great River, occur as crisis deepens in each theatre of action and are only a few days apart). Sam despairs because of insufficient understanding, Denethor because he thinks he understands all too well.

Sam gives up hope: at the closed gate of Morannon, at what Sam perceives as "the bitter end" (II, 310; 289); when what seems to be the only way into Mordor is barred against him and Frodo, despair covers Sam like a shroud.

Denethor, arguing about the disposition of the Ring, says he would not have put it "'at a hazard beyond all but a fool's hope'" (III, 105; 95), courting utter disaster. (Denethor thinks ruin is imminent because he thinks the Seeing Stone has been telling him the entire truth. It has in fact been showing him only enough to make him think the West is losing.) In the Houses of the Dead Denethor cries to Gandalf, "'Pride and despair! . . . The West has failed'" (III, 157; 142).

And what happens in either case? Sam and Frodo go on; Sam even sees an oliphaunt (to his everlasting delight and terror), they meet Faramir, and they receive help and rest and counsel. Gondor is saved despite Denethor: Rohan comes, and the fleet of black sails his *palantír* has shown him is a squadron of friends, not enemies. Aragorn has come to relieve the siege.

As to hope, it does not inspire the actions east of the River Anduin. Frodo must struggle onward whether or not he feels hopeful about his eventual goal. But westward, in the manifold actions leading to the War of the Rings, where the forces of the Free Peoples must contend with the mighty forces of Sauron, hope can ebb and flow. In the early chapters of Books III and V hope seems to be a keyword, a theme, a recurrent notion, positively or negatively.

- Éomer says little hope remains of finding the hobbits when Aragorn explains his mission early in Book III.
- Gandalf returns and speaks hopefully about the future conduct of the campaign; but he cautions that hope is not certainty.
- When Théoden awakens and resumes his kingly mien, men feel hope for Rohan.
- Our hope is in the east, Gandalf tells the king.
- At Helm's Deep, Aragorn calls for stout defense of the citadel throughout the night: "'day will bring hope,'" he says (II, 180; 167).

Then, as war deepens at the opening of Book V:

- Beregond the guard questions if Gondor can withstand Sauron's attack. Yet even if we fall, he tells Pippin, "'Hope and memory shall live still'" (III, 43–4; 40–1).
- Arwen sends a message to Aragorn: "'Either our hope cometh, or all hope's end'" (III, 56; 52).

A concordance could list many more examples, but the point is sufficiently made: this is normal, rational hope, the kind of hope that good Men and Hobbits have; the kind that springs eternal in the human breast.

But the emotion ranges far above and beyond this level:

- Aragorn exclaims that Gandalf has returned "'beyond hope'" (II, *125*; 116).
- When reinforcements (Théoden and Éomer and their troops) appear at Helm's Deep the guard calls it good news and repeats the very words (II, 172; 159).
- When later at Helm's Deep the Huorns obliterate the Orc army, Gandalf takes no credit; it was not his plan, he says, but it worked "'better even than my hope . . .'" (II, 189; 175).

In this question of hope and despair, certainly it is Christian—but not exclusively so—to put oneself lower than one's Creator, and not, by despairing, to set oneself equal to Him. But the idea of something happening "beyond hope," or something coming to pass which was only a "fool's hope" (as Denethor characterizes Gandalf's strategy) seems specifically Christian.

One can say—without prejudice—that the very nature of Christianity is exactly a "fool's hope." The redemption at the center of Christian belief is totally "beyond hope," beyond any rational expectation or probability. It is rationally absurd to suppose that God would become mortal, die, and rise from the dead for us; as Tertulian is said to have remarked, "I believe it *because* it is impossible."

What the Christian is called upon to believe is so far beyond the merely rational as to strain the faith, hope, credulity of any but a fool, just as anyone's belief that Frodo's errand will succeed and destroy Evil is beyond any probability. Robert M. Adams supposes he is offering an adverse criticism when he remarks that Frodo's action of carrying the Ring in the heart of Enemy country does not "really make much practical sense,"[7] but Frodo's action is well out of the reach of practical sense.

Yet Frodo's errand does succeed, so what happens then to rationality, and probability, and practical sense? They are superseded, just as the central miracle of Christianity supersedes historical probability in both the incarnation and the resurrection of Jesus Christ. The saving of Middle-earth is certainly not to be compared in significance to the saving of this world or of the individual soul. There may, however, be applicability (as Tolkien might say). Hope, even a fool's hope, may be justified.

The Land of Dreams

If in *The Lord of the Rings* poems can serve as a form of dramatic punctuation, and Frodo's journey can be a spiritual progress of a particular kind, then dreams can be symbols, images, and types of many kinds of emotions. Being unbounded by space, time, or probability, dreams can be very useful literary items, perhaps especially for writers of fantasy. There we can see dreams used as framing devices, as Alice dreams her adventures in *Alice in Wonderland*; or as plot devices, as Jane Studdock's veridical dreams initiate the action in C. S. Lewis's *That Hideous Strength*, or as purely symbolic devices, as Arren dreams in Ursula Le Guin's *The Farthest Shore* of a ruined cobweb-laden hall which stands for the death of magery in Earthsea. Dreams can foreshadow, prophesy, echo, suggest, or even reveal. Given their evident literary value, and given the space available to him, Tolkien uses dreams with considerable restraint in *The Lord of the Rings*. There are eight fully or partially described dreams in the tale, and all except two of them were dreamed by a hobbit.

One of the exceptional dreams seems to be more a sending than a dream, and it came to Faramir often and to his brother Boromir once. In it the *eastern* sky grows dark, and a voice comes out of the still-lighted *West*, saying: "Seek for the Sword that was broken . . ." (see I, 323; 296 for the full stanza).

That the voice came from the West seems again to suggest the intervention, or at least the prompting, of the Valar. The various elements of the rhyme are explicated at the Council of Elrond. It is significant, perhaps, in the relationship of Faramir and Boromir that although Faramir was eager to seek Imladris, the place of the sword, Boromir prevailed with their father and came instead.

Among all the dreamers in the tale, Faramir perhaps occupies the oddest position. Not only does he often have the riddle-dream just mentioned, he also (as Tolkien's persona in part) dreams an Atlantean dream of Tolkien's own. Tolkien describes how from his earliest years he has had "a terrible recurring dream ... of the Great Wave, towering up, and coming in ineluctably over the trees and green fields."[8] Not only did his son Michael inherit this dream (though for years neither father nor son knew the other had had it), but Tolkien also gave it to Faramir.

Faramir describes the dream to Éowyn as they stand on the ramparts of the Houses of Healing looking northward. It is the very moment of Sauron's destruction; the air is unnaturally still, and they see a vast mountain of darkness rising. Faramir says that his recurring dream reminds him of Númenor, "'... of the great dark wave climbing over green lands ... and coming on, darkness inescapable'" (III, 297; 268).

And yet, as Faramir knows and acknowledges, the dream is not evil: the dream is of the end of evil, whether seen as a picture of the destruction of corrupted Númenor, or as a picture of the fall of Sauron and his realm— ends of two evils that were worse for once having been good, and that were indissolubly linked: the end of the entity, Sauron, whose baleful influence had caused the end of the great kingdom, Númenor.

These dreams aside, all the others are dreamed by hobbits. They fall roughly into three groups: quasi-dreams, real dreams without detail, and real dreams with fairly complete circumstantiality, which serve various narrative purposes.

By quasi-dreams I mean mental phenomena that occur in the borderland between sleep and waking. On the way to the Ford of Bruinen, the wounded Frodo is "half in a dream" and imagining dark wings (I, 273; 250). In the Mines of Moria, Frodo thinks he's dreaming when he sees tiny lights (see I, 414; 379). He is in fact awake, though drowsy, and is seeing Gollum's eyes in the dark. Similarly, Frodo is half-asleep on March 13 of the year after the Quest; he is ill and he is muttering about emptiness and the loss of "It" (III, 376; 339). This small detail shows how profoundly the Ring and its loss have affected Frodo, although he usually has strength enough to put the loss aside.

Real dreams without detail include (among others) Frodo's therapeutic dream as he and Sam approach the Black Gate: no recollection of it stayed with him, but it made him feel happier (see II, 305–6; 285). And as they near Mount Doom Frodo predictably has "dreams of fire" (III, 244; 220).

Of the six real hobbit dreams described in greater or less detail, three belong to Frodo, and one each to Merry, Pippin, and Sam. Merry's dream,

Pippin's dream, and two of Frodo's dreams take place in the house of Tom Bombadil.

The night before the hobbits are to set out for the Old Forest, Frodo dreams of a white tower that he longs to climb in order to look at the Sea; he is awakened before he can do so (I, 154; 142). This is presumably one of the Towers where Frodo and those riding with him as he leaves Middle-earth can look out to Sea as they proceed to Mithlond and the Grey Havens (III, 383; 346). It is the place among the Tower Hills, Gandalf told Pippin, where one of the Seeing Stones was located: near "'Mithlond ... where the grey ships lie'" (II, 259; 240). If this is indeed the same place, the dream is the first in a pattern which hints at Frodo's ultimate fate.

The only other dream with any detail which takes place outside Tom Bombadil's realm is one Sam has as he, Frodo, and Gollum approach the Cross-roads in Ithilien. Sam dreams he is searching around in the garden back at Bag End; but the garden is all overgrown and unkempt, a weary task ahead for Sam. "Presently he remembered what he was looking for. 'My pipe!' he said, and ... woke up" (II, 391; 363–4). Given the hobbits' situation, this seems a commonplace, but appropriate, anxiety dream. Sam has already seen in the Mirror of Galadriel that destruction is going on in the Shire, which someone will have to set to rights; and he is very tired; their journey has already been arduous although the worst remains ahead. It is a very probable sort of dream to be having at this point.

We are left then with the dreams in Tom Bombadil's house. Understandably, Pippin dreams of being shut up in Old Man Willow again, whereas Merry dreams of water, water "rising slowly but surely"; he imagines drowning (I, 178; 164). This may be a precognitive dream, referring to the future occasion when the Ents flood Isengard. When that happened, Merry later tells his friends that "'the water was rising rapidly'" but he and Pippin found a safely elevated spot and watched the water pour in (II, 225; 208).

If Merry's dream is precognitive, there may be something even more peculiar than first appears about Tom Bombadil's little land. It is a place, as we have seen, where the Ring's power is strangely limited or skewed: neither Tom nor Frodo disappears from the other's sight when wearing the Ring.

And Tom has some kind of power over time: he takes the entranced hobbits in narrative back "into times when the world was wider ..." (I, 182; 168). Tom's language (and it is a matter of language) has power over time in that way, being able to take the hobbits back to when the West was not inaccessible to ordinary beings, and in another way, for when he was done, Frodo and his friends could not tell whether hours or perhaps days had passed, so great was the charm of his words.

In a realm like this, it is no wonder that one night Frodo can dream of the past, seeing Gandalf on the Tower of Orthanc, which the wizard had left a week earlier (see Chapter 4), *and* the next night he can dream of a song like a light behind a curtain, and the curtain rolling back, at which "a far green country opened before him under a swift sunrise" (I, 187; 172). Tom's strange little land seems to be a place where time is highly pliable, or where, in dreams at least, one can look through windows opening on either past or future.

A land of dream indeed: the dream of the green country is, in terms of Frodo's life, a dream of the far future, when Frodo arrives in Elvenhome or Eressëa, and "as in his dream in the house of Bombadil ... he beheld a far green country under a swift sunrise" (III, 384; 347). But also, because Elvenhome was removed from the Circle of the World at the end of the Second Age, this is a dream beyond the time of this world, and—even this early in Frodo's Quest—a dream foretelling reward after the suffering of life within Middle-earth.

Notes

1. He is quoted as saying that "a lot of the criticism of the verses shows a complete failure to understand the fact that they are all dramatic verses; they were conceived as the kind of things people would say under the circumstances." See Daniel Grotta-Kurska, *J. R. R. Tolkien: Architect of Middle-earth* (Philadelphia: Running Press, 1976), pp. 117–8.

2. An association item of some interest is the Caedmon recording of several Tolkien poems as set to music by the British comedian/composer Donald Swann. They are sung by the wonderfully named British tenor William Elven; the disc includes Tolkien himself reciting "A Elbereth Gilthoniel" and a setting of Galadriel's Farewell suggested by Tolkien.

3. Religion and myth have received a great deal of attention from readers and critics of Tolkien; I do not therefore apologize for the scant treatment here. People more capable of belief than I am have written learnedly, indeed movingly, about Tolkien's spirituality. See, for instance, Verlyn Flieger's *A Question of Time* and Joseph Pearce's *Tolkien: Man and Myth*, both listed in the Bibliography. William Dowie's essay in the Salu and Farrell collection, and Chapter 3 of Lobdell's *England and Always* are also helpful, as are Tolkien's own letters, especially to Father Robert Murray.

4. The exception: Faramir and his men face west "in a moment of silence" before their meal in Henneth Annûn. They are in effect saying grace, as noted in Chapter 2.

5. *The Tolkien Reader*, p. 55.

6. For these considerations of Frodo and Gandalf, see *Letters*, p. 326 and 237 respectively.

7. Robert M. Adams, "The Hobbit Habit," *The New York Review of Books*, November 24, 1977; rpt. in Neil Isaacs and Rose Zimbardo, eds., *Tolkien: New Critical Perspectives* (Lexington, KY: The University Press of Kentucky, 1981), pp. 168–79.

8. *Letters*, p. 213 and note.

MARK T. HOOKER

Frodo's Batman

But be not afraid of greatness. Some men are born great, some achieve greatness, and some have greatness thrust upon them.
—William Shakespeare, *Twelfth Night*

While *The Lord of the Rings* was not published until the early 1950s, it is nevertheless to some extent a product not of World War II but of the six months during which Tolkien fought with the 11th Lancashire Fusiliers during World War I, before trench fever took him back to England. Tolkien wrote that Sam was "a reflection of the English soldier, of the privates and batmen I knew in the 1914 war, and recognized as so far superior to myself" (Carpenter 91).

For the modern reader, the most likely association with the word *batman* is Batman and Robin of film and comic book fame. Tolkien, however, had another image in mind. Before World War II, when officers were indeed gentlemen, in the British sense of the word, having a soldier-servant was the accepted order of the day. The word *batman* comes not from cricket bats, as some have suggested, but from the French word *bât*, which means *pack saddle*. A batman was, therefore, the man who took care of the luggage carried on the pack-horse or pack-mule. In time, the word also came to mean an officer's valet, who, among other things, also took care of his officer's baggage.

From *Tolkien Studies*, vol. 1, edited by Douglas A. Anderson, Michael D.C. Drout, and Verlyn Flieger, pp. 125–136. © 2004 by West Virginia University Press.

The literature of World War I recounts a number of examples of the loyalty and devotion of batmen to the officers they cared for. An examination of these stories, which were written by British line officers who, like Tolkien, saw combat in World War I, offers an insight into the kind of batmen with whom lieutenant Tolkien came into contact in the 1914 war. We have no evidence that Tolkien read these stories himself, but the characteristics of the batmen described in them are much the same as the characteristics that Tolkien ascribes to Sam. "He [Sam] did not think of himself as heroic or even brave, or in any way admirable—except in his service and loyalty to his master," wrote Tolkien in a letter to a reader (*Letters* 329).

William Noel Hodgson (1893–1916) wrote under the pseudonym "Edward Melbourne." A lieutenant with the Devonshire Regiment, he died in the first day of the Battle of the Somme. He was a Georgian poet in the style of Rupert Brooke, and he also wrote stories and essays about the war. His short story "Pearson"[1] is a tale about his resourceful batman named Pearson (77–81). Lieutenant Colonel Graham Seton Hutchison (1890–1946)—the author of numerous books on World War I—wrote a biography of his batman, Peter McLintock (*Biography of a Batman* 211–22).

The relationship between Hodgson and his batman is the kind that P.G. Wodehouse (1881–1975) parodied in his Jeeves and Wooster stories. Shortly after Jeeves had been engaged, Bertie Wooster tries to establish who is in charge in their relationship by saying that he is not one of those men who becomes an absolute slave to his valet. Jeeves' irreproachably polite reply, however, leaves no doubt as to the absurdity of Bertie's statement ("Jeeves Takes Charge" 8). Hodgson's story, being much more compact, gets straight to the point. Hodgson has learned that it is best to "acquiesce in all that Pearson does":

> He is my servant, and if he were Commander-in-Chief, the war would be over in a week. But I should get no baths, so I am glad he isn't. And I doubt whether he would care to be, himself; at present he is supreme in his own sphere, and knows it and knows that the other servants know it. The only thing that he does not know is his own limitations—nobody else does either—they have never been reached.... A good soldier servant is one of the greatest marvels of our modern civilization. To posses one is better and cheaper than living next door to Harrods. Do you want a chair for the [Officers'] Mess? You have only to mention it to Pearson. Are you starving in a deserted village? Pearson will find you wine, bread and eggs. Are you sick of a fever? Pearson will heal you. From saving your life to sewing on your buttons, he is infallible. (77)

To prove his point about Pearson's ingenuity, Hodgson offers the reader some concrete examples. Having relocated his unit into some filthy trenches, Hodgson soon discovers that he is infested with lice. Pearson's unhesitating reaction to this news is that the lieutenant requires a bath and a change of clothes. He will see to it. Hodgson, bowing to what he perceives as the reality of trench warfare, dismisses Pearson's reply with a joke. If Pearson would be so kind as to call him a cab, he could drop in on his tailors on the way to the Jermyn Street Baths. The reality of trench warfare, however, proved to be what Pearson made of it. A short while later, Pearson called Hodgson back to his dug-out, where a hot bath and change of clothes awaited. To those who have never experienced the privations of combat, Hodgson's description of this exploit as "epic" may seem overblown. It is not. In combat, where clean, dry socks seem worth their weight in gold, a warm bath and a complete change of clothes would ransom a host of kings.

Hodgson's mention of Pearson finding a chair for the Officers' Mess is echoed in the other story he tells about Pearson. The empty house that they had taken over to use as the Officers' Mess had a cold stone floor. In response to a comment by the President of the Mess, Hodgson offhandedly volunteers Pearson to get them a carpet to make the Mess more comfortable. This time it is the President of the Mess who represents the accepted perception of the reality of life in a combat zone in World War I. He doubts that it is possible; after all, "the boy is not a conjurer." Hodgson's belief in Pearson's "genius" prompted him to bet the President of the Mess five francs that Pearson could produce a carpet for the Mess by tea time the next day. The most likely source of carpets in the area was a nearby town that was under daily enemy artillery fire. Pearson asked Hodgson for permission to go to the town to look for a carpet, but Hodgson refused because of the danger. The next day, just before the deadline for the bet, Pearson appeared in the Mess, covered in sweat, carrying a carpet and two rolls of linoleum. He had gone to the town anyway, because Hodgson had not expressly forbidden him to go. "I could not let you lose a bet, sir, for the sake of a little trouble," said Pearson.

As if in anticipation of the incredulous, modern, peacetime reader, Hodgson closes his paean to Pearson with the comment that "there are many like him, I am sure, though I prefer to think of him as supreme. But when next a soldier friend boasts of his servant—as they always do—sooner or later, remember that he is not always such a liar as he appears." Tolkien's readers would do well to remember Hodgson's caution, when they consider Sam's role in Tolkien's works. Tolkien is—as Hodgson put it—"boasting" about the batmen of his acquaintance, all rolled into one fictional character. "You're a marvel," says Frodo to Sam in the Tower of Cirith Ungol, echoing Hodgson's comment about Pearson, when Sam produces the Ring that Frodo had imagined lost (*RK*, VI, i, 188).

Hutchison's batman was named Peter McLintock. He was, said Hutchison, "the best, most intimate friend man ever had" (211). He was "a faithful servant, a friend and counselor, an ever-present companion to give me confidence in the darkness of a dangerous night, and good cheer, when fortune favored a visit to battalion headquarters" (215).

> [Peter's] friendliness took complete possession of the necessary, though often inconvenient, affairs of life. In such things Peter's service was priceless. No matter at what hour I would return to the cubby hole for sleep, it was as dry and as warm as human ingenuity could devise. Eggs and small comforts he conjured from behind the lines without any promptings from me. . . . He would . . . prepare a varied menu from interminable bread, plum-and-apple jam, and the sickly meat and vegetable ration. He would clean my limited wardrobe, wash and mend the socks and shirts, keep me supplied with tobacco, dry my boots and stockings. The batman was *Multum in parvo* to his charge, omnipresent, yet ubiquitous. . . . And he would run when his officer went over the top, and fight by his side. When the officer dropped, the batman was beside him." (219–20)

> Peter's friendship expressed itself in "little acts of vigilant kindness. Opportunities for the rendering of trifling services and for the doing of kindness were for ever present, every hour and every day. The batman's attitude was one of selfsubordination, and he tarried neither to consider the worthiness of his charge nor the nature of the service asked. He gave freely, the man of humble origin and pursuit, to one at least temporarily exalted with authority. By his ready service, words and gestures he won affection, by his forethought and unknown sacrifices he penetrated quietly and unobtrusively into the heart of the master of his goings and of his comings." (221–22).

These two short stories by Hodgson and Hutchison taken together provide a list of traits that any good batman should have. Sam has a great many of them. He does not have the trait of healing, which Tolkien gives to others of more stately bearing, like Elrond and Aragorn. He also has no opportunity to dry Frodo's boots and stockings, since Hobbits do not wear shoes.

Tolkien clearly establishes the relationship between Sam and Frodo as "master" and "servant" by spreading those two descriptors throughout the text. As Frodo prepares to leave the Shire, the excuse given for Sam going with him is that Sam was going "to do for Mr. Frodo" (*FR*, I, iii, 78), which is another way of saying that he is going to be Frodo's valet or butler. At the feast in Rivendell, Sam begs to be allowed "to wait on his master" (*FR*, II, i, 240). Tolkien accentuates this by peppering Sam's speech with plenty of "Mr. Frodo, sir," echoing the customary form of address of a valet to his master and a soldier to an officer. Tolkien also drops a number of hints as to Sam's duties at Bag End as the story progresses. As Frodo awakens in the Tower of Cirith Ungol, for example, Sam tries "to sound as cheerful as he had when he drew back the curtains at Bag End on a summer's morning" (*RK*, VI, i, 187). This phrase evokes an image almost straight out of Jeeves and Wooster. Tolkien makes Sam sound almost like Jeeves, when Sam replies with an unperturbed "Very good, sir!" to Frodo's announcement that he is leaving the Shire for good and that neither of them may ever come back (*FR*, I, iv, 96).

Hodgson's comment about having to give up hot baths were Pearson to become Commander-in-Chief and his story about the clean clothes and the hot bath find a brief reflection in Tolkien's tale in Pippin's off-hand comment upon awakening in the fir-wood after their first night out of the Shire. Pippin commands Sam to have his breakfast ready at nine thirty, and inquires if his bath water is hot yet (*FR*, I, iii, 81). Both requests would be logical, if made of a batman or valet, and Sam takes no offense at them, reflecting Hutchison's description of Peter McLintock's attitude of selfsubordination, which Hutchison said kept him from considering the nature of the service asked or the worthiness of his charge.

While Sam clearly has an attitude of selfsubordination, he, unlike Hutchison's Peter McLintock, does have a considered opinion as to the worthiness of his charge. Sam had always felt that Frodo was so kind that he was in some ways blind to what went on around him. At the same time he held fast to the contradictory opinion, that Frodo "was the wisest person in the world" (with the possible exception of Bilbo and Gandalf) (*TT*, IV, iii, 248). In fact, Sam loved Mr. Frodo (*TT*, IV, iv, 260; *RK*, VI, i, 177). This is a very different picture of the relationship between an officer and his batman than the ones presented in Hodgson's and Hutchison's short stories. Perhaps Pearson and McLintock both loved their charges, too, but their charges were simply not aware of the fact, just as Hutchison was not aware of all the sacrifices that McLintock made for him.

One of Hutchison's "unknown sacrifices" can be found echoed in the chapter "Mount Doom," in which Frodo and Sam are struggling through Mordor toward their final goal, almost out of water to drink. Sam lets Frodo drink from their meager supply of water, but does not drink any himself (*RK*, VI, iii, 213, 216). Frodo is almost unaware of everything at this point (*RK*, VI, iii, 215), but the narrator lets the reader in on Sam's secret. Earlier in the tale, as they are just leaving the Shire, Tolkien has Frodo complain in jest that they have saddled him with all the heaviest things in his pack. Sam stoutly volunteers to take on some of Frodo's burden, saying that his pack is quite light, which the narrator pointedly informs the reader is a not true. At this stage of their journey, Frodo is still alert enough to recognize that Sam is making a sacrifice for him, and makes a resolution to look into it at their next packing (*FR*, I, iii, 80).

Forethought was one of Hutchison's characteristics for Peter McLintock. Sam shows himself worthy of this appellation in the scene in which he is checking the contents of his pack, one that Aragorn notes was "rather large and heavy" (*TT*, III, i, 21). It held Sam's "chief treasure," his cooking utensils, a box of salt, a supply of tobacco, flint and tinder for starting fires, woolen hose, linen, and a number of small things that Frodo had forgotten, that Sam planned to produce in triumph when Frodo asked for them on the trail (*FR*, II, iii, 293). One of these items finds a special resonance in Hutchison's comment about how McLintock kept him supplied with tobacco, as well as in Tolkien's tale, where a whole segment of the "Prologue" is devoted to "pipe-weed" (*FR*, Prol., 17–18). Most importantly for the story, Sam's pack also held a length of Elvish rope, which they would need later in the mountains (*TT*, IV, i, 214–17). At the Breaking of the Fellowship, Sam is the one who "grabbed a spare blanket and some extra packages of food" before they left (*FR*, II, x, 423). All these things point to Sam's forethought.

McLintock's "little acts of vigilant kindness," as Hutchison termed them, can be seen in Sam's actions too. In the morning, after the Hobbits' first encounter with the elves on their way to Rivendell, for example, Frodo awakes to find Pippin already up. Pippin prods him to get up and have some of the food that the elves left them. The bread was as delicious as it was the night before and Pippin would have eaten it all, if Sam had not insisted that he leave some for Frodo (*FR*, I, iv, 95).

Both Hodgson and Hutchison comment on their batman's skill at supplementing their rations. In "Of Herbs and Stewed Rabbit," Sam exhibits the same sort of initiative as was exhibited by the two real-life batmen, by "conjuring up"—as Hutchison put it—some rabbits for Frodo to eat. That Gollum was actually the one who caught the rabbits is unimportant. It was Sam who sent him out to hunt them (*TT*, IV, iv, 260). The same was probably true of Pearson and McLintock. To the batman's charge, it was not important who took the eggs out from under the chicken, but rather who arranged for them to appear unexpectedly on his plate at breakfast.

Hodgson's image of Pearson coming up with "wine, bread and eggs" when he was "starving in a deserted village" finds its reflection in Tolkien's chapter on the Tower of Cirith Ungol. The tower could hardly have been more deserted. It was strewn with the bodies of the Orcs that had killed one another (*RK*, VI, i, 179). Tolkien plays on the emptiness, repeating it for effect. "[I]t was empty, save for two or three more bodies sprawling on the floor.... The dead bodies, the emptiness," intones the narrator. "'I do believe that there's nobody left alive in the place! ... I've met nothing alive, and I've seen nothing,' said Sam" (*RK*, VI, i, 181, 189). The plot line remains the same in Tolkien's version of the tale, but there is a slight adjustment to the details. It is not that Sam found them some food. His find was some clothing for Frodo. It was Frodo himself who found the food among some rags on the floor (*RK*, VI, i, 190). Sam's success in his scavenger hunt for clothes is no less a triumph of "conjuring," as both Hodgson and Hutchison put it, even though he was not the one to find the food.

Hodgson's comment about the range of Pearson's services is likewise echoed in Tolkien's tale. Hodgson pairs saving his life with sewing on his buttons to show the incredibly wide gamut of services that Pearson provided for him. In Tolkien's tale, the explicit comparison is missing, but the attentive reader can easily construct a similar one from the events of the tale. Saving Frodo's life comes most vividly to mind in "The Choices of Master Samwise," in which Sam defends Frodo from Shelob. Sam, in fact, stood ready on numerous occasions to defend Frodo. For example, as the company flees the Black Riders on their way to Buckland, the narrator says that the Black Riders would have to ride over Sam to get to the wagon where Frodo was hidden (*FR*, I, iv, 106). Pippin says, "'Sam is an excellent fellow and would jump down a dragon's throat to save you'" (*FR*, I, v, 114). These efforts at saving Frodo's life can easily be paired with the simple task of having Sam run down to his home to drop off the key to Bag End as they departed (*FR*, I, iii, 79). Sewing on a button or dropping off a key are inconsequential services when compared to saving one's life, but they are part and parcel of the job of a batman.

Tolkien also manages to work in a jest in much the same vein as Hodgson's throw-away line about calling him a cab so that he could drop in on his tailors on the way to the Jermyn Street Baths. In the Tower of Cirith Ungol, after Sam frees Frodo from the Orcs, and they prepare to flee the tower, Frodo, with a wry smile, poses the equally nonsensical question of whether Sam has made inquiries about inns along the way (*RK*, VI, i, 190). In the context of *LotR*, Hutchison's description of the confidence that McLintock's companionship gave him in the darkness of a dangerous night finds a special resonance in Tolkien's tale of a journey into a land of unabated darkness. Hutchison's terse description pales, of course, in comparison to the detail of Tolkien's, but the two, nevertheless, describe the same bond to be found between an officer and his batman in combat.

Understanding this relationship is one of the key difficulties for the modern, peacetime reader. An officer and his batman were from different social classes. While Frodo represents the English officer and gentleman, born to greatness, as it were, Sam—like Pearson and McLintock—was not born to greatness, but had greatness thrust upon him. The change in the relationship between Sam and Frodo as the quest progresses reflects a change in the English class structure that was brought about by World War I. The literate divide, for example, was only one of a number of very real class factors that were a part of Tolkien's time. The need for reading and writing was not at all a universally accepted idea among Hobbits. Bilbo had taught Sam to read and write, but Sam's father was not so sure that it was a good idea (*FR*, I, i, 32).

In his short story "Half and Half," Hodgson explains how the factor of class difference was made less distinct by the war. This is the story of a sergeant from the Highlands, whom Hodgson deftly characterizes by replicating the sergeant's accent, a technique that Tolkien also used, though sparingly. In Tolkien's tale, Sam's father, the Gaffer, and a stranger from Michel Delving both say "jools" instead of "jewels," the crowning touch to a dialogue full of turns of phrase that mark them as men of limited education. Sam's dialogue is peppered with a number of less obvious turns of phrase that clearly mark him as a member of that class as well. Hodgson's story begins with the sergeant asking: "Wull Ah tell ye the tale of Micheal Starr thet wes in oor regiment?" (103). This opening line characterizes the sergeant much more deftly and economically than a long, detailed narration. He was a "man of humble origin and pursuit," as Hutchison termed McLintock.

Having established who the sergeant was, Hodgson turns quickly to the relationship between himself—an officer and a gentleman—and the sergeant. "It was curious," said Hodgson, "how intimate we had become, he and I, although at the time neither of us was aware of the incongruity." The incongruity that Hodgson finds "curious" was that in peacetime, neither the sergeant, nor Hodgson would have had a relationship that allowed them to swap stories in the fashion described in Hodgson's short story. This is the same incongruity that troubles the modern peacetime reader. In the next sentence, Hodgson explains how this change in their relationship had come about. "There are, I suppose, times when an unconscious strain tunes all our natures up to a single note, and though he was as fully armed with the carelessness of experience as I was with the recklessness of ignorance, we must both of us have been at high tension, for as I realized two days later I had had neither bite nor sup for thirty hours and never knew I was hungry." Tolkien shows exactly the same fine edge of the strain of combat in "The Tower of Cirith Ungol," in which, having rescued Frodo, Sam is reminded of food and water by Frodo's wry question about the inns along the way. "I don't know when drop or morsel last passed my lips. I'd forgotten it, trying to find you," says Sam (*RK*, VI, i, 190).

Relationships like these, forged in the strain of combat, changed post-war English society profoundly. In Tolkien's version of this change, Sam becomes Frodo's heir, and goes on to become Mayor of the Shire, the most famous gardener in history, and keeper of the knowledge of the Red Book

(*RK*, VI, ix, 309). It is an interesting change, that has Sam wearing more than one hat, which is an aptly appropriate metaphor for English society, which indeed did, and to some extent still does, judge a man's social status by the hat that he wears. Sam moved up in social status, but kept to his roots. The change in the society of the Shire is also less widespread than in England after World War I. Sam was, after all, the only representative of his class to participate in the perilous adventure that reshaped class relationships. There were a great many more British private soldiers and batmen who went off to war and discovered that things could be different.

Sam's participation in the quest to destroy the Ring was a "punishment" for eavesdropping on Frodo and Gandalf, when they were planning Frodo's departure (*FR*, I, ii, 73). Gandalf does not say what kind of punishment Sam will receive. A reader with no foreknowledge of the tale could suppose that the punishment would be having to leave the Shire (uncommon for Hobbits), or that it would be exhausting, or uncomfortable, or even terrifying, but because Tolkien does not say what the punishment is, the reader—and Sam—are not immediately scared off by it. Sam's reaction to this "punishment" is one of enthusiasm. He is happy to go, because he will get to see "Elves and all! Hooray!" (*FR*, I, ii, 73). It is only later—much like the British soldiers who went off to World War I full of enthusiasm—that Sam will find out how terrifying his quest is. "And we shouldn't be here at all, if we'd known more about it before we started," says Sam to Frodo (*TT*, IV, viii, 320).

Tolkien repeats the plot line of Sam listening at the window later in the episode at the Council of Elrond, but with a slight difference. Sam has taken up his new job of batman, helping and serving Frodo. Elrond's pronouncement upon discovering Sam, therefore, is not a punishment, as was Gandalf's, but an evaluation of his performance in his new role as Frodo's batman (*FR*, II, ii, 284). From this point on Sam is Frodo's "ever-present companion," to use Hutchison's description of his batman, Peter McLintock.

As Frodo and Sam discuss leaving Lórien to get on with their quest, Tolkien shows Sam in the role of counselor, another of Hutchison's descriptions of Peter:

> "You're right," said Sam. . . . I don't want to leave. All the same, I'm beginning to feel that if we've got to go on, then we'd best get it over.
> "*It's the job that's never started as takes longest to finish*, as my old gaffer used to say. And I don't reckon that these folk can do much more to help us, magic or no." (*FR*, II, vii, 376)

Job is a key word in the story, and Tolkien repeats it again and again to help define Sam's character and explain his motivation. The word *job* presents a problem for some modern—especially American—readers who think first of *mac-jobs* and unskilled labor, and only later, if at all, think of the other meanings of the word *job* that were more common in the time that Tolkien was writing *The Lord of the Rings. The Merriam-Webster Dictionary* defines *job* as:

> job \jäb\ n. 1: a piece of work 2: something that has to be done: DUTY 3: a regular remunerative position—jobless *adj.*12

Sam's job has to be understood in the context of the duty of a batman: to serve and protect his charge. The second meaning from *The Merriam-Webster Dictionary—duty—*comes clearly to the fore in "The Tower of Cirith Ungol," in which Sam "turned quickly and ran back up the stairs. 'Wrong again, I expect,' he sighed. 'But it's my job to go right up to the top first, whatever happens afterwards'" (*RK*, VI, i, 184).

As Sam and Frodo draw closer to Mount Doom, Tolkien's attention returns to Sam's job. Even though his death appears to be the most likely outcome, duty and honor require that Sam—like Hutchison's and Hodgson's batmen—go on. "'So that was the job I felt I had to do when I started,' thought Sam: 'to help Mr. Frodo to the last step and then die with him? Well, if that is the job then I must do it'" (*RK*, VI, iii, 211). Tolkien's description of Sam's job here is exactly the same as the job description that Hutchison gives for a batman: "And he would run when his officer went over the top, and fight by his side. When the officer dropped, the batman was beside him."

Hodgson was killed during an attack on German positions south of Mametz. Pearson was found dead at his side. They are buried together with their comrades in arms in the trench they died taking. Peter McLintock died at Hutchison's side and is buried in Ration Farm Military Cemetery, la Chapelle-d'Armentières, France. Tolkien gave the story of his batman a happy ending: Sam returned to the Shire to marry his sweetheart, Rose Cotton.

Sam's job was indeed a "punishment," and in more ways than just the privations that he suffered when he accompanied Frodo to Mount Doom and back. To do his job, Sam had to leave Rose Cotton and she was not particularly pleased with him for that. She viewed the year that he was gone with Frodo as "wasted" (*RK*, VI, ix, 304). This, in general, mirrors a feeling about the service of private soldiers (enlisted men) that was widespread in England in the period following World War I.

Note

1. Dated March 23, 1916.

Works Cited

Carpenter, Humphrey. *J.R.R. Tolkien: A Biography*. London: George Allen & Unwin, 1977.

Hodgson, William Noel. *Verse And Prose In Peace And War*. London: Smith, Elder & Co., 1916, 1917.

Hutchison, Graham Seton. *The W Plan*. London: Thornton Butterworth Ltd., 1929.

———. *Biography of a Batman*. London: Eyre and Spottiswoode. 1929. (Reprinted from the *English Review*, August 1929.)

———. *Colonel Grant's To-morrow*. London: Thornton Butterworth, 1931.

———. *Footslogger: An Autobiography*. London: Hutchison, 1931.

———. *The Sign of Arnim*. New York: Cosmopolitan Book Corporation, 1931.

———. *Warrior*. London: Hutchison & Co. Ltd., 1932.

———. *Life Without End*. New York: Farrar & Rinehart, 1934.

———. *Pilgrimage*. London: Rich & Cowan, 1935. (A guide to the battlefields of France and Belgium.)

———. *According to Plan*. London: Rich and Cowan, 1938.

Wodehouse, P. G. (Pelham Grenville). *Selected Stories*. New York: The Modern Library, 1958.

———. *Jeeves and The Feudal Spirit*. Kent: Hodder and Stoughton, 1977.

———. *Jeeves and The Hard-boiled Egg and Other Stories*. London: Bloomsbury, 1997.

———. *Jeeves Omnibus*. London, Jenkins, 1931,

———. *Life with Jeeves*. Harmondsworth, Middlesex: Penguin Books, 1981.

———. *Right ho, Jeeves*. c. 1922. London: Barrie & Jenkins, 1978.

———. *Stiff upper Lip, Jeeves*. c. 1963. New York: Perennial Library, 1990.

———. *Thank You, Jeeves*. London: H. Jenkins, 1956.

———. *The Inimitable Jeeves*. c. 1923. London: Vintage, 1991.

———. *The Return of Jeeves*. New York: Simon and Schuster, 1954.

———. *Very Good, Jeeves!* London: H. Jenkins, 1958.

JARED LOBDELL

In the Far Northwest of the Old World

My road calls me, lures me
West, east, south, and north;
Most roads lead men homewards,
My road leads me forth.
　　　　　　—JOHN MASEFIELD

And not by eastern windows only,
When daylight comes, comes in the light.
In front the sun climbs slow, how slowly,
But westward, look, the land is bright.
　　　　　　—ARTHUR HUGH CLOUGH

That *The Lord of the Rings* is set in the Northwest of the Old World there is no doubt, and I have no doubt that the setting is important—for two reasons. First of all, this is Tolkien's own country, the England for which he so earnestly desired to create (or sub-create) a mythology. We recall that in the very beginning of *The Lord of the Rings*, in part 1 of the prologue, "Concerning Hobbits," that the days of the Third Age of Middle-earth, "are now long past, and the shape of all lands has been changed; but the regions in which Hobbits lived then were doubtless the same as those in which they still linger: the North-west of the old World, east of the sea" (I, 21).

From *The World of the Rings: Language, Religion, and Adventure in Tolkien*, pp. 71–93. © 2004 by Carus Publishing.

Second, both North and West have a significance—*significatio*—though I hasten to add that, so far as I can see, the significance of the Northwest is simply the significance of the North and the West, and not some superadded "synergistic" compound. When Frodo says Strider is only a Ranger, Gandalf replies "My dear Frodo, that is just what the Rangers are; the last remnant in the *North* of the great people, the men of the *West*" (I, 291, emphasis mine). We should begin, I think, with the dominant myth (if you will forgive me the word)—that is, the myth of the West. We have already discussed Tolkien's three-directional universe, and the great goodness attaching to the West. Let me briefly summarize what we have said, and then go on to say at least a little more.

We have remarked that Aragorn is one of the Men of the West, long-lived, of Elven descent, and "of the blood of the West unmingled," King by right and inheritance. We have remarked the conversation of Treebeard with Celeborn and Galadriel, in which they say that they will meet again not in Middle-earth, but in the land of Tasarinan. We have noted that the meeting is not to take place in Middle-earth, *and* it is not to take place until Númenor is raised up. It will indeed take place in Númenor. We might think Númenor would be part of any Middle-earth, as (we might think) would be any Isles of the Blest, but it is not part of Tolkien's Middle-earth.

If the West is Heaven (or Paradise), then the East in some sense approaches Hell, even though the symmetry is incomplete, and Middle-earth is middle because betwixt West and East. This reading fits in with the land under the wave and Middle-earth as separate entities: by it, the Undying Lands remain forever beyond the circles of the world, reachable only by the Old Straight Track. By it, Númenor (or, rather, the Isle of Elenna) will be raised up, the world—Middle-earth being included in the circles of the world—will be changed, and the dead will be raised (III, 428). This is the framework, but in my reading over *The Lord of the Rings* in preparation for writing this chapter (would it be for the fortieth time, or more?), one thing has struck me with particular force. We are introduced to this, as to much else in the background of *The Lord of the Rings*, by hints and slight mentions, over the three volumes. It is certainly part of Tolkien's mythology for England, and his desire for the fair elusive beauty that some call Celtic. It is unquestionably based on the Celtic Islands of the Blest, on Hy Bréasail, on the drowned lands of Lyonesse, on all the westering motion of the sacred in Celtic lore, on the *imramm* (and he himself published an "Imram" in 1955). But he does not here tell much of the myth (until he gets to the appendices): it is almost as though, by knowing the myth (if we do), we discover it here, underlying and informing the story, until we reach the appendices.

In the opening chapters, in the Shire, we find Bilbo and Gandalf "sitting at the open window of a small room looking out west on to the garden" (I, 49).

The link of garden with west, though minor, is fitting (to cross mythologies, the gardens of Ponemah, perhaps?). Then, while things are beginning to stir, around the time of Frodo's fiftieth birthday, there is this report from Sam:

> "And I've heard tell the Elves are moving west. They do say they are going to the harbours, out away beyond the White towers." Sam waved his arm vaguely; neither he nor any of them knew how far it was to the Sea, past the old towers beyond the western borders of the Shire. But it was an old tradition that away over there stood the Grey Havens, from which at times elven-ships set sail, never to return. "They are sailing, sailing, sailing over the Sea, they are going into the West and they are leaving us," said Sam, half chanting the words, shaking his head sadly and solemnly. (I, 74)

Then, when Gandalf begins to tell Frodo the story of the One Ring (I, 83), he tells him of the Men of Westernesse, elf-friends: "The strength of the Elves to resist [Sauron] was greater long ago; and not all Men were estranged from them. The Men of Westernesse came to their aid. . . . It was Gil-galad Elven-king and Elendil of Westernesse who overthrew Sauron, though they themselves perished in the deed." When the hobbits hear the High Elves singing (I, 117), the song begins with the lines, "Snow-white, Snow-white! O Lady clear! / O Queen beyond the Western Seas!" and ends "O Elbereth! Gilthoniel! / We still remember, we who dwell / In this far land beneath the trees, / Thy starlight on the Western Seas." The linking of the Elves with the West is made, and made again.

Of course, the west (no capital W) may simply be part of a proverbial saying, as in "east or west all woods must fail" (I, 159). But even Tom Bombadil (I, 201) tells the hobbits of the Men of Westernesse, and when they meet with Strider at the Prancing Pony, he speaks of the "Shadow in the East" (I, 229). The opposition of West and East grows clearer. The *Forsaken Inn* is a day's journey *east* of Bree (I, 253). And when Strider comes up to Bilbo and Frodo in Rivendell (I, 306–7), Bilbo calls him Dúnadan. "Why do you call him Dúnadan?' asked Frodo. '*The* Dúnadan,' said Bilbo. 'He is often called that here. But I thought you knew enough Elvish to know *dún-adan*: Man of the West, Númenorean.'" And when the Council of Elrond discusses what to do with the Ring (I, 349), Galdor remarks that his heart tells him that Sauron will expect them to take the Western way—whereas, of course, the way they take is to the East, to destroy the Ring where it was made.

It is, I think, revealing, that the Elven songs in their lines (and especially their concluding lines) come so often to the West: we have quoted one, and here is another. "But from the west has come no word, / And on the Hither Shore / No tidings Elven-folk have heard / Of Amroth ever more" (I, 442).

And another (though here not in the concluding lines): "*Andúne pella Vardo tellumar / nu luini yassen tintilar i eleni / ómaryo airetári-lírinen*" ("beyond the West beneath the blue vaults of Varda wherein the stars tremble in the song of her voice, holy and queenly"—I, 489). And, of course, when Galadriel declines the Ring, "'I pass the test,' she said. 'I will diminish, and go into the West, and remain Galadriel'" (I, 474). And just to be sure there is no doubt, when they are going down the Great River that divides Osgiliath, and Legolas shoots the great black winged creature, "it fell out of the air, vanishing down into the gloom of the eastern shore" (I, 501). And "the Enemy holds the eastern bank" of the river, and "the Orcs prowl on the east shore" (I, 504, 505).

I have not, of course, touched on every reference to West or East (or even west or east) in *The Fellowship of the Ring*, but I have not missed a great number of them, either. The line is clearly drawn, and the link of the Elves and the west well-forged, but it has scarcely been dinned into our ears, at least in the first two books (book 1 and book 2 make up *The Fellowship of the Ring*, volume I of *The Lord of the Rings*,). In the next two (books 3 and 4, making up the second volume of *The Lord of the Rings*, *The Two Towers*), the number of references is scarcely greater, though one may add in some countervailing references to the East. In Aragorn's apostrophe to Gondor (II, 29), apparently an Elvish invocation, he asks, "O! Gondor, Gondor! Shall Men behold the Silver Tree, Or West Wind blow again between the Mountains and the Sea?" When Merry and Pippin are talking to Treebeard, he remarks, on the changing times, "Mordor is a long way away. But it seems that the wind is setting East, and the withering of all woods may be drawing near" (II, 95). We note also that the songs of the Ents about the Entwives "have not come west over the Mountains to the Shire" (II, 98), reminding us that the Shire is indeed not only in the North but also in the West of Middle-earth. And then (II, 101, 102) we hear an Elvish song of the Ents and Entwives, how "When woodland hills are green and cool, and wind is in the West, / Come back to me! Come back to me, and say my land is best" and then, in the final strophe, "Together we will take the road that leads into the West, / And far away may find a land where both our hearts may rest." Once again, this is the West as seen by the Elves.

Not all references to east or west are fully relevant here. When Legolas says (II, 121) that if they had left the Great Plain and struck west on the second or third day they would have struck Fangorn together, that is *west* but not West. Even when the Sun falls down the sky into the West in a great fire and blood-red burning (II, 139), it is the West (the sacred direction), but not a reference, we might say, to the True West, and the same holds, I believe, when (II, 140) the waxing moon sinks into the cloudy West. Then we have a curious form of the legend or *mythos* of the West, as among the Men of Rohan, in the song of the Rohirrim that Aragorn sings (II, 143), "The days have gone down in the West behind the hills into shadow, / Who shall gather the smoke of the dead wood burning, / Or behold the flowing years from the Sea returning?" I call this curious because it may be a combination of the fact that the day (the sun) sinks into the west, and the idea of the sacred West taken over from the Men of Gondor, *Dúnedain*—as the Saxons might have taken over such a thing from the Celts. But it is not the story of the Men of the West, unmingled. Yet in context, though "pagan," it has at least a suggestion of it.

Théoden, regaining his life, stands with Gandalf, "and together they looked out from the high place toward the East," while "doom hangs still on a thread" (II, 154). When Shadowfax bears Gandalf, and Éomer cries out "Were the breath of the West Wind to make a body visible, even so would it appear," there again the West is both the significant (if "pagan") direction for the Rohirrim, and the sacred West of the *Dúnedain* (II, 164), nor is it accidental that the Rohirrim under Théoden ride West (II, 165)—"*Westú Théoden hál*." On the other hand, the speech of the Dunlendings "once was spoken in many western valleys of the Mark" (II, 180)—but that was because the Dunlendings were there when Eorl the Young came to the aid of Gondor and was given their eastlands (where the unfaithful Dunlendings dwelt), whose western border was the Westfold from which Erkenbrand rides with Gandalf Mithrandir (II, 186). And then we come to Isengard— "long had it been beautiful; and there great lords had dwelt, the Wardens of Gondor upon the West, and wise men that watched the stars" (II, 204). But Isengard was not its only name: its citadel was Orthanc, "the name of which had (by design or chance) a twofold meaning; for in the Elvish speech *orthanc* signifies Mount Fang, but in the language of the Mark of old the cunning mind" (II, 204)—a double word or meaning, in two languages (one from the West), rather like Eärendil.

So much for book 3, and when we get into book 4 we can expect fewer references to the West or the west, for this is Sam and Frodo going into the Land of Mordor. But we can expect references to the East (or east), which may, after all, be taken as implicit references to the West (or west). "A chill wind blew from the East" as Sam and Frodo stood on the brink of a tall cliff, after "they had worked steadily eastward," and now "South and east they stared" (II, 265). There are orcs, out prowling on the east bank of the river (II, 266). Frodo tells Sam (II, 267) he feels "all naked on the east side." Trees were dead and gaunt, "bitten to the core by the eastern winds" (II, 268). Then, in a line that reminds us of what is at the anthropological root (so to speak) of the Celtic West, the "hurrying darkness, now gathering great speed, rushed up from the East and swallowed the sky" (II, 270).

But after the storm has passed, clear sky "was growing in the East once more" (II, 273). What that clear sky presages just then we do not know, but even in the East there may be a signal of hope. What comes next is Gollum, who clenches "his long hand into a bony fleshless knot, shaking it towards the East" (II, 282).

When Frodo and Sam are with Gollum, in the passage of the marshes, they all three shrink from the Ringwraith. But Gollum shrinks also from the white-face moon, until she goes down, "westering far beyond Tol Brandir" (II, 300): we know—though he does not—that the moon and the Ringwraiths are enemies, not friends. And when (II, 312) they are looking at the roads to the Gate of Mordor, they run northwards and eastwards and southwards: the southwards road runs briefly west ("Westward, to his right, it turned"), but then "southwards into the deep shadows." Frodo sees "Men of other race, out of the wide Eastlands, gathering to the summons of their Overlord" (II, 313). The hobbits take refuge in a little valley, a dell: "the sun moved, until at last the shadow of the western rim of their dell grew long"—and then, the "dark was deep when at length they set out, creeping over the westward rim of the dell" (II, 324), as though toward the sun's destination (though in fact they go eastward toward Mordor). And Sam is heartened, when "he saw the sun rise out of the reek, or haze, or dark shadow, or whatever it was, that lay ever to the east, and it sent its golden beams down upon the trees and glades about him" (334).

When Frodo and Sam encounter Faramir, they go with him to Henneth Annûn, the Window of the Sunset, facing west, where his men are gathered, their refuge and place of strength (II, 358). They come to table with Faramir and his men. "Before they ate, Faramir and all his men turned and faced west in a moment of silence" (II, 361). But otherwise, while they are with Faramir, they go neither west nor east, though they look to the West.

Even when they take up their weary journey again, while Gollum mutters "Long way to go still, south and east" (II, 387), they see, as a sign, their first night again on the road, the Mountains of Gondor, glowing, "remote in the West, under a fire-flecked sky" (II, 387). Under Gollum's guidance, they work "eastwards, up the dark sloping land" (II, 389). In the morning, "no day came. . . . In the East there was a dull red glare under the lowering cloud" (II, 390). Then, the "red glare over Mordor died way. The twilight deepened as great vapours rose in the East" (II, 391). And when Gollum has led them to the Stairs of Cirith Ungol, reluctantly, "Frodo turned his back on the West and followed as his guide led him, out into the darkness of the East" (II, 396). At the Bridge, when the Wraith King is seeking the hobbits, he turns away in haste. "Already the hour had struck, and at his great master's bidding he must march with war into the West" (II, 401). Sauron looks toward the West, where he does not belong, which is not his, while slowly, step by step, the Ringbearer moves ever Eastward. "Big things going on away west," as Shagrat the orc says to Gorbag the orc, but "in the meantime enemies have got up the stairs" (II, 442).

Then, in the fifth book (at the beginning of *The Return of the King*), we are back westward with the rest of the Company, and as we might expect, the references to the West and to the west both increase. Pippin (III, 20) catches a "glimpse of high white peaks . . . as they caught the light of the weltering moon" (note the contrast with Gollum). "Anduin, going in a wide knee about the hills of Emyn Arnen in South Ithilien, bent sharply west" (III, 23, and one might think, "bent sharply West"). As Pippin looks out over morning and the world (III, 40), there is promise of what is coming in a "stiffening breeze from the East." "Things move in the far East, beyond the Inland Sea" (III, 43). The last succoring troops enter the citadel, and "in the West the dying sun had set all the fume on fire, and now Mindolluin stood black against a burning smoulder flecked with embers" (50).

"The night was old and the East grey" when Merry and Legolas and Gimli "rode up at last from Deeping Coomb and came back to the Hornburg" (III, 56). Aragorn takes the Paths of the Dead and comes ere midnight the third day to the Stone of Erech. Of which "those who still remembered the lore of Westernesse told that it had been brought out of the ruin of Númenor and set there by Isildur at his landing" (III, 74). Merry rides to Dunharrow with Théoden, who tells him "Long years in the space of days it seems since I rode west," and they come down into the valley "where the Snowbourn flowed near the western walls of the dale, and . . . [so] the King of the Mark came back victorious out of the West to Dunharrow" (III, 78). It has occurred to me that "the hobbit on his little shaggy grey pony, and the Lord of Rohan on his great white horse" (III, 77) recapitulate Ceddie Errol on his pony and the Earl of Dorincourt on his great horse in *Little Lord Fauntleroy*, which was of course an omnipresent vision in the world of Tolkien's youth.

At Dunharrow, he is met by the chieftain Dúnhere. "At dawn three days ago . . . Shadowfax came like a wind out of the west to Edoras, and Gandalf brought tidings of your victory" (III, 79). Some out of the great concourse of men gathered at the Dunharrow hail "the king and the riders from the West with glad cries" (III, 79), but it is still a solemn and quiet assembly for the war coming out of the East. At the Siege of Gondor (III, 114), though "the enemy was checked, and for the moment driven back, great forces were flowing in from the East." There are "Men of a new sort . . . broad and grim, bearded like dwarves, wielding great axes. Out of some savage land in the East they have come, we deem" (III, 115). They despair for Rohan, but (III, 126), "Horns, horns, horns. In dark Mindolluin's sides they dimly echoed. Great horns of the north wildly blowing. Rohan had come at last." Rohan is guided by old Ghán through the Stonewain Valley, while "eastward and southward the slopes were bare and rocky" (III, 132).

Then, as Rohan had come in the hour beyond hope, there comes a greater. For

upon the foremost ship a great standard broke.... There flowered
a White Tree, and that was for Gondor; but Seven Stars were
about it, and a high crown above it, the signs of Elendil that no
lord had borne for years beyond count.... Thus came Aragorn son
of Arathorn, Elessar, Isildur's heir, out of the Paths of the Dead,
borne upon a wind from the sea to the kingdom of Gondor....
East rode the knights of Dol Amroth driving the enemy before
them.... South strode Éomer and men fled before his face....
There came Legolas and Gimli wielding his axe, and Halbarad with
the standard, and Elladan and Elrohir with stars on their brow, and
the dour-handed Dúnedain, Rangers of the North, leading a great
valour of the folk of Lebennin and Lamedon and the fiefs of the
South. But before all went Aragorn with the Flame of the West,
Andúril like a new fire kindled, Narsil re-forged as deadly as of old;
and upon his brow was the Star of Elendil. (III, 150)

When Merry and Éowyn are in the Houses of Healing, injured by the
Enemy's weapons, awaiting Aragorn's coming, "soon they began to fall down
into darkness, and as the sun turned west, a grey shadow crept over their
faces" (III, 136). But even now, and even as they begin their healing, we are all
awaiting the last throw. "Two days later the army of the West was all assembled
on the Pelennor" (III, 195). On the third day out from Minas Tirith, the army
began its northward march. "The weather of the world remained fair, and the
wind held in the west, but nothing could waft away the glooms and the sad
mists that clung about the Mountains of Shadow" (III, 198). And then we
are back with Frodo and Sam, and they see the darkness breaking up out in
the world. "It was the morning of the fifteenth of March, and over the vale
of Anduin the Sun was rising above the eastern shadow, and the southwest
wind was blowing. Théoden lay dying on the Pelennor Fields" (III, 240). As
Sam and Frodo crawl ever closer to their goal, they take the northward road,
"maybe the way their hunters would least expect them to take" (III, 241),
avoiding the direct eastward road. As they move slowly along, they see that on
"its outer marges under the westward mountains Mordor was a dying land,
but it was not yet dead" (III, 243).

It is not long after that the "wind of the world blew now from the
West, and the great clouds were lifted high, floating away eastward; but still
only a grey light came to the dreary fields of Gorgoroth" (III, 245). As they
climb Mount Doom, in "the morning a grey light came again, for in the high
regions the west wind still blew, but down on the stones behind the fences of
the Black Land the air seemed almost dead" (III, 258). The desperate journey
goes on, as the Ring goes south and the banners of the kings ride north, and
there "came at last a dreadful nightfall; and even as the Captains of the West

drew near to the end of the living lands, the two wanderers came to an hour of blank despair" (III, 261). They "could not follow this road any longer; for it went on eastward into the Great Shadow" (III, 262). Finally Sam looks down on Sauron's Road to the Sammath Naur: "Out of the Dark Tower's huge western gate it came" (III, 269). Over this road Sam carries Frodo: "after climbing eastward for some time it bent back upon itself at a sharp angle and went westward for a space" (III, 271), and in that westward space, Gollum returns to them, and his attack spurs Frodo on to the Crack of Doom—where, finally, as we know, he fulfills his mission, and the Ring falls into the Crack of Doom (or rather, Gollum falls into the Crack, holding the Ring). Gandalf lifted up his arms and called once more in a clear voice. "Stand, Men of the West! Stand and wait! This is the hour of doom." And even as he spoke the earth rocked beneath their feet. Then rising swiftly up,

> far above the Towers of the Black Gate, high above the mountains, a vast soaring darkness sprang into the sky, flickering with fire. The earth groaned and quaked. The Towers of the teeth swayed, tottered, and fell down; the mighty rampart trembled; the Black Gate was hurled in ruin.... "The realm of Sauron is ended!" said Gandalf. "The ring-bearer has fulfilled his Quest."... The Captains bowed their heads, and when they looked up again, behold, their enemies were flying.... But the Men of Rhûn and of Harad, Easterling and Southron, saw the ruin of their war and the great majesty and glory of the Captains of the West. And those that were deepest and longest in evil servitude, hating the West, and yet were men proud and bold, in turn now gathered themselves for a last stand. (III, 279–80)

One particularly interesting reference to the East comes when Éowyn complains to Faramir that her window in the Houses of Healing does not look eastward (III, 294). This is after we (but not they) have learned of the destruction of Sauron, and we have here, I think, both a precognition—or recognition—of that destruction and, still more perhaps, a looking toward the sunrise (even, it may be, the sunrise of the new age). It is a short while later that the Eagle, flying (and is this really an aggelos = *angelos* = angel?), bears "tidings beyond hope to the Lords of the West," commanding "Sing and be glad, all ye children of the West, / for your king shall come again, / and he shall dwell among you, / all the days of your life" (III, 297–98).

When he has been crowned, Aragorn tells Gandalf that he would, if he could, still have his counsel, but Gandalf tells him, "The burden must lie now upon you and your kindred" (III, 308). To which Aragorn replies, "But I shall die.... For I am a mortal man, though being what I am, and of the race of the West unmingled, I may have life far longer than other men, yet that is but a little while; and when those who are now in the wombs of women are born and have grown old, I too shall grow old" (III, 308). And die. And so will Arwen, who has chosen the doom of Lúthien, not to go into the West, "But in my stead you shall go, Ring-bearer, when the time comes, and if you then desire it. If your hurts grieve you still and the memory of your burden is heavy, then you may pass into the West, until all your wounds and weariness, are healed" (III, 312). Until that time, as Aragorn tells Frodo, for him "in all the lands of the West there will ever be a welcome" (III, 311).

The North (where the line of Isildur has been preserved) and West (where it now reigns) are linked in the great pageant before Midsummer's Day.

> It was the day before Midsummer when messengers came from Amon Dîn to the City, and they said there was a riding of fair folk out of the North, and they drew near now to the walls of the Pelennor. And the King said: "At last they have come. Let all the City be made ready!" Upon the very Eve of Midsummer, when the sky was blue as sapphire and white stars opened in the East, but the West was still golden, and the air was cool and fragrant, the riders came down the North-way to the gates of Minas Tirith. First rode Elrohir and Elladan with a banner of silver, then came Glorfindel and Erestor and all the household of Rivendell, and after them came the Lady Galadriel and Celeborn, Lord of Lothlórien, riding upon white steeds and with them many fair folk of their land, grey-cloaked with white gems in their hair; and last came Master Elrond, mighty among Elves and Men, bearing the sceptre of Annúminas, and beside him on a grey palfrey rode Arwen his daughter, Evenstar of her people. (309–10)

When the travelers ride back on the North-way, the hobbits with them, they "had journeyed thus far by the west-ways, for they had much to speak of with Elrond and with Gandalf, and here they lingered still in converse with their friends" (III, 325). But now we are coming close to the ending of the story, or rather, of this part of the story. It is not long until the hobbits return to find the garden at Bag End "full of huts and sheds, some so near the old westward windows that they cut off all their light" (III, 367)—Saruman's work. And then at the death of Saruman (III, 370), "about the body of Saruman a grey mist gathered, and rising slowly to a great height like smoke from a fire, as a pale shrouded figure it loomed over the Hill. For a moment it wavered, looking to the West; but out of the West came a cold wind, and it bent away, and with a sigh dissolved into nothing."

There is not much more to tell here. When Sam planted the small nut with a silver shale from Galadriel's box, there grew in the Party Field (III, 375), "the only *mallorn* west of the Mountains and east of the sea, and one of the finest in the world." And when Sam and Frodo ride out their last time together to meet the Elves, Frodo sings, "A day will come at last, when I / Shall take the hidden paths that run / West of the Moon, east of the Sun" (III, 381). And the Elves answer, "We still remember, we who dwell / In this far land beneath the trees / The starlight on the Western Seas" (III, 381). And when Frodo takes ship and "on the shores of the Sea comes the end of our fellowship in Middle-earth" (III, 384), then "the ship went out into the High Sea and passed on into the West"—"But to Sam the evening deepened to darkness as he stood at the Haven; and as he looked at the grey sea he saw only a shadow on the waters that was soon lost in the West."

Here we see again a linking of light and shadow with the west (and east), though not perhaps as we would expect. Note that from Saruman's view, and ours in Middle-earth, the westward windows of Bag End will let in light from the west, if not the West. But when Sam is far westward of Bag End, at the Grey Havens at the long Firth of Lune, then the ship bearing Frodo sails like a shadow into the shadows of the West—not because the West is a land of shadows but because the sailing is secret from all but the Fellowship, as Sam and Frodo and the Elves pass unseen through the Shire. There is no contradiction here—indeed Frodo carries with him into the West Galadriel's light which comes from the West. But this is a hidden path that runs East of the Moon, West of the Sun, and the Starlight on the Western Seas is remembered, not visible.

The wind blows from the West, blowing away the wrack of Saruman's spirit as it has blown away the wrack of clouds above the Field of Gorgoroth. The West is golden as the East is sapphire and white. Summary will not do justice to the varying implications of the West in *The Lord of the Rings*. We have set out much here in detail, and yet, when all is said and done, there remains another quest for us. Or at least a question. Is this simply a matter of detail? Will summary not do justice because the act of summarizing will eliminate necessary detail and connotation? Is there indeed an underlying meaning to Tolkien's West, as we suggest there is to his North? Is this West, as we have suggested, a Celtic West?

Because we (who have been reading these books for years) are so used to the significance of Tolkien's West, and because we know that Tolkien's mythology for England was designed to show that fair elusive beauty that some call Celtic—and because, for me at least, "Numinor" was the True West or ever I read Tolkien (because I read of Numinor in C. S. Lewis's *That Hideous Strength*)—it would be easy to speak of the significance of the West in the Celtic world when we are really speaking of the significance of the West in *Tolkien's* "Celtic" world. It is advisable, I think, to examine a book from Tolkien's student days, to see what we can learn from it of the West in the Celtic world view, as it was understood then. The book is Thomas W. Rolleston's *Celtic Myths and Legends*.

Rolleston believed that there were three "Celtic" peoples: there were the autochthonous small dark pre-Celtic Megalith builders who brought the ancient religion from the south, who buried their dead, and who were "Celticized" by their Celtic compatriots or conquerors or overlords; there were the Celts of the plains, who burned their dead and who intermingled with the Megalith builders not through conquest but simply through settlement—and who may also have been "Celticized" rather than true Celts; and finally there were the Celts of the mountains, the "warlike Celts of ancient history" (57), who considered burning the dead a disgrace, the Celts of the bards and druids, "dauntlessly brave, fantastically chivalrous, keenly sensitive to the appeal of poetry, of music, and of speculative thought" (57). Of particular interest to us in our present inquiry is Rolleston's discussion of the Celtic "ship symbol" (most especially in burial sites)—which he connects, through the Megalith "Celts" to the "ship symbol" of Egypt and the doctrine of the Transmigration of Souls (71–84, 88–89).

The sun rises, of course, in the east and goes down into the west, bearing the day with it to the Western realms beneath the horizon or beyond the ocean. The "solar ship" marking at New Grange in Ireland (Rolleston 1911, 72) shows the sun, the ship, and passengers—as with certain Egyptian solar barks (75): one of these barks shows a single figure on a bier, while others are crowded with figures. The statement is clear. As the ship of the sun carries the day to the realms beyond, so it carries the dead (or sometimes the gods) to those same realms, with the day. The Egyptians (so far as we can tell) believed in the immortality of the soul, but also in its migration, or transmigration; the Celts (so far as we can tell) believed in the immortality of the soul, but also in its migration, or transmigration.

Because the final redaction of our Celtic stories comes from the far western edge of the Celtic lands, where—beyond Ireland the furthermost—is the sea, we find there a stronger linking than else where of sea boats and the boats of the soul, and indeed between the sea and the sacred. In the story of Tuan, son of Starn, the brother of Portolan and the son of Sera, Tuan lives as a sea eagle all through the days of the Sons of Miled and the Tuatha De Danann, then as a salmon of the sea, until he becomes Tuan the son of Carell, and speaks to us in "The Legend of Tuan mat Carell" in *The Book of the Dun Cow* (Rolleston 1911, 97–101). So when the Elves and Gandalf and Gimli and Frodo and Sam take ship at the Havens and depart for the True West, they are the departed or the saints (like Brendan) journeying for Hy Breasaíl, the Sons of Don voyaging to the Summer Country, the men and ladies who sailed the soul—and they are in the right line from the ancient voyagers.

Or perhaps, if we accept Tolkien's chronology, the ancient voyagers are in the right line from them (a faint breath reaches even the late generations). It should be noted, however, that immortality is of the Elves, but the transmigration of souls of the autochthonous dwarves. And we might remark here, also, that the ancient (pre-Christian) Celtic beliefs and images linger in the Celtic stories of Christian saints.

Perhaps we should quote here from the rather Chestertonian lines of Tolkien's poem on St. Brendan ("Imram") published in *Time and Tide* in 1955 (I say Chestertonian, but there is at least—to me—a hint of Kipling. Or even of Walter de la Mare):

> ... When Shannon down to Lough Derg ran
> under a rain-clad sky
> Saint Brendan came to his journey's end
> to find the grace to die.
> 'O tell me, father, for I love you well,
> if you still have words for me,
> of things strange in the remembering
> in the long and lonely sea,
> of islands by deep spells beguiled
> where dwell the Elvenkind:
> in seven long years the road to Heaven
> or the Living Land you find?'

> . . . .

> 'The Star? Why, I saw it high and far
> at the parting of the ways,
> a light on the edge of the Outer Night
> beyond the Door of Days,
> where the round world plunges steeply down,
> but on the old road goes,
> as an unseen bridge that on arches runs
> to coasts that no man knows.'

> . . . .

> In Ireland over wood and mire
> in the tower tall and grey
> the knell of Clúain-ferta's bell
> was tolling in green Galway,
> Saint Brendan had come to his life's end

under a rain-clad sky,
journeying whence no ship returns;
and his bones in Ireland lie.

We are, of course, looking at *The Lord of the Rings*, and not at later illuminations of Tolkien's meaning, but this is scarcely a later illumination. I quote it because it places the Elves and the sea and the ships and the Old Straight Road that are all part of Tolkien's Middle-earth strictly in the context of Irish legend, and at the very time he was publishing *The Lord of the Rings*. Or perhaps not quite in the context of Irish *legend*. It is worth noting that when Rolleston (309–31) published an *imram*, he chose "The Voyage of Maeldûn"—which is quite evidently legend—from *The Book of the Dun Cow* (from the Whitley Stokes translation in the *Revue Celtique* in 1889), rather than the *Navigatio Sancti Brendani*, which at least claims to be history. And Tolkien, after all, is working in the realm of feigned history. In fact, in choosing the story of Maeldûn, Rolleston specifically notes that it tells "of adventures lying purely in regions of romance, and out of earthly space and time" (309). But for all that, Ailill father of Maeldûn came from the islands at the mouth of Galway Bay, Maeldûn's voyage to Leix took him through the western islands, and the island of the Monk of Tory (327–29) gave shelter to a man of Donegal who voyaged in the western sea—so that even if it was in a region of romance out of space and time, nonetheless Maeldûn, like Brendan, voyaged in the west before he came back eastward to Ireland.

The Celtic land of the dead in the west is the land of youth (in the west): it is not certain whether the ancient custom of laying graves in England east and west has to do with this (see Hazlitt 1905, 286ff). It may have to do with ships as coffins and their launching. There is a saint's life here that seems relevant. The saint in question (Cutha or Cuthbert), after his death, goes voyaging in his stone boat (coffin) for several centuries, with his body uncorrupted. He lives on an island where wheat (the grain of the living) will not grow, but barley will grow (the grain of the dead). It might even be profitable to compare his adventures to those of Brendan, if not of Maeldûn, though that will not be our task here.

Those who wish to study Tolkien's Northernness may have a more complex task than those who wish to study his Westernness—or, perhaps, his *Westernesse*. Hobbiton is in the North, though not so far as Norbury of the Kings. Northern rusticity is in part the subject of Tolkien's study in the *Transactions of the Philological Society* (1934) on the Northern "rim ram ruf by lettre"—but the whole Tolkienian attitude toward the North is to be found more through *Finn and Hengest*, and still more in Christopher Tolkien's edition of *The Saga of King Heidrek the Wise*, where the North also and especially preserves what has been lost elsewhere. The action of *The Lord of the*

Rings indeed mostly takes place in the northwest corner of Europe, and has a British or English feel to it, though Gondor (home of the Sunnlendings) is well south of that northwest. Indeed, Tolkien wrote, in a letter to Charlotte and Dennis Plimmer of February 8, 1967:

> The action of the story takes place in the North-west of "Middle-earth," equivalent in latitude to the coastlands of Europe and the north shores of the Mediterranean. . . . If Hobbiton and Rivendell are taken (as intended) to be at about the latitude of Oxford, then Minas Tirith, about 620 miles south, is at about the latitude of Florence. The Mouths of Anduin and the ancient city of Pelargir are at about the latitude of ancient Troy. Auden has asserted that for me "the North is a sacred direction." That is not true. The North-west of Europe, where I (and most of my ancestors) have lived, has my affection, as a man's home should . . . but it is not "sacred," nor does it exhaust my affections. (Tolkien 1981, 376)

Of course, the sacred direction (if any) is the West. But the memory of the West is, in *The Lord of the Rings*, preserved in the North, as the memory of Gothic battles in *Heidrek's Saga*, and of Frisian days in *Finnsburh* and *Beowulf*. And as with the *sogür*, the preservation is factual—matter-of-fact—not Romantic. Of course, the North also preserves Evil, the Barrow-Wights, and Old Man Willow.

The North preserves what is lost elsewhere. I can see in the story of Arvedui Last-King the echoes of the polar expedition of Sir John Franklin, and the expeditions after him: they provide a good—indeed the best—Victorian example. In fact, one of the great stories of disaster in the North is that of the loss of Sir John Franklin, sent out with the *Erebus* and the *Terror* in 1845 and all trace of his expedition then lost for twelve years—when (in 1857–58) the record was found of his death in 1847 and the disastrous end of the expedition in 1848. In 1852, one of the more incompetently commanded of the various Franklin search expeditions (and the last mounted by the Admiralty), under Sir Edward Belcher, abandoned all four search ships including the *Resolute*, which made its own way out of the ice and sailed without guidance more than a thousand miles, where it was boarded by American whalers and sailed back to England (see Mowat 1973, 249ff). The Search for Sir John Franklin was a staple of Victorian news and current history, and a basis for novels and stories into the twentieth century. Ships lost in the ice and wrecks preserved in the ice entered the English consciousness in those years 1845–57, if not before.

Even more to the point, perhaps, is the role of the North in *The Saga of King Heidrek the Wise*. This is one of the *fornaldarsògur*, the Sagas of Ancient Times, and is in fact one of the class of *fornaldarsògur* based to some degree at least on older poetry, so that scattered throughout are references to ancient customs and practices of the pagan age (C. Tolkien 1955). The importance of this particular example of the *fornaldarsògur* to our investigation here may also lie in the form, in which the references to ancient customs are set out in verses inlaid in the prose—rather like what Tolkien has done in *The Lord of the Rings*. Be that as it may, we should look at the examples in *Heidrek* to see—as we will also with *Finn and Hengest*—just how strong and lasting this preservation may be.

The most significant of these preservations of ancient times is, I think, the "Battle of the Goths and the Huns" (though the riddles of Gestumblindi are at least a candidate for that title). Here are the opening lines of what is apparently a very ancient song or poem (45), far more ancient than *Heidrek the Wise*. "The pike has paid / by the pools of Grafá / for Heidrek's slaying / under Harvad-fells" (45). (This "Harvad" is an ancient Germanic form of the name that is now generally given as *Carpathian*.) And in the prose passage following there is the name *Danparstòðum*, clearly referring to the River Dnieper in Russia. Here, preserved in a Northern saga of the 1200s is a record of a battle in the Russian/Carpathian borderlands some eight centuries before. (It is worth remarking, I think, that the next reference to the Dnieper refers also to "hrís þat it maera, / er Myrkviðr heitir"—the renowned forest that is named Mirkwood [49].)

Besides the Battle of the Goths and the Huns, and the riddles of Gestumblindi, *Heidrek the Wise* also preserves a description of the game of "Hnefatafl," clearly similar to *taflborð* and thus to the Welsh *Tawlbwrdd* (88). But this, though useful in corroboration for the preservation of old times in Northern memory (and as hinting at unguessed links between Welsh and Norse), is by no means significant in the same way as the battle and the riddles. Of course, this is not our only Northern preservation recorded in scholarly work, either from Professor Tolkien or from Christopher. In putting together for publication Professor Tolkien's *Finn and Hengest. The Fragment and the Episode*, Alan Bliss observed that his lectures on Finn and Hengest displayed "to a high degree the unique blend of philological erudition and poetic imagination which distinguished Tolkien from other scholars" (1983, v)—a unique blend directed, so to speak, at the question of the past—a past not from the North-embedded (even "alive") in a Northern text.

This entire book is a brilliant use of philological and linguistic analysis as an aid to history, though Bliss does suggest (as against Tolkien's view) that Hengest may have been a prince of the Angles rather than of the Jutes. But he accepts Tolkien's central arguments, based on the preserving text, (a) that there were Jutes on both sides of the fights at Finnsburh and elsewhere, and (b) that the Hengest of the conquest of Kent in England was the Hengest who fought at Finnsburh on the continent a few years earlier. This may all seem to be somewhat apart from our concerns here (though it is certainly relevant to the preserving North), but one point in any case should be emphasized. This book is a wonderful excursion into the world of the North, Beowulf, Finn, Hengest, Hnaef, Scyld Sceafing—even to considering Hamlet son of Eärendil (this, admittedly, in the editor's appendix). But unless I have missed a few passages, the only ones *invoking* the North refer to the freezing of the northern seas (122) and the northern custom of fosterage (emphasized by the editor, p. 159, if not by Tolkien). The passage on the freezing is worth quoting, for Tolkien's tone.

> The function of this passage [ll. 1131ff] is two-fold: (1) Primary—
> the explanation of why Hengest (and company) did not sail away,
> at least as soon as their hurts were healed. . . . I take it they were
> capable of departing singly, or together. Winter prevented them,
> impassable storms, followed by the freezing of the northern
> waters: but spring came at last to end that winter, as it still does.
> (2) Secondary—doubtless . . . largely unconscious: a symbol or
> parallel to the moods of men, the winds to their troubled hearts,
> the ice to their forced inactivity . . . in a hostile land—the spring
> to the release of passions once more. (1983, 122)

I am reminded of John Buchan's great descriptions of the Canadian north in *Sick-Heart River*. What is important is that this is the North felt as part of one's own experience—internalized, we might say. In C. S. Lewis, for example, even in so deeply felt a passage as his description of his first reading of Tegner's *Drapa*, he recollects the pang of joy, but he is not (I think) exercising the Coleridgean feeling intellect that is at the heart of Tolkien's North. That is, Tolkien has internalized what the North means, the freezing, the daily struggle in small things, the matter-of-factness of the *sogür*, the annual rebirth (in *The Lord of the Rings*, carried beyond as the rebirth even of an *Annus Mirabilis* and a whole New Age), the rocks and crags of Britannia's North. It is part of another story dear to him, of the English language, and another also—for did not Christ and his disciples speak with a Northern (Galilean) accent and provincial speech, but the kingship of Israel likewise was preserved there in the North, unseen for centuries?

And then there is Tolkien's great neglected 1934 essay on "Chaucer as Philologist." I am intending elsewhere to look more fully at that essay, particularly in the context of a kind of joint investigation of Chaucer by Tolkien, C. S. Lewis, and Nevill Coghill, in the early 1930s. Its importance here is that it illuminates, at the time of beginnings of *The Lord of the Rings*, Tolkien's understanding of the North as preserver of old forms and old words, but also the idea of separate development of forms in the North, of the sort later mentioned in the second part of appendix F in *The Lord of the Rings* (III,

513). There it is explained that it was "one of the peculiarities of Shire-usage that the deferential forms [of the second-person pronoun] had gone out of colloquial use. This was one of the things referred to when people of Gondor spoke of the strangeness of Hobbit-speech. Peregrin Took, in his first few days in Minas Tirith, used the familiar form to people of all ranks, including the Lord Denethor himself. This may have amused the aged Steward, but it must have astonished his servants" (III, 513–14).

As we noted at the beginning of this Chapter, it is in the appendices that we find more of the story and significance of the West set out (as well as of the North). It is also in the appendices that we find the end of this part of the story—whether in the Tale of Arwen and Aragorn (III, 428), or the end of the Tale of Years (III, 472), or one of the last notes in the *Red Book* (III, 451). It used to be argued, in Tolkien circles, in the young days of the 1960s, whether the last words of the story were "'Well, I'm back,' he said" (III, 385)—or "There at last, when the mallorn-leaves were falling, but spring had not yet come, she laid herself to rest upon Cerin Amroth; and there is her green grace, until the world is changed, and all the days of her life are utterly forgotten by men that come after, and elanor and niphredil bloom no more east of the sea" (III, 428)—or "Then Legolas built a grey ship in Ithilien, and sailed down Anduin and so over sea; and with him, it is said, went Gimli the Dwarf. And when that ship passed and end was come in Middle-earth of the Fellowship of the Ring" (III, 472).

In all these endings there is the fair elusive melancholy that some call Celtic, though I would say there is true Dickensian pathos only in "'Well, I'm back,' he said." ("Arter all, Samivel, she died.") If this is indeed the mythology for England of which Tolkien spoke—and it is—then the Celtic ambiguity by which the land of death is the land of youth, by which one voyages West in a stone coffin or a coracle or a ship of the sun, by which the immortal Elven ships and cloaks are grey with invisibility, is at its heart. The Tale of Years tolls like the Westron bell in the drowned lands, whether Lyonesse or Westernesse or Númenor of the great wave. There is always the hinted melancholy of "Westron wind, when wilt thou blow?" Even the subtitle of the Tale of Years is "chronology of the westlands" (III, 452). But before we come to that Tale, we learn of Númenor and the *silmarilli*, and the three marriages of Elves and Men (III, 388ff).

Fëanor created the Three Jewels, the *Silmarilli*, which were stolen by Morgoth the Enemy and brought to Middle-earth, to his great fortress of Thangorodrim. The Eldar and Edain fought against Thangorodrim and were utterly defeated. These Edain were three peoples of Men, who coming first to the West of Middle-earth and the Great Sea, became allies of the Eldar against the Enemy. Idril of the hidden Elven city of Gondolin wed Huor of the House of Hador, the third House of the Edain: their son was Eärendil the Mariner. He wedded Elwing, daughter of Dior, son of Lúthien Tinúviel (daughter of Thingol Greycloak of the Eldar and Melian of the Valar) and Beren of the First House of the Edain. The sons of Eärendil and Elwing were Elros and Elrond, the Half-Elven. "Eärendil wedded Elwing, and with the powers of the *silmaril* passed the Shadows and came to the Uttermost West, and speaking as ambassador of both Elves and Men obtained the help by which Morgoth was overthrown" (III, 389).

For their sufferings against Morgoth, the Edain were granted (by the Valar, the Guardians of the World), a land over sea to dwell in, removed from the dangers of Middle-earth. Most of them set sail over sea, therefore, to the Isle of Elenna, where they built Númenor, and whence they were forbidden to sail further West. The first King of Númenor was Elros, called Tar-Minyatur. The fourth King was Tar-Elendil, in whose reign the first ships of the Númenoreans came back to Middle-earth, and from whom descended the Lords of Andúnië in the west of the land. Tar-Elendil's daughter's son, Valandil was the first of these Lords, from whom descended Amandil Last-Lord and his son Elendil the Tall, who escaping from the wrack of Númenor with nine ships, was cast up on Middle-earth. "There they established in the North-west the Númenorean realms in exile, Arnor and Gondor" (III, 393). Through ten High Kings of Arnor, and fifteen Kings of Arthedain (ending with Arvedui Last-King), and sixteen Chieftains of the Dúnedain (Aragorn II being the sixteenth), the line of Elendil continued, and in it the line of Elros Tar-Minyatur, until at length Aragorn wedded Arwen, the daughter of Elrond, and the long-sundered branches of the Half-Elven were reunited. But both Aragorn and Arwen were of the blood of Tuor and Idril, and of Beren and Lúthien, and thus of Melian of the Valar. It could be said that as much of the West as was alive in Middle-earth came together at their wedding. The past walked in the present, the West as alive in the world, and that brought in the Fourth Age, in hope.

For with Tolkien, I think, even recapturing the past is a kind of advance. (Come to think of it, that is a theme in some of those writers with whom Tolkienian fantasy is connected—Kipling in *Puck of Pook's Hill* and *Rewards and Fairies*, and E. Nesbit in *The House of Arden*.) Learning the past is a kind of recapturing the past—Frodo and Sam grow through learning the past; in fact, it is only because of what they (and Bilbo) have learned, I believe, that they can come to Rivendell, and then to Lothlórien. But after the learning comes the true advance—Aragorn remembers, then takes, the Paths of the Dead, and then comes victory. The Ring cut by Isildur from Sauron's hand, bitten by Gollum from Frodo's hand, is destroyed because the Captains of the West knew the past, and because the line of the Kings (with Aragorn's knowledge, and his powers) was preserved in the North, so that in the Circles of the World, the Three Ages came full circle.

It is at the great set pieces in the narrative of the Great Days, the coming of Aragorn (III, 150), the overthrow of Sauron (III, 279–80), the coming of Arwen on Midsummer Eve (III, 309–10), that we see North and East and South and West laid out before us, in full—I might even say almost heraldic—significance. And we know that they are not accidental directions, but inherent in the very nature of the world's four corners. Perhaps from the boat that sailed the sun, perhaps from the ice of the north, perhaps from the hot blood of the south, but from whatever root, each has its sacral, if not its sacred, value. We need not go further into that—except perhaps to say that we who are the English-speaking inheritors of the World of the Rings will find our West going westward from England (and Ireland), our South going southward from England, our East going eastward from England. For the mind of this world is an English mind, the tongue our English tongue, the tale an English tale, and the trees are English trees.

MARJORIE BURNS

Spiders and Evil Red Eyes:
The Shadow Sides of Gandalf and Galadriel

Though Tolkien's fiction is by no means as unsophisticated as critics often believe, it is still true that Tolkien preferred to separate his good characters from his bad. We have no doubt that Aragorn, even as Strider, is a man to be counted on and that Gollum, though 'he may yet be saved,' is a doomed and untrustworthy wretch. It is equally clear that Théoden belongs on the side of the good though he initially appears weak and floundering. Even Boromir, Tolkien's most deliberate attempt to create a morally troubled personality, gives us little difficulty. As the picture of a soul in doubt, he never quite succeeds. It is too easy to feel (and to feel without deep concern) that Boromir is destined to fall. Still, by creating characters of this sort, Tolkien knew exactly what he was doing. He was well aware that, in real life, good and evil are never so clearly defined as fiction permits them to be and that fantasy, even more than other genres, tends to present human nature in elemental, uncluttered forms.[1] At its best, such simplification allows for a clearer presentation of basic human types, but simplification of this sort may also leave the reader feeling that reality has been sacrificed in the name of clarity.

How then can a writer, a serious writer deeply concerned with human intricacies and matters of bona fide moral choice, create fantasy characters who represent all the complexities and multiplicity of the human temperament? It is not an easy problem, and Tolkien attempts to solve it by more than

From *Perilous Realms: Celtic and Norse in Tolkien's Middle-earth*, pp. 93–127. © 2005 by Marjorie Burns.

one approach: by allowing for occasional moments of doubt, temptation, or irritability in his good characters and by creating moments when his fallen characters waiver and reconsider the choices they have made, as Gollum does on the Stairs of Cirith Ungol when he looks upon the sleeping Frodo and Sam. But Tolkien's most common and most effective means of adding moral complexity is to link ideal characters with specific negative ones, thereby suggesting a darker, undeveloped side. By creating such connections and by having his negative figures shadow—and at times almost *stalk*—his most admirable individuals, Tolkien establishes character teams whose members, taken together, represent the intricacy and inconsistency that lies within any human being.

It is easy to see how Tolkien matches Frodo with Gollum, showing us, at one moment, Gollum in the guise of an 'an old weary hobbit' and, in another, Frodo speaking of his 'precious' and clutching at the Ring. There are times, then, when we are encouraged to see Frodo and Gollum as two opposing extremes of a single struggling soul, united by the burden and seduction of the Ring to the point where it makes good symbolic sense to have Faramir bind them with what are virtually marriage vows. In a similar way, Denethor and Théoden are another matched pair. One is a failed steward who wishes to be king; the other is a weakened king who regains his earlier powers. Their names too hint at a connection. A subtle shifting of syllables and the two are nearly the same.

Tolkien, however, also uses character splits and character multiplicity in far more complicated ways. This is particularly so for Gandalf and Galadriel. Like Frodo and Théoden, Gandalf and Galadriel are each matched with and balanced by negative figures from within Tolkien's own literature, Gandalf rather obviously with the wizard Saruman but also with Sauron, the Dark Lord (as well as with that fire spirit, the Balrog, in one brief scene). Galadriel, the giver of light and life, is more subtly matched—with 'Shelob the Great,' that proponent of death and darkness, 'an evil thing in spider-form' (*TT*, 332). The connections, however, are more intricate than this. Gandalf and Galadriel (and their negative counterparts) are not the products of Tolkien's imagination alone. They owe a good part of their presentation and behaviour to figures—particularly highly ambiguous figures—drawn from mythology and from earlier literary works before Tolkien's time.[2]

Though the Arthurian figure of Merlin no doubt contributed to Gandalf, though Tolkien himself cited a painting, *Der Berggeist* (The Mountain Spirit), as an 'origin of Gandalf,'[3] and though Gandalf is not quite the same in *The Hobbit* as he is in *The Lord of the Rings*, it is Norse mythology that most consistently influenced his character. The very name *Gandalf*, taken from *The Poetic Edda's* 'Catalogue of Dwarfs,' is a strong indication of Gandalf's Norse connections. But as far as character goes, it is Odin, the primary Norse god (an exceptionally ambiguous god), who is most consistently linked to Gandalf and who works in the background in multiple ways to add the greatest depth to Gandalf's personality.

This comparison to Odin may at first seem a highly unlikely one; Gandalf is unquestionably one of Tolkien's good, peace-seeking characters and Odin is best known for his role as a battle god. But it is important to realize that the Odin of Norse belief was by no means a consistently negative figure. It is more appropriate to say that he was perceived as an untrustworthy deity, one whose favour was uncertain and could suddenly be removed, as it is in the story of Harald Wartooth, who is first aided by and then killed by Odin through a blow from Harald's own weapon, or as it is in the account of Sigmund the Völsung, who initially seems favoured but whose death occurs on the battle field when Odin shatters his sword.

The titles or attributes (there are many) applied to Odin or substituted for his true name are indicative of the god's variable character. The most extensive list comes from *The Poetic Edda*'s 'Lay of Grímnir,' where Odin himself claims an impressive number of titles and attributes. The following are from Lee M. Hollander's 1928 *The Poetic Edda* (with Hollander's untranslated names included and his doubtful translations marked as such).[4] 'Grím is my name,' Odin begins, and then goes on to cite further names: Wayweary War-god (?), Helm-Bearer, the Welcome one, the Third, Thuth, Uth, Helblindi, One-Eyed, the Truthful, the Changeable, Truthfinder, Glad in Battle, Hnikar, Bileyg, Fiery-Eyed, Bale-Worker, Wise in Lore, Grímnir, Glapsvith, The Much Experienced, Long-Hood, Long-Beard, Victory Father, (Spear-)thruster, Father of All, Father of the Battle-slain, Attacker by Horse (?), Lord of Boat-loads, Ialk, Kialar, Inciter to Strife (?), Vithur, Óski, Ómi, Equally High, Biflindi, Bearer of the (Magic) Wand, Greybeard, The Wise, Ygg, Thund, Wakeful, Skilfing, Wayfarer, God of Gods, God of Goths (of men?), Ófnir, The Entangler, He Who Lulls to Sleep or to Dreams.

A good many other names and other renditions could easily be added. Of particular interest are Paul B. Taylor's and W.H. Auden's 1969 translation of the *Elder Edda* (Poetic Edda) dedicated to J.R.R. Tolkien.[5] Taylor and Auden list Odin's names from 'The Lay of Grímnir' as follows: Grím, Traveler, Warrior, Helmet Wearer, Agreable, Third, Thud, Ud, High-One, Hel-Blinder, Truth, Change, Truth-Getter, Battle-Glad, Abaser, Death Worker, Hider, One-Eye, Fire-Eye, Lore-Master, Masked, Deceitful, Broad-Hat, Broad-Beard, Boat-Lord, Rider, All-Father, Death-Father, Father of Victory, Stirrer-of-Strife at Things, Equal-High, Shaker, Shout, Wish, Wand-Bearer, Grey-Beard, Wise, Sage, Ygg, Wakeful, Heavens-Roar, Hanged, Skilfing, Goth, Jalk, Unraveler, and Sleep-Bringer. From *Cassell's Dictionary of Norse Myth and Legend*, which lists over 150 Odin names and titles, come the following additions or variant translations: One Who Rides

Forth, Wanderer, Deceiver, Battle-Wolf, Raven God, Shaggy-Cloak Wearer, Truth-Getter, Drooping Hat, Treachery-Ruler, Terrible, and Gelding (an attribute that has given scholars much to puzzle over).[6]

A mixed review to say the least! Nonetheless it should already be evident that a number of these epithets (or ekenames or byenames) are strikingly appropriate for Gandalf, most obviously so Long-Hood (translated as 'Broad hat' in Taylor and Auden and as 'Drooping Hat' in *Cassell*), Long-beard, Greybeard, Bearer of the (Magic) Wand, One Who Rides Forth, Wayweary and Wayfarer and Wanderer. In eddic tales these attributes are applied to Odin when he travels—as he frequently does—through his own middle-earth, the middle-earth of Norse mythology, disguised as a grey-bearded old man, carrying a staff and wearing either a hood or a cloak (nearly always blue) and a wide-brimmed, floppy hat. The cloak, the staff, the wide-brimmed hat, the figure of an old bearded man are Gandalf precisely. Even the blue cloak makes an appearance by the end of *The Lord of the Rings*, most noticeably when Gandalf astounds the Bree folk 'with his white beard, and the light that seemed to gleam from him, as if his blue mantle was only a cloud over sunshine' (*RK*, 274), an image quite appropriate to Odin, who also dresses in blue and who—in addition to all else—is a god of the sky.[7]

For both Odin and Gandalf such manifestations serve as forms of disguise. Odin is a god masquerading as a grey-bearded but vigorous man; Gandalf is one of the Istari sent from Valinor 'in simple guise, as it were of Men already old in years but hale in body, travellers and wanderers' (*UT*, 393). He is, in Tolkien's own words, a figure of 'the Odinic wanderer' (*Letters*, 119). When Frodo describes Gandalf as 'an old man in a battered hat' leaning on 'a thorny staff' (*FR*, 375), he is giving us a purposefully limited description. He is depicting Gandalf the way Gandalf appears to those who do not know him well, to those who do not recognize his wizardry or his rank. When Gandalf first returns to Gimli, Legolas, and Aragorn after Moria, they see him not as Gandalf but as a grey-bearded old man, cloaked and hooded, wearing 'a wide-brimmed hat' and leaning on a staff (*TT*, 95–6). He is at that moment very much like Odin in Odin's wandering old man guise.

There are, of course, obvious limits to similarities between Gandalf and the Scandinavian Odin. For one, unlike Odin, Gandalf is not a god but an emissary of Manwë, the godlike chief Vala, who is himself based on an idealized Odin and who, like Odin and Gandalf, associates with eagles and is sometimes described as wearing a cloak of blue.[8] But what seems more to separate Gandalf from the Norse god are the sinister and negative attributes associated with Odin, attributes such as Inciter to Strife or Entangler (in Hollander) or Evil-Doer and Terrible (in *Cassell*), none of which seems in anyway appropriate to Tolkien's admirable wizard (who— unlike the god Odin—invariably puts himself on the line for others rather than for personal gain). The remaining titles do not, however, go to waste. For one, in an ameliorated, modified way, certain of Odin's less desirable traits are still present in Gandalf's character. Though Tolkien more than once claimed that Gandalf is essentially an 'angel,'[9] Gandalf is neither saintly nor always peaceable. There is a certain amount of self-satisfaction, irascibility, and sarcasm within Gandalf's character, all of which adds to his appeal. Under necessity, Gandalf shows a warrior side; and his wizard's staff, though innocuous in appearance, is in reality an object of power, as it is in Théoden's hall or in stands against Orcs and wolves. It is, then, like various sticks, wands, or staffs that the wandering Odin carries, a weapon in disguise. (In the Norse *Flateyjarbók*, for example, a hooded and disguised Odin hands Eric, King of the Swedes, a slender stick which becomes a javelin when thrown over his enemies.) Finally, those who misunderstand Gandalf's mission refer to him as a herald of war and evil times; 'Master Stormcrow,' Gríma Wormtongue calls him, and 'Ill-news' (*TT*, 117), titles far more appropriate to Odin in his role as promoter of war, the Odin whose ekenames include Raven god, Battle-Wolf, and Father of the slain.

There are, as well, particular characteristics associated with Odin that may not appear specifically in Gandalf but which appear in other characters within Tolkien's story, negative characters who are themselves connected with Gandalf and who therefore, in a roundabout, second-hand way, serve again to link Gandalf back to Odin and at the same time suggest moral failings that might have developed within Gandalf's character. These negative figures are the two primary villains in *The Lord of the Rings*, Saruman, the fallen wizard, who would emulate Sauron himself, and Sauron, the creator of the Ring. Much like Odin in his less savory role, but quite unlike Gandalf, Saruman and Sauron (with their significantly similar names) both exhibit ruthlessness and single-minded lust for power and control; they are both figures who deceive, figures who destroy rather than preserve. Sauron, as 'the Deceiver' or 'the Base Master of Treachery' is particularly well matched by those aspects of Odin that name him as Deceiver or Treachery-Ruler. Nor is it merely a generalized preference for tyranny and destruction that connects Sauron and Saruman with the Scandinavian god. Certain animals, certain similarities in clothing (worn by Saruman), and certain fragmentary body images (affiliated with Sauron) also recall Odin. At the same time, these shared animal associations (as well as the clothing) are also connected to Gandalf.[10]

More than once, Tolkien purposely confuses Gandalf and Saruman (both of whom dress, Odin-like, in cloak and wide-brimmed hat). After the escape from Moria and Gandalf's supposed death, the remaining members of the Fellowship are uncertain whether it is Saruman or Gandalf they have seen. 'Like, and yet unlike,' Gimli says (*TT*, 183). Éomer later describes Saruman as an 'old man hooded and cloaked, very like to Gandalf' (*TT*, 39), and Gandalf himself informs us that, in his new incarnation as Gandalf the White, he has indeed become Saruman—Saruman 'as he should have been' (*TT*, 98). (The ambivalence of grey, we should notice, has now been left behind.)

Links between Gandalf and Sauron and the Dark Lord are less obvious. Though Tolkien once considered a final confrontation between Gandalf and Sauron and claimed 'it would be a delicate balance' (*Letters*, 332), connections between the two are less blatant than they are between Gandalf and Saruman. Sauron is, after all, more concept than substance, less easily pictured and therefore (visually at least) less easily compared. After the drowning of Númenor, Sauron is deprived of the 'shape in which he had wrought so great an evil' and can 'never again appear fair to the eyes of Men.' Nonetheless, something of a physical presence remains: 'His spirit arose out of the deep and passed as a shadow and a black wind over the sea, and came back to Middle-earth and to Mordor that was his home. There he took up again his great Ring in Barad-dûr, and dwelt there, dark and silent, until he wrought himself a new guise, an image of malice and hatred made visible; and the Eye of Sauron the Terrible few could endure' (*Silmarillion*, 280–1).

In *The Lord of the Rings*, Sauron is pictured in much the same nebulous or fragmented manner, as a 'shadow,' a 'black hand,' a 'finger,' an 'arm.' More than anything else, however, he is an eye, a single 'dreadful eye,' a 'lidless eye,' that projects its searching hostility westward over Middle-earth. Orcs in his service wear an emblem of the eye, and carvings or painted signs of the 'Red Eye' mark where they have been. 'The Red Eye will be looking towards Isengard,' Aragorn says, referring to Sauron's watchfulness (*TT*, 169). To Frodo the Eye appears in Galadriel's mirror as 'rimmed with fire' (*FR*, 379).

If we remember that one of Odin's epithets is the fiery-eyed and that he, like Sauron, lost something of his physical self in his search for greater power, another link suggests itself. Where Odin gives up an eye to gain wisdom from the Spring of Mimir (thus. earning the epithet, One-eyed), Sauron—in his efforts to 'make himself master of all things in Middle-earth' (*Silmarillion*, 289)—loses the greater part of his physical self (thus becoming little more than an Eye, a searching sleepless Eye). Beside the Red Eye or the Lidless Eye, Sauron is referred to as the Great Eye, the Eye of Barad-dûr, the Evil Eye, the Nameless Eye.

Both Odin and Sauron have rings with supernatural powers. In Norse mythology one of the few objects associated with Odin is the ring Draupnir, an arm ring that magically produces eight more rings, all equal in weight, every nine nights. In Tolkien's books, Sauron's One Ring has the power to dominate the three, seven, and nine lesser rings associated with the One.

Animal affiliations also tie Odin to Sauron—as well as to Gandalf and Saruman. The animals most closely associated with Odin are Sleipnir (his eight-legged, otherworldly horse) and the three beasts of battle that are traditional to northern literature: the eagle, raven, and wolf. Wolves sit at Odin's feet and are fed the flesh of the battle-slain; every day two ravens fly outward, gathering news of the world and returning with it to the god; in *The Poetic Edda* a hovering eagle and a wolf are associated with Valhalla, Odin's battle hall (where resurrected warriors feast and carouse through the night).[11]

The eagle associated with Valhalla has both positive and negative connotations, representing both the power and threat of war and the power of transference between spiritual states or worlds. In 'The Mead of Poetry,' Odin escapes back to Asgard (the world of the Aesir gods) from Jotunheim (the Middle-earth land of giants) by turning into an eagle; Suttung, the giant who pursues him, is also in eagle form. In 'The Theft of Idun's Apples,' the giant Thiazi disguises himself as an eagle in order to seize the goddess Idun and carry her away.

In similar ways, Tolkien's eagles rescue Gandalf and his associates in both *The Hobbit* and *The Lord of the Rings*; in similar ways, worlds are bridged through the eagles' flight (most obviously so at Mount Doom when Sam and Frodo are lifted away from Mordor's realm of death). In *The Silmarillion*, Thorondor, 'King of Eagles, mightiest of all birds that have ever been' is the primary rescuer (110). It is Thorondor who transports Fingon to Thangorodrim (where the captive Maedhros is freed). It is Thorondor and his vassals who save Tuor and the remnant of Gondolin on a high mountain pass, and it is Thorondor who carries Lúthien and Beren away from Morgoth's dungeon-fortress (and away from a fiery setting reminiscent of Mount Doom).[12]

But eagles in Tolkien's worlds can be threatening and 'cruel' as well as helpful, and in this they come closer to the eagles of Norse mythology. In *The Silmarillion* (before the Drowning of Númenor), Manwë, the chief of the Valar (and the one who sends Gandalf to Middle-earth), warns the Númenoreans of their impending doom by sending visions of 'the Eagles of Manwë' or 'the Eagles of the Lords of the West' (277). And while the eagles we meet in *The Hobbit* and *The Lord of the Rings*, the 'proud and strong and noble-hearted' (*H*, 93) ancient race of the north, serve again and again for eleventh-hour rescues, they nonetheless remain creatures that understand violence and are quick to join battle or to seek out enemies. Even in their propensity for timely rescue there are hints of a darker side, a sense that they are at the least a race readily and almost supernaturally aware of death and events that threaten death—a quality they demonstrate by joining in the Battle of Five Armies after 'smelling battle from afar' (*H*, 244).

Like his eagles, Tolkien's ravens represent both battle and transference; and, again like his eagles, they are for the most part given a positive role. As pure-bred members of the raven race (not to be confused with crows), they appear only in *The Hobbit*, where they are unquestionably useful, knowledgeable creatures, much like Odin's wise and far-flying, shaman-sent ravens, Huginn and Muninn (Thought and Memory). In this role they help to fulfil the quest that Gandalf promoted and arranged. It is the ancient raven Roäc (son of Carc) that informs Bilbo and the dwarves of Smaug's death but tells them as well that hosts of elves and carrion birds 'hoping for battle and slaughter' are already on the way (219), an announcement that firmly marks Roäc as a harbinger of war, part of the raven's traditional role in both Norse and Celtic belief.

In *The Lord of the Rings*, ravens (kindly or otherwise) are absent, but the darker side of their nature, their role as war or carrion birds, still remains and manifests itself in the raven's close relative the crow (giving us yet another example of how Tolkien tends to share out a mixed reputation and create two separate halves of a whole). We are already given a good idea of Tolkien's raven/crow split in *The Hobbit* when Balin explains to Bilbo that crows are 'nasty, suspicious-looking creatures,' name-callers and rude, but that ravens have excellent memories, 'hand on their wisdom to their children,' and have long been friends of the dwarves (217–18).

By *The Lord of the Rings*, the nastiness of crows has been greatly intensified. We now hear about 'the crows of Saruman' or Saruman's 'own crows' and spying 'regiments of black crows' that are known as *crebain*, 'a kind of crow of large size' (*TT*, 154, 186; *FR*, 298). The physical difference between these birds and the raven is negligible, a moral distinction more than anything else.

Saruman's spying crows are not expressly focused on Gandalf or watching him alone, and yet they too create an indirect connection between Gandalf and Saruman, a connection that circles back again to Odin and his carrion birds. In Rohan's golden hall, Gandalf is five times associated with the crow or with birds that eat the battle-slain. 'Troubles' will follow Gandalf 'like crows,' says Théoden; he then refers to the wizard as 'Gandalf Stormcrow.' The false counsellor, Wormtongue, continues the association, twice more applying the term 'Stormcrow' to Gandalf and claiming he is one of the 'carrion-fowl that grow fat on war' (*TT*, 117). Though the intent (most certainly from Wormtongue) is to insult or ridicule Gandalf and to undermine his warning of the coming 'storm,' these references to crows and greed and the promotion of war would be far more appropriate applied to Saruman, that overly ambitious instigator of war who keeps both crows and Wormtongue in his service— and both in spying roles. The link is subtle but significant. If Gandalf is a positive version of Saruman (Saruman 'as he should have been'), then it is fully appropriate that a denigrated version of Gandalf be descriptive of Saruman. And the common factor, leading back again to Odin in this scene, is the image of the raven/crow carrion bird of war.

Wolves are the last of the traditional Norse war beasts associated with Odin, and Tolkien uses their characteristics in a particularly innovative way. In eddic accounts, Odin keeps and feeds two wolves, Freki and Geri (both names indicative of greed). The two are pets, though pets of a remarkably hostile kind. This fraternizing with wolves, however, does not immune Odin from their dangers; it is the giant, humanized wolf, Fenrir, that ultimately destroys Odin, devouring him in the apocalyptic battle of Ragnarok. Wolves, then, are both Odin's associates and his enemy, and both of these aspects occur in Tolkien's *Lord of the Rings*. Sauron and Saruman (with their attributes of a negative Odin) either keep wolves and Wargs[13] in their service or use the image of the wolf as a symbol of havoc and terror. The massive, black battering ram, Grond, that shatters Gondor's city Gate (a ram forged 'in the dark smithies of Mordor') is 'shaped in the likeness of a ravening wolf' (*RK*, 102). And Gandalf, escaping from Orthanc, is pursued by the wolves of Saruman.

In both *The Hobbit* and *The Lord of the Rings*, Gandalf takes the lead defensive role in scenes with Wargs and wolves. Like Odin (who is the first of the gods to rush into battle at Ragnarok and who does so to engage in battle with Loki's wolf-son, Fenrir), Gandalf responds dramatically and aggressively to wolves. In *The Hobbit*, Gandalf is the one who understands the 'dreadful language' of the Wargs (here defined as 'evil wolves over the Edge of the Wild'), and it is Gandalf who sends burning pine-cones 'whizzing down among the circle of the wolves,' setting them on fire (90–2).

This enmity with wolves is even more evident in *The Lord of the Rings* where the Fellowship is confronted by a lead wolf, the 'Hound of Sauron,' and his pack, and where Gandalf seems 'suddenly to grow,' becoming 'a great menacing shape,' and strides with a burning brand and a voice like thunder, crying, 'Naur an edraith ammen! Naur dan i ngaurhoth!' (*FR*, 312).[14] Though Tolkien turns the outcome around and allows Gandalf to survive, the very suggestion that wolves are looking to devour Gandalf hints at Odin's fate. 'Whatever may be in store for old Gandalf,' says Sam, 'it isn't a wolf's belly,' a sentiment which he repeats immediately after the battle: 'What did I tell you, Mr. Pippin? . . . Wolves won't get him' (*FR*, 311–12).

If we move beyond *The Hobbit* and *The Lord of the Rings*, there are more connections still. In *The Silmarillion* and the *legendarium* Christopher Tolkien published in the twelve-volume *History of Middle-earth*, wolves kept by both Morgoth and Thû (a variant name for Sauron) come even closer to eddic accounts. Morgoth, the prime force of evil in these accounts, sends demons in 'wolvish form and flesh' to hunt down enemies, and he keeps one wolf, Carcharoth, the Red Maw (sometimes called 'Everhungry' or 'Jaws of Thirst'), by his throne, just as Odin keeps Freki and Geri. Again, in a way highly reminiscent of Odin, Morgoth, 'with his own hand,' feeds Carcharoth on the 'flesh of Elves and Men' (III, 288). Sauron (who is called 'Lord of Wolves' and who imitates Morgoth in the *legendarium* much as Saruman imitates Sauron in *The Lord of the Rings*) also keeps a favoured wolf (or werewolf) by his chair, and this wolf, Draugluin, is fed as well 'on flesh of Man and Elf' III, 252).

One animal remains, Sleipnir, Odin's eight-legged otherworldly horse, born to the trickster, Loki (who temporarily assumes the form of a mare). Like Odin's other animals, Sleipnir has positive and negative sides, both of which appear in Tolkien's literature. Though Sleipnir is sometimes depicted in battle scenes (most frequently in art) and is a horse for heroes to ride, he is not so often associated with war as he is with transference between various planes and worlds, a shamanistic act that both Odin and Gandalf perform and which is indicated in eddic tales by Sleipnir's ability to carry his riders above the earth or away from Asgard and downward to lower worlds. In most such accounts, Sleipnir transports gods to and from the spirit world of the dead; and, likely enough, it is this persistent association with the underworld that gives Sleipnir his somewhat ambiguous character.

H.R. Ellis Davidson's interpretation of Sleipnir (an interpretation that is generally accepted today) speaks directly to Sleipnir's underworld association. If Sleipnir's eight legs represent the eight legs of the four men who carry a corpse in its coffin on the way to burial, then a ride on Sleipnir's back represents a 'ride' into the land of death. And this explains why Odin has Sleipnir carry him to the depths of Niflheim to learn the meaning of Balder's dreams or why Hermod too rides Sleipnir to the underworld, seeking Balder's return from the dead.

It is not difficult to see the parallels in Gandalf's Shadowfax. Where Sleipnir is grey, Shadowfax has a coat that 'glistens like sliver' (FR, 276); he is described as 'a shade' or a 'shadow' and most often depicted at night or in scenes of mists and greys. His very name (shadow mane) suggests a twilight, darkened world. And Shadowfax's otherworldly powers are hinted at in a number of other ways. He is 'the chief of the Mearas,[15] lords of horses' (TT, 108). He is descended from a sire that 'knew the speech of Men' (TT, 38); and, like Sleipnir, he appears immune from terror and attuned to the world of the dead. 'Among all the free horses of the earth,' only he can withstand the Nazgûl horror, remaining as 'steadfast as a graven image' in Minas Tirith's street of tombs (RK, 103). The last we see of him is the leap he makes over a dike before racing—Gandalf on his back—'like a wind from the North' towards the mists of the Barrow downs (RK, 276).[16]

Though Shadowfax never literally runs above the earth or through the air as Sleipnir is capable of doing, he is described as having a 'flying' pace, and he is repeatedly associated with the wind (moving as 'a wind over the grass' or as swiftly 'as the flowing wind'). At the start of The Return of the King, after the beacons of Gondor are lit, this sense of a ride expressed in terms of otherworldly flight is particularly strong: 'Three riders swept up and passed like flying ghosts in the moon and vanished into the West. Then Shadowfax gathered himself together and sprang away, and the night flowed over him like a roaring wind' (RK, 20).

In Norse belief Sleipnir's ability to move through the air is depicted positively. In later beliefs, however, this same ability became associated with those terrifying storm-riders and lost souls who sweep through the night in the tradition of the Wild Hunt. And here again Tolkien separates the good from the negative. Pleasing images of Sleipnir appear in Shadowfax, who can run like the wind, 'flying' over plains and 'spurning the earth'; negative images appears in the Nazgûl flying beasts that move through the sky bearing Sauron's key emissaries with a presence that reduces the staunchest warriors to impotent terror and, on one occasion, causing blindness (one of Odin's less commendable tricks).

Associations such as these, both positive and negative, greatly extend Gandalf's character, granting him a complexity, depth, and potentiality that would otherwise not have occurred. Through images from Norse mythology, Gandalf (the Grey Pilgrim, the preserver, the proponent of mercy, free will, and truth) is linked to and balanced by his negative doubles, by Sauron and Saruman (the destroyers, the unpitying proponents of war, slavery, and deceit). At the centre of all this splitting and reallocation lies Odin, the god who held the highest position in early Norse belief, the god who walked the earth as Gandalf and Saruman do, the god who associated with eagles, ravens, wolves, and a highly magical horse, the god who was known for his contrary, unreliable ways.

In much the same way that Tolkien adds to Gandalf's character through parallel figures from both his own and other literatures, Tolkien develops Galadriel beyond the strictures of her idealized role within *The Lord of the Rings*. For Gandalf (and his negative counterparts), the central ambivalent figure Tolkien borrows from is the Scandinavian Odin from Norse mythology; for Galadriel, however, Tolkien turns instead to Celtic tradition, drawing extensively from concepts of the early Celtic goddess in her multiple forms and from various enchantress descendants of these unreliable but often enthralling Celtic deities. Certainly, much of what is typical of Celtic goddesses and Celtic enchantresses is also typical of goddesses and enchantresses in other literatures; but the settings, characters, and incidents Tolkien imitates most closely suggest the Celts. And all of this is most prominent in the story of Galadriel.

Since an impressive collection of influential figures lies behind Galadriel, her development (and the development of her negative counterparts) is considerably more complex than that of Gandalf, Sauron, and Saruman, who are primarily based on images of the Norse Odin alone. The particular complexity of Galadriel derives not only from the greater number of figures in her past but also from the greater number of literary and historical periods to which these figures belong. Nor is Galadriel the only magical or quasi-magical woman created by Tolkien and based on Celtic tradition. The Galadriel we meet in *The Lord of the Rings* is a late and fairly subdued interpretation of a Celtic type that Tolkien borrowed from throughout his writing career.

The Celtic goddess herself is the logical place to begin. Like Odin, she is not a simple personality. She is a proud, jealous, and vengeful goddess, a goddess who represents both fertility and war, a goddess who appears either alluring or hideous in the extreme. She is, in fact, a composite of several goddess figures (which accounts for much of her conflicting character), and these contributing figures are themselves likely to differ from tale to tale, from region to region, and most definitely over time—as various goddesses are confused with one another or are split into separate entities. With such a variety of shifting, syncretic material at hand, it is no surprise that explanations or interpretations differ to some extent from one scholar to the next; but among those scholars who were most renowned during Tolkien's career and who most influenced his thinking, there is, at least, a consensus about the nature of these early deities and a similarity of scholarly approach.

Among the most prominent and the most representative of these multiple Celtic goddesses are Dana, the Great Mother; Rhiannon, a horse and fertility goddess; and the troubling trio of Badb, Macha, and the Morrígan, three figures who primarily 'prophesied carnage and haunted battlefields.'[17] In spite of her title, *The Great Mother*, Dana has never drawn the attention of writers and scholars the way other goddesses, particularly war goddesses, have; and among the Celtic war goddesses, it is the Morrígan who dominates, so much so that the trio of Badb, Macha, and the Morrígan were known collectively under the plural *morrígna*. Because of her 'position of peculiar prominence' (and because of her various powers and her legacy in Arthurian tales), the Morrígan is the Celtic goddess who most directly influenced Tolkien's Galadriel.[18]

At first, differences between the Morrígan, who often appears as a crow, and the fair, golden, peace-loving Galadriel may seem insurmountable. Where the sometimes alluring, sometimes hideous Morrígan is referred to as the Queen of Demons (in her more vicious and vindictive modes), Galadriel seems anything but demonic; she is, in fact, the most revered Elf in *The Lord of the Rings*, and the reverence she elicits can be measured by Tolkien's comment, in a 1963 letter, that he owed much of Galadriel's 'character to Christian and Catholic teaching and imagination about Mary' (*Letters*, 407). Nonetheless, the primary framework behind Galadriel, and behind the Elves in general, is not a Christian one (though Christian virtues prevail), and hints of the less-than-ideal do in fact hover around Galadriel's character. For one, her name is associated with fear, and those who have never met her tend to consider her perilous or worse. But it is not only rumours about 'the Sorceress of the Golden Wood' or 'the Mistress of Magic' that permit us to see Galadriel—however tentatively—in another, less reassuring light; there is, as well, one moment when Tolkien carries this image further and allows the possibility of Galadriel's rumoured demonic side to be revealed. This is when Frodo offers Galadriel the Ring and she briefly envisions herself as Middle-earth's Queen, 'beautiful and terrible as the Morning and the Night! Fair as the Sea and the Sun and the Snow upon the Mountain! Dreadful as the Storm and the Lightening! Stronger than the foundations of the earth. All shall love me and despair!' (*FR*, 381).

Nor is this all. If we look beyond the boundaries of *The Lord of the Rings*, there are other indications of Galadriel's less than peaceable side. In *The Silmarillion*, we learn that Galadriel was the sole 'woman of the Noldor ... among the contending princes' who rebelled against the ruling Valar and departed for Middle-earth. Though she, unlike others, swore no oaths, she nonetheless 'yearned to see the wide unguarded lands and to rule there a realm at her own will' (83-4).

But Galadriel (or, to be more accurate, Galadriel as she developed in the drafts of Tolkien's *legendarium*) is even less consistent and less straightforward than this gelled version from the published *Silmarillion* would seem to indicate. Altogether, according to Christopher Tolkien, the inconsistencies surrounding Galadriel are 'severe' and the 'reasons and motives given for Galadriel's remaining in Middle-earth are various.' Furthermore, the story of her marriage is highly confusing, so that no part of the history of Middle-earth is 'more full of problems than the story of Galadriel and Celeborn' (*UT*, 225).

In a letter written in 1967 (four years before comparing Galadriel to Mary), Tolkien cited Galadriel as not only a participant but as one of the 'chief actors in the rebellion,' indicating she was far more directly involved than she appears to be in the *Silmarillion* (*Letters*, 386). And in a late draft that Christopher Tolkien feels was 'certainly written' after *The Road Goes Ever On*[19] (placing it in the mid- to late 1960s), an even more dissatisfied and forceful personality emerges than we see in *The Lord of the Rings*, in *The Silmarillion*, or in any *History of Middle-earth* account. We learn here that Galadriel's 'mother-name' (a name given in infancy or childhood through the insight of one's mother) was 'Nerwen' ('man-maiden'). She is described as 'strong of body, mind, and will, a match for both the lore-masters and the athletes of the Eldar in the days of their youth,' and her restlessness is extreme. Even in the Blessed Realm, she finds 'no peace'; and though deep within her a 'noble and generous spirit' remains, she is 'proud, strong, and self-willed' and 'dreams of far lands and dominions that might be her own to order as she would without tutelage.' Because of her 'pride,' she rejects 'the pardon of the Valar' (offered to all who had fought against Morgoth) and is 'unwilling to return' or to 'relent' (*UT*, 225–8). Galadriel is, then (at least in this rendition), not merely the sole woman to join the rebels in either a passive or active role but a restless, ambitious, almost masculine individual whose desire to have her own way and establish her own rule adds to the disruption begun by Fëanor, the lead rebel Elf. In these ways she comes considerably closer to the strife-promoting, easily vexed Morrígan than we might initially believe.

But the Morrígan's powers are not limited merely to battle and disruption. Like Odin, she also manifests a number of positive attributes, 'notably' (in the words of Lucy Allen Paton) 'knowledge of the future, the ability to create effects of nature, and versatility in shape-shifting,'[20] attributes which may have their own elements of danger but which are far more likely to be seen as favourable. There are other indications of a better side as well. The Morrígan initially assists the Irish hero Cúchulainn (until he spurns her advances); and at the end of his life, when it seems clear he will die in battle, she attempts to change fate and to save him once again. These few acts of sponsorship and remorse are hardly enough to recommend the Morrígan's character, but there are other indications that the goddess once played a larger, more positive role. There is a well-known tale of her mating with the Dagda, the Good God, the god whose sack releases a river of grain and whose magical cauldron provides food and poetical inspiration and restores life to the dead. It is hard to imagine any union with the Dagda which is not an auspicious one; moreover, in her mating with the Dagda (which occurs at a waterway), in her seductress tendencies in general (again associated with waterways), in the existence of place names such as the Morrígan's Garden or the Paps of the Morrígan, there is good evidence that the Morrígan played a fertility role as well as a battle one.

Similar powers and similar images are attached to Galadriel who likewise has her garden, who sees far (in both distance and depth), and who is strongly associated with water (most noticeably through her wearing of Nenya, the Elven Ring of Waters). If, in fact, Roger Sherman Loomis is correct that the Morrígan and her counterpart, the Welsh Modron, derived primarily 'from an ancient Celtic divinity of the waters,'[21] an element strongly associated with fertility, it is particularly appropriate for Galadriel (as a literary descendant of such a goddess) to wear the Elven Ring, Nenya, and to live in a realm heavily bordered by both rivers and streams.[22]

There are, however, clear limits to Galadriel's fertility role, and these limits should come as no surprise when we remember that Tolkien, though he died in 1973, was born in Victorian times. In Galadriel the more fleshly aspects of the Celtic goddess figure have been conspicuously removed. And those early Celtic goddesses were unquestionably of the flesh. They are shown longing, mating, and even giving birth—a far cry from what *The Lord of the Rings* shows us of Galadriel, who, in her somewhat removed role as Arwen's grandmother, seems distanced from the biological by an intervening generation and not so much a creator or procreator as a preserver of what has been.

Or so it would seem. We have to watch Tolkien carefully here. As he does with Gandalf, Tolkien is quite capable of suggesting complexities that are easily overlooked if we are unaware of related literatures and mythologies or if we fail to read carefully. Before Galadriel is dismissed as an overly restrained fertility figure held back by lingering Victorian ideals, we should think for a minute about the box of soil that she gives to Sam, soil that sends out waves of riotous fertility throughout the Shire, in tree and grass, in vegetation in general, and—most significantly—in the birth of hobbit young. It may be a comfortable, distanced, domesticated manifestation of the flesh that Tolkien gives us here, but it is enough to show that the role of generative goddess nonetheless remains and in more than vegetative forms.

Now another step must be taken. It is generally understood that the Morrígan is a principal, if not *the* principal, mythological ancestress of the Arthurian fay (or fairy), a figure best exemplified and most familiar in Arthur's adversary and sister (or half sister), the strangely contradictory, evil/good, shape-changing enchantress Morgain la Fée, generally known in English tradition as Morgan le Fay, a figure of such lasting importance that she is still referred to as 'Morgan the Goddess' (stanza 98), in the fourteenth-century *Sir Gawain and the Green Knight*, a title that 'helps' link Morgan with the Morrígan, as Tolkien was well aware.[23] Like the Morrígan, who both aids and harms the Irish hero, Cúchulainn, Morgan both aids and harms Arthur; and again like the Morrígan, who fails in her attempt to seduce Cúchulainn, Morgan fails in her seduction of Lancelot, and there are scholars who believe she attempted (perhaps successfully) to seduce Arthur as well.[24]

The story of the Morrígan's evolution into this most notorious and fascinating of Arthurian characters is not a simple one. It took several languages, several cultures, and a number of centuries to unfold. For our own purposes, it is important to realize that the shift was a phenomenon that deeply interested scholars early in the twentieth century, at the very time Tolkien was beginning to develop a mythology for England based on that 'elusive beauty' attributed to the Celts.

Here is how Lucy Allen Paton, in her highly influential 1903 book, *Studies in the Fairy Mythology of Arthurian Romance*, describes the fay (or 'fairy queen'): 'The fay of Arthurian romance is essentially a supernatural woman, always more beautiful than the imagination can possibly fancy her, untouched by time, unhampered by lack of resources for the accomplishment of her pleasure, superior to human blemish, contingency, or necessity, in short, altogether unlimited in her power.'[25] And Roger Loomis—in a passage more mindful of Morgan's two-sidedness—writes the following (1956): 'Morgann may be the most beautiful of nine sister fays, or an ugly crone. She may be Arthur's tender nurse in the island valley of Avilion, or his treacherous foe. She may be a virgin, or a Venus of lust.' He then quotes Mark Twain's Connecticut

Yankee, who says, 'I have seen a good many kinds of women in my time but she laid it over them all for variety.'[26]

If we ignore Morgan's less pleasing traits, similarities to Galadriel are readily evident, some of them subtly different from what we saw in the Morrígan, others basically the same. The most obvious similarities are Galadriel's beauty, her power and superiority, and her escape from the effects of time. But the fairy queen's ability to overpower men is decorously suggested in Galadriel as well. In part this is implied by the lesser role Celeborn, Galadriel's husband, appears to play in the story. More indicative, however, is the way in which those males who meet her fall inevitably under her spell, a pattern of behaviour that Tolkien renders more acceptable by depicting its effects predominately though Gimli, an individual so removed from Galadriel by race and status (as well as stature) that any question of carnality can safely be put aside.

Certain other matters are significant. If we add Tolkien's early use of *fairy* instead of *elf* to his occasional use of *Queen* or *Elven-queen* for Galadriel,[27] ties between Galadriel and the Arthurian fairy queen become still more evident. Furthermore, the Fairy Queen figure traditionally lives in an isolated, magical realm. This is where she takes her chosen males. It is to such a realm (the Island of Avalon) that Morgan le Fay takes Arthur to be healed of his battle wounds, for—at this point in Arthur's life—she is his benefactor rather than his enemy.

Lothlórien is clearly similar. Not only is Lothlórien 'an island amid many perils' (*FR*, 363), but Gandalf, at Galadriel's request, is carried there to be healed of his injuries after Moria. Though Tolkien does not specify that it is Galadriel who tends Gandalf, from all we have seen of Lothlórien and of Galadriel, there is no one else likely to fill this role, the role that traditionally falls to the Fairy Queen.[28]

And there is more. During the nineteenth century, interest in Arthurian themes underwent a considerable revival, a revival initially most evident in Victorian poetry. The best known and most influential of these poets was Alfred, Lord Tennyson, whose first notable success (an Arthurian collection entitled simply *Poems*) appeared in 1842 and whose *Idylls of the King* appeared in 1859. Other poets followed Tennyson's lead. In 1852 Matthew Arnold published his *Tristram and Iseult*, in 1858 William Morris began his Arthurian career with *The Defense of Guenevere*. By the 1880s, Algernon Charles Swinburne—who disliked Tennyson's Victorianized version of the tales—began his own Arthurian cycle with 'Tristram of Lyonesse.'

Artistic interpretation followed closely behind. In her book, *The Legends of King Arthur in Art* (1990), Muriel A. Whitaker notes that 'between 1860 and 1869 alone fifty or sixty paintings on Arthurian subjects were exhibited' throughout England (214). Among such paintings (or drawings, tapestries, glass windows, sculptures, woodcuts, and carvings) images of the enchantress had a particularly strong appeal. Morgan le Fay appears repeatedly, as does Merlin's nemesis, Vivian—also called the Lady of the Lake or Nimue (or variations on these names). And Tennyson's offshoot enchantress, the Lady of Shalott (an ingenious blending of the traditional tower-imprisoned maiden with the woman of disquieting power), also instigated an impressive artistic flurry—mostly through depictions of her elegantly reposed body drifting to Camelot or scenes of her standing at her loom, where she often appears as unsettling as Vivian or Morgan le Fay.[29]

But fascination with enchantresses was by no means limited to works on Arthurian themes. The end of the century saw an increase in femme fatale figures in a variety of settings and forms. Among these man-confounding, latter-day enchantress figures (whose intensity increased as the century advanced), one *fin de siècle* seductress particularly influenced Tolkien's depiction of Galadriel—She from H. Rider Haggard's late-nineteenth-century book of the same name. Though She (or, more properly, Ayesha) appears in a novel set in nineteenth-century Africa,[30] rather than in an England of Arthurian times, she is nonetheless closely related to those Arthurian women of power who haunted the Victorian mind and who appeared again and again in Victorian poetry and Pre-Raphaelite art.

As John Rateliff explains in a 1981 article on Tolkien and *She*, Tolkien was quick to deny the influence of modern works yet openly admitted his early fascination with Haggard's book.[31] Even without this admission on Tolkien's part, the influence of *She* is undeniable. The novel clearly left its mark on Galadriel, as well as on Tolkien's Queen Melian (discussed below). Like Haggard's immortal ruler, whose beauty sends men to their knees, Galadriel inspires fear or devotion or sometimes a mixture of the two. Galadriel and Ayesha both see more deeply and know more than the men who encounter them on quests. Galadriel and Ayesha are both associated with weaving and oversee maidens trained in the art. Both have remained in isolated, sheltered realms, avoiding the changes of time. Both serve as preservers or healers; both allow those who visit them to look into a dish of water that shows scenes of what has occurred, what is presently elsewhere occurring, or (in Galadriel's case) 'things that yet may be' (*FR*, 377). And both deny that the working of these visions should rightly be ascribed to magic. The water in Galadriel's basin is drawn from a silver stream, flowing from a fountain on the hill of Caras Galadhon; and the visions that appear in this 'Mirror' are, as she tells Sam, 'what your folk would call magic, I believe; though I do not understand clearly what they mean' (*FR*, 377). Ayesha too explains that the images seen in her 'font-like vessel' are not produced by magic. 'There is no such thing as magic, though there is such a thing as knowledge of the secrets of Nature.'[32] In the end, each travels out of her sheltered and sheltering realm, and each as well loses power and diminishes (Ayesha literally shrinking and shrivelling in a highly dramatic scene).[33]

Galadriel, however, is not the only woman to whom Tolkien gives power based on water enclosed within a vessel or flowing from a fountain or stream. Goldberry, the River-Woman's daughter, is also a water enchantress. In Tolkien's 1934 poem, 'The Adventures of Tom Bombadil,' Goldberry is the 'little water-lady' and her home is in a 'deep weedy pool,' where Tom finds her sitting among the rushes 'singing old water-songs.'[34] In *The Fellowship of the Ring*, her singing is like 'glad water flowing,' and it brings visions to the hobbits, visions of 'pools and waters wider than any they had known' (143).

Goldberry is Tolkien's happiest interpretation of a woman imbued with watery powers (or, for that matter, imbued with any form of magical or near-magical power). Truer to the two-sided, perilous woman of fairy tradition is a water-enchantress who appears in another of Tolkien's early poems, 'The Lay of Aotrou and Itroun' (first published in 1945 but completed fifteen years before).[35] In this reworking of a Breton (hence Celtic) lay, a lord is destroyed by a 'Corrigan' or 'the Corrigan,' which T.A. Shippey cites as a Breton term for 'a witch, or fairy, or shape-shifter with malevolent powers.'[36] In Tolkien's rendition, the Corrigan sits before her cave, waiting by a fountain, 'the fountain of the fay' (line 284).[37]

Similarities between Tolkien's enchantress, the Corrigan, and the Irish goddess, the Morrígan, are suggested not only in the close spelling of their title-like names but also in their shared powers and potential viciousness. Like the Morrígan, Tolkien's witch, or 'fay,' is a shape-changer, a figure of either horror or beauty, a would-be seductress, and a source of both death and fertility. Like the Morrígan, she is associated with water and depicted near water. Her magic, described as a pale watery potion, is held in a glass phial of 'gleaming grace' (a phial much like the phial of Galadriel).[38]

But more needs to be said about the relationship between Ayesha, Haggard's nineteenth-century enchantress, and Tolkien's Galadriel. Though similarities in their beauty, their powers, and their visionary use of water are evident, there are obvious differences as well. Galadriel may diminish on Middle-earth, but nothing suggests she will be a lesser figure once she comes again to the West. There is a sense of near-divinity in Galadriel that evades Ayesha in spite of her powers and in spite of comments suggesting that Ayesha is, or almost is, divine. Where Galadriel is clearly on the side of the good, Ayesha is amoral at best; 'My life has perchance been evil, I know not—for who can say what is evil and what good?'[39] Where Galadriel maintains an aura of almost spiritual purity, Ayesha is strongly motivated by earthly love. Altogether, the golden-haired Galadriel is considerably upgraded from the saucy, spoiled, arbitrary, wilful, dark-haired, anima-figure, She, who is nonetheless one of Galadriel's prototypes.

Still, the division is not quite so simple. Once again, in a removed and inconspicuous way, Tolkien allows his source's negative qualities to remain, and once again he does so through a shadow character. Just as Odin is a prototype for both Gandalf and Sauron/Saruman, She (with her Celtic goddess attributes) is a prototype for both Galadriel and another character in Tolkien's *Lord of the Rings*: Shelob,[40] who lies waiting 'in spider form' in the tunnels of Torech Ungol (a character matching others have seen before).[41]

Just as Sauron and Saruman carry the burden of Odin's less admirable side (a side that cannot be openly developed in Gandalf's character), Shelob embodies those characteristics of Haggard's latter-day Celtic goddess, or latter-day Arthurian fay, that cannot be directly revealed in Galadriel—all of which strengthens and defines the best of Galadriel. The more she stands in opposition to Ayesha (at her worst) or to Shelob (who could hardly be worse), the more exalted and deserving Galadriel must appear.

Like Shelob, She—notice the similarity in names—has lived for long, immortal years in the tunnels and caverns and passageways of Kôr, a mountain realm hollowed out by an ancient, now-departed race.[42] Both Shelob and She live in darkness, and both are strongly associated with death—Shelob desiring 'death for all others' and finding her greatest pleasure in the act of taking life, and She (who wears 'corpse-like wrappings,' who lives among the dead, whose eating room is an ancient embalming chamber) easily inflicting death upon those who oppose her will. Though Ayesha has remained a virgin, waiting for the reincarnation of her beloved (whom she murdered in a fit of jealous passion two thousand years ago), she is snakelike, seductive, and openly sexual in her approach, while Shelob, with her 'lust' and 'appetite,' suggests a particularly unattractive sexuality. Though Ayesha, unlike Shelob, is initially beautiful and has remained so for the extended years of her life, she ends as a species of horror, losing in a matter of minutes the girlish face and form she maintained for centuries.

A short aside seems called for here. It has been easy enough for critics to see a Freudian intent in Tolkien's description of Shelob, particularly (as certain critics have noted) in the 'bitter spike' of Sam's sword ('deep, deep it pricked') and in the graphic descriptions of Shelob's 'soft squelching' body with its 'shuddering belly' like 'a vast bloated bag, swaying and sagging between her legs' (*TT*, 334 and 338). But to go far with this, to reduce Sam's and Frodo's use of phial and sword against Shelob to a thinly disguised sexual encounter, seems highly unfair to Tolkien, who was, after all, not just exaggerating Ayesha's negative qualities to create his giant spider but was also borrowing from traditional confrontations with monsters that dwell beneath the surface of the earth—the Minotaur, Fafnir, Smaug, or Beowulf's dragon, for example—but more specifically from confrontations where the monster in question is female. Grendel's mother ('grim and greedy fiercely ravenous' (*Beowulf*, lines 1498–9), living in her high-roofed hall deep beneath the waters) is one such monster, as is Milton's personification of Sin, with her 'Caves' and 'Death' and vile broods of young (Book II of *Paradise Lost*). And behind Milton's seventeenth-century figure of Sin lies Edmund Spenser's sixteenth-century figure of Errour, the 'monster vile,' half serpent, half woman, who appears early in Book I, Canto I of the *Faerie Queene* (stanzas 11–26). Both Errour and Shelob vomit (Errour expelling allegorical books and papers, frogs and toads, and Shelob merely 'darkness'); both excrete foul fluids from their wounds; both attempt to use a 'sting.' Like Shelob ('the mostly loathly shape' that Sam had ever seen), Errour ('most lothsome, filthie, foule, and full of vile disdaine') lives within a 'hollow cave' or 'darksome hole' and hates light 'as the deadly bale'; like Shelob, (whose ample procreation produced Mirkwood's spiders and more), Errour daily breeds 'a thousand yong ones.' And again like Shelob, Errour raises 'her beastly body . . . high above the ground' before leaping upon her sword-wielding challenger, the Red Cross Knight, and binding him: 'That hand or foot to stirr he strove in vaine' (stanza 18).[43]

But still there is more. Spenser's monster is preceded by an even earlier British monster rushing out from her cave with the intent to kill, and this earlier account links us back again to the Celts and the Morrígan (and, likely enough, to Brittany's cave-dwelling Corrigan as well).[44] In 1903, and continuing until 1935, Edward Gwynn translated and published *The Metrical Dindshenchas*, from manuscripts dating back as early as 1160 and as late as the fifteenth century (though the stories themselves are much older this). Among the verses Gwynn translated is a poem lamenting the death of 'noble' Odras; 'a lady of the land was she, and mighty, deedful, radiant, danger-loving, the fair and shapely spouse of stout Buchat, lord of cattle.'[45] At the poem's culmination, the 'horrid' Morrígan, 'the envious queen,' 'the shape-shifting goddess,' emerges from the Cave of Cruachan, 'her fit abode,'[46] and with 'fierceness unabating' chants 'every spell of power' over the sleeping Odras. The images we are given of Shelob issuing from her 'black hole' with murderous intent and then 'bending over' the prostrate Frodo are intriguingly similar.

There is a distinction, however. Unlike Beowulf or Spenser's knight or Frodo and Sam, the one attacked by the monster in the Odras poem is female. Nonetheless, this distinction itself may be meaningful. If Tolkien did indeed borrow from the Irish story of 'Odras' for the monster he placed in opposition to Galadriel, then the open matching of the Morrígan in monstrous form ('fierce of mood' and 'full of guile') against a radiant, fair, deedful lady is perfectly suitable.

We need now to return to Tolkien's own literature and *The Lord of the Rings* to see what it is that forms a connection between Shelob and Galadriel and how this connection strengthens and defines the best of Galadriel. In spite of their clear physical separation on the map of Middle-earth, Tolkien does indeed develop a bond between the two, a bond created most obviously, but not only, through a balance of opposition. Where Galadriel preserves, where Galadriel sustains life in Lothlórien and extends this power to the Shire, Shelob brings death and desires death, 'mind and body,' for all. Where Galadriel, after one moment of imagining herself as a queen (a very Ayesha-like queen), chooses to dwindle, to diminish so that others may live and grow, Shelob wishes only to increase, to swell and bloat by feeding on the lives of other beings. Where Galadriel, whose name may be translated as 'Maiden crowned with gleaming hair' (*Letters*, 428), seems almost too removed from the physical to have borne a child, Shelob is all body, a foul bag of vile and oozing flesh; breeding 'bastards of the miserable mates, her own offspring, that she slew' (*TT*, 332). Galadriel gives light; Shelob is darkness itself. (Ayesha, as a pivotal, middle figure, merely avoids the light.) And the light that Galadriel gives through the gift of the phial is the light that Sam and Frodo use to counter the darkness of Shelob's lair.

But again—as with Gandalf's two shadow figures—it is not only opposition that matters here. Both Shelob and Galadriel have long histories that stretch back to the beginnings of Tolkien's mythology, histories that may be equally long. ('Galadriel,' wrote Tolkien in 1954, 'is as old, or older than Shelob'—*Letters*, 180). They both, then, have ties that connect them to the First Age, and they both settle into enclosed and limited domains on Middle-earth, domains where others come to them.

More striking, however, are specific titles and images that Tolkien applies to both. Each is referred to as 'lady' or 'her ladyship' (Shelob, ironically). In her spider form, Shelob is the epitome of the entrapping female, 'weaving webs of shadow' (*TT*, 332) and 'great grey net' (*TT*, 331). In this she fulfils the negative rumours of Galadriel, who is herself a weaver, one whose powers are superstitiously misunderstood or purposefully misrepresented. 'Then there is a Lady in the Golden Wood, as old tales tell!' Éomer exclaims. 'Few escape her nets, they say.' Those in her favour, he adds, are 'net weavers and sorcerers, maybe' (*TT*, 35). This sentiment is echoed by Wormtongue in Théoden's hall: 'Then is it true, as Éomer reported, that you are in league with the Sorceress of the Golden Wood? . . . It is not to be wondered at: webs of deceit were ever woven in Dwimordene' (*TT*, 118).

Though Tolkien occasionally uses 'net' or 'web' to refer to male workers of sorcery (particularly the Dark Lord), spinning and the weaving of nets or webs have long been most strongly associated with female arts or powers. By granting the power of weaving to Vairë, the Vala 'who weaves all things that have ever been in Time into her storied webs' (*Silmarillion*, 28), by giving 'webs' and 'spider-craft' to his Corrigan, by creating Shelob and her vast webs, and by associating Galadriel with webs that both entrap and the 'web' of those garments she and her maidens weave, Tolkien is borrowing from the long-standing tradition of female spinning and weaving and the magic and danger these activities suggest—from the story of Arachne (changed to a spider through a goddess's jealousy), to the spinning, measuring, thread-cutting Fates (whose mother was Night), to Penelope (who repeatedly wove and unravelled her father-in-law's shroud), to the doomed 'fairy' Lady of Shalott (who 'weaves by night and day a magic web')[47] to Ayesha who has her weavings and whose entrapping powers are referred to as 'the web of her fatal fascinations.'[48]

Darkness and death are prevalent in these stories of weaving by female hands. Threads are cut; a shroud is woven; the fairy Lady of Shalott (spoken of in 'whispers') will leave her loom and die. In Tolkien's creation myth, Vairë, the Weaver, is spouse to Námo, keeper of the Houses of the Dead. In his Breton lay, the web-working Corrigan brings death to Aotrou and Itroun. In *The Lord of the Rings* the web-spinning Shelob, in her darkened, entrapping tunnels, desires death for all but her own beloved self; and even in Lothlórien, though we are assured at length that the cloaks Galadriel 'herself and her maidens wove' are no more than fair, serviceable garments ('and the web is good'), something unsettling remains. 'It was hard to say of what colour [the cloaks] were: grey with the hue of twilight under the trees they seemed to be; and yet if they were moved, or set in another light, they were green as shadowed leaves, or brown as fallow fields by night, dusksilver as water under the stars' (*FR*, 386).

The colours are somber, shifting, uncertain, and muted by twilight, dusk, or night. The brown described is the brown of fields, but the fields in question are 'fallow,' and the green is the green of 'shadowed' leaves. (Even the repetition of *under* is vaguely disquieting.)

Though Tolkien softens and diffuses passages of this sort by others in which Lothlórien is referred to as the Golden Wood, the land of 'sunlight and bright day,' the land where 'gold and white and blue and green' dominate (365), hints of a darker, more threatening side persist. We are told that 'on the land of Lórien no shadow lay' (364); yet shadows, 'deepening' or looming, persistently intrude, and the green hill of Cerin Amroth is the shape of a burial mound. In this way, what is bright, ageless, and secure in the land is countered and balanced by what is muted, ancient, and imperilled.

In the realms of (and characters of) Tolkien's other good or auspicious enchantresses, this sense of underlying peril, of troubling, twilight powers, is even more pronounced. The darkened, misty realm of his mysterious but helpful Faërie Queen is perilous to mortals in Tolkien's 'Smith of Wootton Major.' Even Tolkien's heroic Lúthien (also called Tinúviel) carries an air of danger, shadow, and risk; but it is Melian, Lúthien's mother, who is the most vivid of Tolkien's enchantresses. Melian (whose name is based on words meaning 'love' and 'dear gift') is a Maia who loved 'deep shadow' and who therefore left Valinor in the early days for the forests of Middle-earth (V, 220).[49] Melian is a dark, bewitching, and unapologetic worker of spells. She is, in fact, the most traditional enchantress in Tolkien's literature (and the one who will serve as Galadriel's final comparator).

Not only does the haunting, 'elusive beauty' of the Celtic world, with all its familiar perils, surround Melian as it does Galadriel, but her story and Galadriel's are significantly similar. Both Melian and Galadriel originate in Valinor, where Melian is initially described (in a 1917 draft) as a 'sprite' singing in the gardens of Lórien, the garden from which Lothlórien took its name (II, 8). Both Melian and Galadriel are drawn to Middle-earth, where each creates and protects an isolated, tree-filled realm. Both are healers and preservers. Both have great wisdom and foresight. Both allow *lembas* to be dispensed to strangers. Both, at moments, are seen as divine or nearly divine.[50] Each marries and remains more influential and more intriguing than her husband. Each husband has silver hair. Melian's daughter, Tinúviel, and Galadriel's granddaughter, Arwen, both love mortal men against the wishes of their fathers. Where Melian is 'Queen Melian,' Galadriel is 'like a queen' and now and then openly called a queen. Where Melian hopes 'to avert the evil that was prepared in the thought of Morgoth' (*UT*, 63) and comprehends the danger and lure of the Silmarils, Galadriel (who earlier opposed Morgoth) is an adversary of Sauron in *The Lord of the Rings* and is quick to recognize the dangers and attraction inherent in the One Ring. Both at last leave their protected realms in Middle-earth to return to the West, and each does so without her husband's company. (Thingol, Melian's husband, is no longer living; Celeborn chooses to stay behind.)

Their stories overlap in actuality as well as in parallel incident. Before establishing Lothlórien, Galadriel (in *The Silmarillion*) remains for a time in Doriath, Melian's enchanted realm. Here she meets Celeborn, and here Melian teaches her 'great lore and wisdom concerning Middle-earth.' The two of them 'speak together of Valinor and the bliss of old,' and Galadriel ultimately trusts Melian enough to reveal to her the story of the Silmarils (115 and 126). To add to this, Tolkien toyed with the idea of bringing their lives even closer together. In a rejected draft of *The Lord of the Rings*, Galadriel explains to the Fellowship that she came to Middle-earth during 'the days of dawn,' by passing 'over the seas with Melian of Valinor' (VII, 265). In yet another draft, Tolkien temporarily considered making Galadriel 'a handmaiden of Melian the Immortal' (XII, 185).

Where the two mostly differ is in matters of intensity. A greater sense of otherworldly danger and beguilement surrounds Melian. Doriath, with its inner stronghold of Menegroth, The Thousand Caves, is unquestionably deeper, darker, and more foreboding than Lothlórien and comes closer, in these ways, to the hidden turbulent world of Haggard's enchantress, She. In fact, Melian's affinity with Ayesha is greater than Galadriel's in a good number of ways. In a *legendarium* draft written in 1917 (or shortly after), Melian, like Ayesha, is described as 'slender and very dark of hair' with skin that is 'white and pale.' Like Ayesha, Melian is overtly desirable. Her garments, like Ayesha's, are 'filmy' and 'most lovely,' and her singing and dancing is like 'strong wine.' When Thingol first comes upon her, she is (so it 'him seemed') 'lying on a bed of leaves' (II, 42). Such open hints of sexual attraction are not to be found in descriptions of Galadriel in any version or draft. Moreover, magic—suggested but denied in Lothlórien—is open and prevalent in Melian's realm. Galadriel is spoken of as a sorceress only by those who do not know her or by her enemies, but Melian is a 'fay' in the earliest renditions and remains an enchantress in all other accounts.

Even in the toned-down later drafts and the published *Silmarillion*, there is no question of Melian's powers. Her singing in the depths of a 'starlit wood' bewitches Elwë (later Thingol) for 'long years' (*Silmarillion*, 55). Through her, 'great power' is 'loaned' to Thingol; and after he and she become King and Queen in Doriath, she is the one who places a protective barrier, an 'unseen wall of shadow and bewilderment,' around the borders of their land (*Silmarillion*, 97). This 'girdle of enchantment, the Girdle of Melian' (*Silmarillion*, 340) is consistently spoken of in terms of magical weaving, so that in the earliest 'Silmarillion' (1926–30) 'fay Gwedheling the Queen' (as she is here called) had 'woven much magic and mystery' about the halls of Thingol (IV, 59) and in the published *Silmarillion* (somewhat weakened by the passive voice) 'the power of Melian the queen was woven about [the borders of Doriath]' (151).[51]

Malevolent female power is also matched against Melian. In her story it is Ungoliant, in the shape of a light-devouring spider 'of monstrous form,' who weaves her 'black webs' and 'dark nets of strangling gloom' and so fills the role given to Shelob (Ungoliant's 'last child') in *The Lord of the Rings*. The two, Ungoliant and Shelob, are, in fact, nearly identical and not only in their malevolence, web making, and attachment to darkness; they also share a tendency to devour their own young and to pair themselves with villains (Ungoliant overtly with Morgoth in *The Silmarillion* and Shelob more loosely with Sauron in *The Lord of the Rings*). They are, in fact, so much the same, that in Tolkien's earliest drafts of *The Lord of the Rings* it is Ungoliant, 'mistress of her own lust' (*Silmarillion*, 73), the 'Gloomweaver,' who confronts Frodo and Sam.[52]

Ungoliant's powers, then, are balanced against Melian's, just as Shelob's are balanced against Galadriel's. Nonetheless, there are important differences both in the staging and the outcome of these polarities. Galadriel and Shelob are never physically placed next to one another: they are never mentioned as known adversaries and are never openly opposed. But in Melian's story, monstrous female power and positive female power are obviously and quite intentionally set side by side. After Ungoliant parts company with Morgoth—driven off by his Balrogs—she lives in Ered Gorgoroth (the Mountains of Terror), where nothing but a 'no-land' (Nan Dungortheb, Valley of Dreadful Death) lies between her and Melian's magically guarded realm. The lines of opposition between Melian and Ungoliant are clearly defined, so clearly defined that confrontation would seem inevitable. Yet no confrontation occurs. Tolkien simply establishes a balance of female good and evil and leaves it at that.

It is not until *The Lord of the Rings* that Tolkien allows his lady-and-the-spider drama to unfold, and even then he fulfils the drama only symbolically. In this, however, Tolkien's instincts are correct. For one, by replacing Galadriel with a symbol of her power, Tolkien greatly increases the significance of the confrontation with Shelob. Galadriel's phial, in the words of Christopher Tolkien, is a 'huge power, a veritable star in the darkness' (IX, 13) and its history extends well beyond the boundaries of Middle-earth and well beyond the time period or characters we meet in *The Lord of the Rings*. The phial that holds Shelob at bay contains the light of the Silmaril that adorned Eärendil's ship before Elbereth placed it in the sky as a star; and the light that came from this remaining Silmaril came first from the Two Trees of Valinor, the trees that Ungoliant destroyed by drinking up their light. The story of Galadriel's phial thus stretches from the days of creation to the end of the Third Age, adding not only far greater meaning to the confrontation with Shelob but bringing together forces from the highest level of Valinor to the hobbits of Middle-earth.

There is this as well: by using her phial (in hobbit hands) rather than Galadriel herself and by bringing her into the tunnels in visionary form, Tolkien allows Galadriel to participate in Shelob's defeat while at the same time saving her from the sullying horror that direct confrontation would bring:

> Then, as he stood, darkness about him and a blackness of despair and anger in his heart, it seemed to him that he saw a light: a light in his mind, almost unbearably bright at first, as a sun-ray to the eyes of one long hidden in a windowless pit. Then the light became colour: green, gold, silver, white. Far off, as in a little picture drawn by elven-finger, he saw the Lady Galadriel standing on the grass in Lórien, and gifts were in her hands. *And you, Ring-Bearer*, he heard her say, remote but clear, *for you I have prepared this*. (*TT*, 328–9)

Melian, on the other hand, is given no resolution at all (not even the surrogate resolution granted to Galadriel), and her story—even more than Galadriel's—can be seen as one of missed opportunity.

In a sense, both stories fall short—if each story is looked at alone. When both are taken together, however, and seen as two parts of a single, though variable, tale, each version gains in depth and possibility. Galadriel's participation (symbolized through her phial and vision) gives Tolkien a means of moving beyond the impasse he created with Melian and Ungoliant; and Melian's story, with its blatant positioning of the enemy, clarifies Tolkien's concept of female power in its two moral extremes: the power that affirms life and the power that takes life away.

With their shared opposition to spiders and villains, their similar strengths and working with webs, their histories and settings and connections to Valinor, Melian and Galadriel are very much two interpretations of a kindred character. In Melian, however, all the contributing figures of power (with their various twists and traits) are more easily discerned, all the goddesses and enchantresses, all the female monsters (*monstresses*, we might say) are far more evident. Darker, more dynamic, more openly magical than her Lothlórien counterpart, Melian is both Tolkien's most authentic portrayal of a ruling Celtic fay and the final key to Galadriel. Through Melian, Galadriel's story is all the better revealed but not simplified. Galadriel's literary history remains a highly difficult one, a history so widespread and multiply connected that it makes good sense to end with the following summary.

Beginning with Galadriel—the Galadriel of *The Lord of the Rings*—and moving backwards (initially tracing only the good that makes up her character), we come first to Tolkien's Melian of the Thousand Caves. Behind Melian (enchantress and sometimes fay) lie the more auspicious traits of Haggard's enchantress She (living in the tombs of Kôr), a woman of immortal power whose better side was inspired by both Victorian and medieval versions of Morgan le Fay, as Morgan appears in her wise, cooperative guise, a guise which is itself based on the Celtic Morrígan's favourable attributes of perception, regeneration, and fertility.

Now—after a moment's pause—we start over again, this time moving forward from the Morrígan's dark, destructive side, which is manifested in the Corrigan of Brittany and in the negative aspects of Morgan le Fay, keeping in mind that Morgan le Fay was one of the prime seductive enchantresses to haunt the Victorian mind, a haunting which created Ayesha (or She), whose destructive side and association with darkness and death appear in both Ungoliant and Shelob, who (circling back again to an earlier stage) share much with the 'Odras' Morrígan, a type that may well have influenced Spenser's Errour and Milton's Sin, two figures that clearly left their mark on Tolkien's Shelob the Great. And there you have it in a nutshell (of large coconut size), the mixing and matching of goddess, fay, and beast in Galadriel's family tree.

Without all this background, without an awareness of all that Tolkien wrote and knew and repeatedly drew upon, it would be easy to miss connections between Shelob and Galadriel, to limit, at best, our perception to their extreme disparity; and yet what Tolkien has created in these two is a striking, ingenious bond that allows him not only to exalt Galadriel and intensify Shelob's corruption but also to suggest—ever so slightly—the possibility of transgression and degeneration within Galadriel.

Notes

1. In 'real life' (Tolkien wrote to his son Christopher during the Second World War) things are not 'as clear cut as in a story' (*Letters*, 78). Shortly afterwards (still in May of 1944) he again wrote Christopher, this time saying that in real life 'men are on both sides: which means a motley alliance of orcs, beasts, demons, plain naturally honest men, and angels' (*Letters*, 82).

2. Clive Tolley presents an excellent example of the 'enticement' Tolkien feels for 'ambiguous character' in 'And the Word Was Made Flesh,' 13–14. What Tolley shows, among a good number of other things, is the way in which Tolkien re-apportions conflicting traits among his own characters by taking the complex, morally compromised figure of Unferth from *Beowulf* and turning him into the consistently treacherous Wormtongue. (Another likely source, though not an ambiguous source, for Wormtongue's character is Bikki, the wicked counsellor of the aged king Jörmunrekk in the eddic poem *Sigurdarkvida in Skamma*.)

3. For information about and a copy of this painting by the German artist Josef Madlener, see Anderson, *The Annotated Hobbit*, 38.

4. *The Poetic Edda*, trans. Lee M. Hollander (Austin: University of Texas, 1928), 72–4. It is difficult to know which translation to use. Scholars translate Odin's names in different ways, and we do not have a translation by Tolkien or know what translation he would have preferred; he read in the original Old Norse. I have settled on Lee Hollander's somewhat old-fashioned 1928 translation. Hollander published a revised edition in 1962, but the earlier book seems more consistent with what Tolkien might have known.

5. *The Elder Edda: A Selection*, trans. Paul B. Taylor and W.H. Auden (London: Faber and Faber, 1969), 69–70.

6. *Cassell's Dictionary of Norse Myth and Legend*, ed. Andy Orchard (London: Cassell, 1997).

7. As early as 1966, John Sprott Ryan noted Gandalf's Odin-like attire and his Odin-like dealings with ravens and eagles, in 'German Mythology Applied—The Extension of the Literary Folk Memory,' *Folklore* XXVII (Spring 1966): 45–59. The most perceptive early critic, however, was William H. Green, who (in his 1969 dissertation) not only recognized similarities in Gandalf's and Odin's old man guises and in their connections to eagles but also in their horses and battles (Moria and Ragnarok). Green, though he does not elaborate on Tolkien's tendency for moral division, was also the first to note that certain of Odin's negative characteristics are allotted to the Dark Lord.

8. The connection between Odin and Manwë is one Tolkien himself alludes to in early notebooks cited in *The Book of Lost Tales* (II, 290). Here Tolkien writes that the 'fairies' (who later became the Elves) 'identified' Odin with Manweg (Manwë). A detailed account of Odin imagery and Odin references in *The Silmarillion* and *The History of Middle-earth* (and the ways in which Gandalf is a Middle-earth representative of Manwë) can be found in Marjorie Burns' 'Gandalf and Odin,' *Tolkien's Legendarium: Essays on The History of Middle-earth*, ed. Verlyn Flieger and Carl F. Hostetter (Westport, CT, and London: Greenwood

Press, 2000), 219–31. A comparison of the full Norse pantheon with Tolkien's individual Valar appears in Marjorie Burns's 'Norse and Christian Gods: The Integrative Theology of J.R.R. Tolkien,' *Tolkien and the Invention of Myth: A Reader*, ed. Jane Chance (Lexington: University Press of Kentucky 2004), 163–78.

9. See, for example, *Letters*, 159n. and 202.

10. Interestingly enough, Norse mythology itself plays with similar doubling. As H.R. Ellis Davidson suggests, there are ways in which 'Loki as the ambivalent mischief-maker' can be seen 'as a kind of Odin-figure in reverse,' 'a kind of shadow Odin,' a parody of Odin. When we look at Loki from this perspective, much about this enigmatic, trickster god—his shamanism, his shape-changing, his journeys and links to the dead, his role in Sleipnir's creation, and his fathering of the giant wolf Fenrir (destroyer of Odin)—makes a kind of mystical, backhanded sense (181). And beyond Loki is Loki's own parody, Utgard-Loki, the giant, ultra-version of Loki that Thor and Loki confront in one of the eddic tales. H.R. Ellis Davidson, Gods and *Myths of Northern Europe* (Harmondsworth, England: Penguin, 1964), 181.

11. Lee M. Hollander, in his translation of *The Poetic Edda*, interprets the *Edda*'s somewhat cryptic allusion to eagle and wolf to mean their 'carved images' decorate 'the gable ends' of Valhalla, so symbolizing Odin's 'warlike activities' (64).

12. *The Silmarillion*, 110, 182, and 243.

13. For the origins of Tolkien's Warg in the Old Norse *vargr*, meaning both 'wolf' and 'outlaw,' see T.A. Shippey, *J.R.R. Tolkien: Author of the Century* (London: HarperCollins, 2000), 30–1.

14. Ruth S. Noel interprets 'Naur an edraith ammen!' as a 'spell producing fire' and translates 'Naur dan i ngaurhoth!' to mean, more specifically, 'Fire take the werewolves!' in Ruth S. Noel, *The Languages of Tolkien's Middle-earth* (Boston: Houghton Mifflin Company, 1974, 1980), 37–8.

15. *Mearas* is Anglo-Saxon for 'horse,' appropriately so since the names of the Rohirrim (the Rohan people) are based on 'forms like (but not identical with) Old English' (*Letters*, 175).

16. In a 1965 letter, Tolkien wrote that Shadowfax is 'an Elvish equivalent of ordinary horses' and that he 'certainly went with Gandalf [across the Sea], though this is not stated' (354). To add to this, in a rejected epilogue to *The Lord of the Rings*, Sam explains to his children that Shadowfax went on the ship with Gandalf. 'Of course,' says Sam, 'Gandalf couldn't have a' left him behind' (IX, 120).

17. Rees and Rees, *Celtic Heritage*, 36.

18. Lucy Allen Paton, *Studies in the Fairy Mythology of Arthurian Romance*, 2nd ed., ed. Roger Sherman Loomis (New York: Burt Franklin, 1960), 11. Paton's book was first published in 1903.

19. J.R.R. Tolkien and Donald Swann, *The Road Goes Ever On: A Song Cycle*, 2nd ed. (London, Boston, and Sydney: George Allen and Unwin, 1978).

20. Paton, *Studies in the Fairy Mythology of Arthurian Romance*, 12.

21. Roger Sherman Loomis, *Wales and the Arthurian Legend* (Cardiff: University of Wales Press, 1956), 126. Though Loomis makes broad theoretical sweeps, he draws together much of the prevalent thinking of Tolkien's time. Tolkien knew Loomis's work and cites him in the introduction to the Tolkien and Gordon edition of *Sir Gawain and the Green Knight* (xii).

22. It matters little that, in early drafts, Galadriel holds the Ring of Earth rather than the Ring of Water. Either will do to suggest fertility. (See VII 260 and 265.)

23. *Sir Gawain and the Green Knight*, ed. Tolkien and Gordon, 115. *Morrigu* or *Morrigain* are how Tolkien and Gordon render her name.

24. Lucy Allen Paton cites a late-nineteenth-century Breton tale relating how 'Morgan became enamoured of Arthur,' carried him to Avalon, and 'made him forget Guinevere' (*Studies in the Fairy Mythology of Arthurian Romance*, 34n.).

25. Paton, *Studies in the Fairy Mythology of Arthurian Romance*, 4–5.

26. Loomis, *Wales and the Arthurian Legend*, 105.

27. See, for example, *Letters* (146), *The History of Middle-earth* XII (185), or *The Two Towers*, where Gimli refers to 'Queen Galadriel' (152). Elsewhere Tolkien insists she should not be called a queen (*Letters*, 274, for example).

28. A further reference to Galadriel's likely role in the healing of Gandalf appears in a 1954 letter, where Tolkien links Gandalf's recovery with 'Galadriel's power' (*Letters*, 203).

29. Muriel A. Whitaker, *The Legends of King Arthur in Art* (Rochester, NY: D.S. Brewer, 1990), 214. See as well Debra N. Mancoff, *The Return of King Arthur: The Legend Through Victorian Eyes* (New York: H.N. Abrams, 1995), and Debra N. Mancoff, *The Arthurian Revival in Victorian Art* (New York: Garland, 1990) for excellent examples (in text and plate) of the Victorians' fascination with the Arthurian world and its enchantress fays. Particularly indicative are William Holman Hunt's well-known renditions of the Lady of Shalott (his illustration of 1857 and the 1886–1905 reworking in oil), Frederick Sandys's *Morgan-le-Fay* (brush point rendered into oil in 1862–3) or his splendid *Vivian* (1863), and Sir Edward Burne-Jones's paintings of Vivian with Merlin (1861–74) or his paintings of Morgan le Fay appearing dangerous and scheming in an 1862 watercolour and attentive and helpful in an 1880–98 oil of the queens who watch over the wounded Arthur.

30. H. Rider Haggard, *She*, in *The Works of H. Rider Haggard* (New York: Walter J. Black, Inc., 1928).

31. John Rateliff, '*She* and Tolkien,' *Mythlore* 8, no. 28 (Summer 1981): 6–8. Tolkien's statement that *She* interested him 'as much as anything' when he was a boy can be found in 'An Interview with Tolkien,' 40 (by Resnick).

32. Haggard, *She*, 256.

33. The 'fairy' Lady of Shalott also shares a number of traits and images with both Ayesha and Galadriel: she too lives in isolation—on a protected, enchanted island. She too sees through her mirror ('shadows of the world'). She too is a weaver and a woman of great beauty and power, a woman spoken of as dangerous and strange. She too is depicted (in Hunt's well-known renditions) with dark, free-flowing hair, hair as abundant and uncontained as Ayesha's rich 'masses' of 'raven black.' She too relinquishes power, as Galadriel does, and, like Ayesha, her life as well (though Haggard later resurrected Ayesha and used her in further books).

34. J.R.R. Tolkien, *The Adventures of Tom Bombadil and Other Verses from The Red Book* (Boston: Houghton Mifflin Company, 1963), 11 and 15. The story of Tom's wooing of Goldberry first appeared in the *Oxford Magazine* in 1934 and was later republished in a 1962 British edition and again in *The Tolkien Reader* (1966).

35. J.R.R. Tolkien, 'The Lay of Aotrou and Itroun,' *Welsh Review* Vol. 4, no. 4 (December 1945): 254–66.

36. Shippey, *Author of the Century*, 293.

37. The original Breton lay and other similar tales and lays appeared in collections published in the late nineteenth century, collections that Tolkien most certainly knew. See Jessica Yates, 'The Source of "The Lay of Aotrou and Itroun,"' *Leaves from the Tree: J.R.R. Tolkien's Shorter Fiction* (London: Tolkien Society, 1991), 63–71. Though variations on the

tale are found as far away as Scandinavia, the Breton version discussed by Yates is the one that appears most directly connected to Tolkien's Corrigan.

38. William Morris has his own fountain enchantresses. In *The Wood Beyond the World*, there are two magical women—one, 'the Mistress,' whose dwelling is an artificial Paradise with a fountain of gold in its centre, the other 'the Maid,' who is discovered within a circle of oak trees near a natural fountain. The Mistress casts 'her net' to entrap the hero (and others); the Maid, who is called 'the land's increase,' is the one who sets him free. If we remember that Galadriel ('the Lady in the Golden Wood' and the preserver of Lothlórien) also has a fountain in the centre of her realm and that Éomer, in his ignorance, believes that 'few escape her nets,' it seems likely enough that Morris also influenced Tolkien's Galadriel. *The Complete Works of William Morris*, vol. 17 (New York: Russell and Russell, 1966).

39. Haggard, *She*, 255.

40. Since *lob* is an obsolete word for spider (*lobbe* in Old English), *Shelob*, means, simply enough, *she-spider*.

41. In a 1974 essay, comparing G.K. Chesterton's poem *The Ballad of the White Horse* with *The Lord of the Rings*, Christopher Clausen commented on Galadriel's light and the image of Galadriel that comes to Sam within Shelob's tunnels. See Christopher Clausen, '*Lord of the Rings* and *The Ballad of the White Horse*,' *South Atlantic Bulletin* 39, no. 2 (May 1974): 10–16. Five years later, two other critics went a step further by noting the ways in which Galadriel is not just opposed to Shelob but matched and contrasted with her in several precise capacities. See Anne Cotton Petty, *One Ring to Bind Them All: Tolkien's Mythology* (University AL: University of Alabama Press, 1979), 53; and Peter Damien Goselin, 'Two Faces of Eve: Galadriel and Shelob as Anima Figures,' *Mythlore* 6, no. 3 (Summer 1979): 3–4.

42. In early drafts of *The Silmarillion*, Tolkien himself uses the name 'Kôr' (diacritical mark and all) for his City of the Elves and for the hill where that City lies. See Volume I, throughout.

43. That the Red Cross Knight and Sam both use swords (so giving fodder to Freudians) is inevitable. What other weapon would they be likely to use? This is not to deny sexuality is present. It is, if only in the vile and excessive breeding both monsters display, but sex itself does not take place with Errour or Shelob, anymore than it does when Beowulf kills Grendel's mother with a mighty sword. For a thorough response to those who misunderstand sexuality in Tolkien, see Daniel Timmons, 'Hobbit Sex and Sensuality in *The Lord of the Rings*,' *Mythlore* 23, no. 3 (Summer 2001): 70–9.

44. The Celts, however, do not have it all; in a 1989 article on Tolkien's monsters, Joe Abbott notes that the hero of the *Ala Flekks Saga* encounters the 'troll-woman Night' within a cave as dark and foul as Shelob's. See Joe Abbott, 'Tolkien's Monsters: Concept and Function in *The Lord of the Rings*. (Part II) Shelob the Great,' *Mythlore* 60 (Winter 1989): 41.

45. *The Metrical Dindshenchas*, Part IV, trans. Edward Gwynn (1924; repr., Dublin: W. and G. Baird Ltd, 1991), 196–201.

46. The Cave of Cruachan, also called the Hell's Gate of Ireland, is a familiar gateway to the Other-world, one that appears repeatedly in tales where magical beings or magical animals (generally highly destructive ones) enter into our world. In one account, the hero, Nera, is shown a horrifying vision of severed heads that lie within the cave; in other accounts, destructive birds or pigs emerge from the Cave of Cruachan, and in yet another tale, magical cats are set loose from the cave and attack three warriors. A similar image of murderous, cave-dwelling cats appears in Tolkien's 'Lay of Aotrou and Itroun.' (See Rees and Rees, *Celtic Heritage*, for further details on the Cave of Cruachan and other supernatural caves.)

47. See lines 37–8.

48. Haggard, *She*, 272.

49. The Maiar and Valar are both 'Holy Ones,' created by Ilúvatar, 'Father of All,' before the making of the World. The Maiar, however, are of lesser degree than the Valar.

50. Sam, for example, prays, or as good as prays, to Galadriel, 'the Lady,' asking for 'light and water' on the way to Mount Doom, and Melian (in the earliest 'Silmarillion' of 1926–30) is given an almost goddess-like role as one of the 'divine maidens of the Vala Lórien' and as the 'divine mother' of Lúthien. (See IV, 13, 23, and 55.)

51. Both the titles *fay* and *queen* and the names Tolkien originally considered for Melian are good indications of an Arthurian heritage. In early drafts, she is variously referred to as Wendelin, Gwendeling, Gwenniel, Gwenethlin, Gwendhiling, and Gwendelin, as well as Gwedheling, names with a clear Arthurian ring (II, 244).

52. See I, 152–3, II, 160, and VIII, 196–9.

ANDREW LYNCH

Archaism, Nostalgia, and Tennysonian
War in The Lord of the Rings

Despite Tolkien's personal experience of modern war, his fantasy epic is surprisingly different in image, diction, and ambience from literature associated with World War I. Its war rhetoric resembles more than anything else the moralized combat of Victorian medievalist literature.

Through his long-running *Idylls of the King*, whose composition stretched from the 1830s to the 1880s, Alfred Tennyson became a major influence on the Victorian shift toward the symbolic in medievalist representations of warfare. Seeing his own era as morally superior to Geoffrey of Monmouth's or Malory's, Tennyson committed himself to capturing the true "spirit" or "ideal" of Arthurian chivalry without much of its troubling military substance, omitting any but legendary history and far reducing the characteristic medieval interest in the detail of wars and tournaments. Partly through the huge success of Tennyson's "parabolic" Arthuriad, in the later Victorian period war became the main selling-point of medievalism as symbolic heroism and chivalry, even though, viewed in the cold light of history, medieval war could also be seen as barbarous violence, an indictment of its age. An elderly character in one of Charlotte Yonge's late novels nicely sums up the conflict:

From *Tolkien's Modern Middle Ages*, pp. 77–92. © 2005 by Jane Chance and Alfred K. Siewers.

[Y]ou will laugh, but my enthusiasm was for chivalry, Christian chivalry, half symbolic. History was delightful to me for the search for true knights. I had lists of them, drawings if possible, but I never could indoctrinate anybody with my affection. Either history is only a lesson, or they know a great deal too much, and will prove to you that the Cid was a ruffian, and the Black Prince not much better.[1]

One outcome of such tension, between the Middle Ages as half-symbolic chivalry and medieval violence as barbaric "Other" to the modern, was the increased ideological vulnerability of the symbolism to adverse critiques of medieval history. Medievalist fictions had to find ways to cope with that difficulty, by giving war a more positive and widely applicable narrative treatment. I wish to suggest in this essay that the war discourse of J.R.R. Tolkien's *The Lord of the Rings* can best be understood within this late-nineteenth-century context. As a war story, *The Lord of the Rings*, I argue, is more of a late utterance in a Victorian medievalist poetic, usually thought to have died out after 1916, than either a medieval or a mid-twentieth-century text.

Tolkien's relation to the war of his own century is problematical. Famously, he made others take all responsibility for any connection between *The Lord of the Rings* and World War II. The book was, he said, purely a "feigned" "history," "with . . . varied applicability to the thought and experience of readers."[2] Yet he hinted that it might have been generally influenced by his dreadful experience in the Great War, more than fifty years before[3]—"By 1918 all but one of my close friends were dead"—and by an even earlier trauma: "The country in which I lived in childhood was being shabbily destroyed before I was ten" (*LR* foreword, xv).

It is not surprising that Tolkien should rate his memories of the Great War as more important than any contemporary reference. The nobility of long memory and the obliviousness of the present time to past sacrifices are major themes in *The Lord of the Rings*, which Tolkien made as deeply nostalgic and past-oriented as he had judged *Beowulf* to be.[4] It abounds in laments for lost landscapes and departed glories, and dwells repeatedly on scenes of decay and desolation. Indeed, given Tolkien's association of the Great War with English rural destruction as his two founding traumas, one might well have expected that a horrific version of modern war would complete *The Lord of the Rings's* indictment of the twentieth century. This is not the case. Early attempts to read the novel as a political allegory probably arose because much of its discourse of war seemed so distant from most twentieth-century sensibilities. Hugh Brogan has written that for "Tolkien, a man whose life was language, . . . [to] have gone through the Great War, with all its rants and lies, and still come out committed to a 'feudal' literary style . . . looks like an act of deliberate defiance of modern history."[5] Tolkien's references to his own war memories are definitely not "feudal" in style—"the animal horror of the life of active service on the earth—such as trench life as I knew it" (*Letters*, 72).

And yet, despite the author's language here and in the 1968 foreword, *The Lord of the Rings* does not mainly represent war as an "oppression" or "hideous experience" that wastes young lives (*LR* foreword, xiii). Instead, Tolkien principally makes the War of the Ring into a theater of heroic action in which the military prowess of groups and individuals is recognized as necessary, ennobling, and deeply effective. His war may be "grim" and "terrible," but it is often valorous and lofty in style, and of the major friendly characters, only Boromir and Théoden actually die in its fighting. Certainly, the novel also shows evidence of more common modern attitudes. Tom Shippey has commented on the post-heroic, "modernistic style of courage" exemplified by the Hobbits.[6] Brian Rosebury,[7] Brogan, and John Garth have all suggested ways in which Tolkien's Great War memories might have influenced horrific and menacing narrative details. Yet Garth's recent book, while fully documenting the evils Tolkien experienced in the trenches and his distaste for war propaganda, still concludes that *The Lord of the Rings* "tackled the themes that Wilfred Owen ruled off limits: deeds, lands, glory, honour, might, majesty, dominion, power."[8] My focus here is on what cultural factors might have helped to make up such an idealized discourse of war in Tolkien, especially the high style of war narrative he often employs within *The Lord of the Rings*.

It would be natural to suppose that Tolkien, as a learned medievalist, dealt with the memory of "hideous" modern war by transforming it into a superior version directly along medieval lines. In this connection, there have been important studies of his indebtedness to various medieval literatures,[9] and, in obvious ways, Tolkien's war looks "medieval." The heroes in *The Lord of the Rings* fight with favored weapons of the Middle Ages— swords, spears, axes, and bows; they offer and fulfil military service as part of feudal or family obligation; there is a preponderance of medieval combat types, especially siege warfare, sword fights, cavalry charges, and battles in open field; there are numerous single combats within battles that broadly resemble those in medieval historiography and romance; battle description is dominated by features such as distinctive armor and livery, famous swords, and horses with special names, banners, heralds, war cries, horns, and so on. There is continued reference to great "tales" of war, in various medieval forms: chronicle, elegy and heroic lay. And yet, Tolkien's wars are not quite like those in the medieval stories he salutes, in either their overall narrative function or their specific rhetoric.

Of course, medieval literary sources and analogues can often be sighted in Tolkien's war narrative, but they become strangely transmuted in the process. For example, he commonly employs a paratactic sentence structure, which joins up its elements by a chain of "and's" and "then's." In Sir Thomas Malory's *Le Morte Darthur* this is the standard narrative method: matter-of-fact, highly physical, and centered on particular exploits. Malory's paratactic structure is congruent with a whole narrative procedure that takes the reader directly from one deed of arms to the next. Tolkien's major extended battle descriptions, such as the Pelennor Fields episode (*LR* 5.6, 821–22), are quite different in overall effect, although one could easily point to individual features that look "medieval." To begin with, there is a good deal of parataxis, but whereas in *Le Morte Darthur* parataxis is the staple of battle narrative, here it is a high style that embraces both simple actions ("and he spurred to the standard") (*LR* 5.6, 821) and sometimes elaborate figuration: "and the drawing of the scimitars of the Southrons was like a glitter of stars"; "and more skilled was their knighthood with long spears and bitter" (*LR* 5.6, 821). Tolkien's alliance of paratactic structure with highly charged imagery and lyrical cadences will recall the King James Bible or verse derived from it, like Lord Byron's "The Destruction of Sennacherib" or Lord Macaulay's narrative poems, much more than it does Malory or any Old or Middle English prose. The symbolic coloring of the Pelennor scene (white and green, scarlet and black), the complex transferral of literal color to metaphorical use ("red wrath," "white fury . . . burned the hotter"), and the lofty similes ("like a glitter of stars, . . . like a firebolt in a forest") (*LR* 5.6, 821) indicate their origin in a post-medieval, romantic mindset. Tolkien makes the battle a panoramic, semisymbolic clash of good and evil, quite unlike the basic functionalism of most medieval English war writing with its principal interest in individual "deeds" of arms and the fortunes of the fight and with occasional evocations of the general battlefield atmosphere.

The style and certainly the individual word choices of Tolkien's description of the Pelennor Fields come closer in places to the effect of Old English and Middle English alliterative verse. "Long spears and bitter" recalls collocations like *Beowulf* 2703b–2704a, "waell-seaxe gebraed, / biter and beaduscearp" ("drew the deadly knife, keen and battle-sharp"),[10] or *The Battle of Maldon* 110b–111a, "bord ord onfeng, / biter waes se beadu-raes" ("Shield received spear-point; savage was the onslaught").[11] In bare meter, at least, "and his spear was shivered as he threw down their chieftain. [/] Out swept his sword, and he spurred to the standard, [/] hewed staff and bearer, and the black serpent foundered" (*LR* 5.6, 821) could almost be lines from the Alliterative *Morte Arthure*.

But in overall effect, Tolkien's writing reads quite differently from any of these medieval poems. This is partly because he has such a mixture of different styles, and they have a fairly consistent style. Another difference occurs because in a twentieth-century prose fiction such abundant parataxis, sentence inversion, and metricality must strike the reader as elements of stylistic individuality, choices to heighten literary "tone," rather than as integral features of a narrative medium that the writer shares as normal with a contemporary audience. Tolkien's war narrative seems to try for elevation by sounding archaic, whereas if Malory or *Maldon* sound lofty to a modern reader (and Malory sometimes does not), they will seem to manage that effect just by being themselves, strikingly different from modern writing, but in modes we imagine to be familiar to the original audience while still sufficiently intelligible to us. They exemplify Virginia Woolf's dictum: "To believe that your impressions hold good for others is to be released from the cramp and confinement of personality."[12]

Tolkien, by contrast, well aware that his impressions did *not* hold good for most literary contemporaries, consciously wielded archaism as an anti-modernist cultural weapon. The insistent archaism of battle scenes in *The Lord of the Rings* reveals his cultural campaign to restore a sense of heroic potential to English life, which is symbolically enacted through the novel's revival of earlier English usages. Tolkien attempts to share his heroic mindset with others by employing archaic language as if it were actually contemporary and colloquial. Even small features of Tolkien's high style, such as the elision of the indefinite article in a phrase like "with great press of men" (*LR* 5.6, 821), stand out as effortfully grand. A reader expects in modern English usage, at a deeper, less negotiable level than individual lexical choices, the form "with a great press of men," so what Tolkien offers as a casual, natural parlance cannot be accepted as such. "Great press" is colloquial thirteenth-to sixteenth-century English, but in a modern work its presence creates a complex secondary effect, revealing the writer's impossible desire for archaic forms to pass as both ordinary *and* lofty.

Naturalization of the archaic as a high style was Tolkien's deliberate program, which he once defended in an unfinished letter: "If mod. E. [modern English] has lost the trick of putting a word desired to emphasize (for pictorial, emotional, or logical reasons) into prominent first place, without addition of a lot of little 'empty' words (as the Chinese say), so much the worse for it. And so much for the better for it the sooner it learns the trick again. And *some* one must begin the teaching, by example" (*Letters*, 225–26). Although inversion of sentence order and other archaisms might seem appropriate in formal speeches between characters drawn from a past age, archaism has a different effect in a simple narrative utterance like "great press," which, if it *were* natural in form to a modern narrator, as it was to the Wife of Bath,[13] would be quite prosaic. It can only be "high" in Tolkien *because* it is archaic, and so the archaism, implicitly proposed as more impressive than what he called "our slack and frivolous modern idiom" (*Letters*, 225–26), is seen to be valued for its own sake.

The frequent archaism, much greater than Tolkien's normal practice, in the battle scenes of *The Lord of the Rings* indicates the special status he gave to military prowess. Battle is consistently made a high subject.[14] Although the love of war for its own sake clearly worried Tolkien, as many critics have noticed, he still very often employs inversion and/or parataxis as a means of ennobling battles and military symbols—"Great was the clash"; "Fewer were they"; "Out swept his sword" (*LR* 5.6, 821); "Very bright was that sword when it was made whole again; the light of the sun shone redly in it, and the light of the moon shone cold, and its edge was hard and keen" (*LR* 2.3, 269).

What helped to form this high style of war? Perhaps one answer lies in the closeness in balance and cadence of the lines on the sword Andúril just quoted to some lines in Tennyson's "The Passing of Arthur": "On one side lay the Ocean, and on one / Lay a great water, and the moon was full."[15] Tennyson was clearly one model for Tolkien's poetry before and around the time he enlisted, as Rosebury notes, and as can be seen in numerous instances quoted by Garth.[16] We need not suppose that the trenches destroyed that influence. Research by historian Jay Winter has suggested that the Great War did not suddenly inaugurate mass modernity by breaking all links with the past, as used to be claimed. Rather, many people, perhaps most, coped with war trauma by performing the work of memory and mourning with their prewar cultural resources. In Winter's words, "The Great War, the most 'modern' of wars, triggered an avalanche of the unmodern."[17] Tolkien's Middle-earth narratives, begun in wartime, might well be understood in this context. It was he who called the Shire "more or less a Warwickshire village of about the period of the Diamond Jubilee" (*Letters*, 230). When he found himself, as a war casualty, faced with the need to invent "a myth for England," it should not be surprising if he was influenced by the very popular "Return of the King" myth presented in Tennyson, Victoria's laureate, who died the year Tolkien was born.[18]

Generally speaking, Tolkien's narrative can be seen as a way of "getting over" the war through its assertion of strong continuities with the nineteenth century. Tolkien does not show nostalgia for the medieval past as a separate period in itself, a lost domain, but he mourns the sudden modern loss of a sense of continuity with that past. In seeking to reconnect the present to the Middle Ages, he therefore binds himself to intervening ages as well, when it was better remembered. So, in *The Lord of the Rings* a privileged discourse of "tree" and "root" connects Norse mythology, English folk-tale, genealogy, and linguistic derivation, and naturalizes their continuing connection with the English landscape. Language, landscape, and identity become intimately close. *Beowulf*, for Tolkien, was a timeless, and therefore a contemporary text for England: "It was made in this land, and moves in our northern world beneath our northern sky, and for those who are native to that tongue and land, it must ever call with a profound appeal—until the dragon comes" ("Beowulf," 33–34).

So much in Tolkien's battle to restore cultural continuity is imaginatively projected in this way from a romantic reading of early heroic narratives that his work might seem to exemplify the nostalgia double bind described by Susan Stewart in *On Longing*:

> Nostalgia, like any form of narrative, is always ideological: the past it seeks has never existed except as narrative, and hence, always absent, that past continually threatens to reproduce itself as a felt lack. Hostile to history and its invisible origins, and yet longing for an impossibly pure context of lived experience at a place of origin, nostalgia wears a distinctly utopian face, a face that turns toward a future-past, a past which has only ideological reality. This point of desire which the nostalgic seeks is in fact the absence that is the very generating mechanism of desire.[19]

In Stewart's terms, one might see a fear of experiential inauthenticity behind Tolkien's grand narrative, fear driving the continuing consolidation of his linguistic and narrative environment against his experience of an environment doubly destroyed. Certainly, within *The Lord of the Rings*, critiques of the heroic view based on empirical history and material culture are branded as loss of faith and associated with demoralized minds like Saruman: "Dotard! What is the House of Eorl but a thatched barn where brigands drink in the reek, and their brats roll on the floor among the dogs?" (*LR* 3.10, 567).

Yet if, for Tolkien, the gap Stewart postulates between history or lived experience, on the one hand, and ideology, on the other, threatens a horror—the debasement of an idealized environment by sordid materialism—it also provides an endless opportunity for fiction. Within the never-sated narrative space, archaism, nostalgia, and the elegiac mode are deployed as active forms of cultural continuity. Tolkien virtually situates himself *within* the tradition of Old English writing, with *The Wanderer* and much of *Beowulf*. In "The Homecoming of Beorhtnoth Beorhthelm's Son," he delights in pointing out that the most famous lines from *The Battle of Maldon* (312–13), spoken in the face of certain defeat—

Hige sceal þe heardra, heorte þe cenre,
mod steal þe mare þe ure maegen lytlað.
[Will shall be the sterner, heart the bolder, spirit the greater as our strength lessens.]

—are "not 'original' [to the man who speaks them], but an ancient and honored expression of heroic will."[20] For Tolkien, to assert these lofty battle sentiments yet again is no mere literary quotation but the conscious renewal of a heroic tradition in the face of imminent loss.

Repetition, which for Stewart is a sign of the otherness of experience mediated through narrative and of the inauthenticity of lived experience, for Tolkien acknowledges the loss of the heroic past in a form that consoles it by asserting a community of interest with the vanished heroes and all those who have since believed in them. Consciousness of loss and absence provides prestigious roles for figures who connect present and past: the mage who can interpret ancient vestiges; the survivor who keeps faith with his dead comrades; the exile in whom memory preserves a lost noble world. With these prestigious adversarial roles comes a sense of cultural work as the battle to reimpose on the world an ideal order that is intuited to be lacking. The conception of heroism in *The Lord of the Rings* feeds directly on the difficulties in realizing such an order:

> "Few now remember them," Tom murmured, "yet still some go wandering, sons of forgotten kings, walking in loneliness, guarding from evil folk that are heedless."
> The hobbits did not understand his words, but as he spoke they had a vision as it were of a great expanse of years behind them, like a vast shadowy plain over which there strode shapes of Men, tall and grim with bright swords, and last came one with a star on his brow. Then the vision faded and they were back in the sunlit world. (*LR* 1.8, 142–43)

That "few" are aware of these guardians, that they walk "in loneliness," completes an impression of their necessity and rightness, their supreme importance within an imperialist system of meaning. The past is "shadowy" only because the present is "heedless," ignorant, and ungrateful. The import of the vision may seem remote from the material "sunlit world," but it portends a steep learning curve for the Hobbits toward a potential re-ennoblement of the modern life they represent. In that process, the "bright swords" of war become paramount.

Tolkien's conscious reassertion of archaism in the face of modernity is itself a reprise of the young Alfred Tennyson's original framing of "Morte d'Arthur," in "The Epic":

> Why take the style of those heroic times?
> For nature brings not back the mastodon,
> Nor we those times; and why should any man
> Remodel models?[21]

Tennyson's anxiety about reviving a past style was partly disingenuous. Despite the frame of authorial self-doubt, the imagined audience of "The

Epic" act like proto-Inklings: after discussing "the general decay of faith / Right thro' the world," they listen in deep silence to "Morte d'Arthur," and one, at least, dreams that night of a modern Arthur returned, "With all good things, and war shall be no more." Implicitly, as in Tolkien, the problematical archaism of Tennyson's medievalist venture is shown to be its main point, a sign of the struggle to keep faith with a heroic potential against the apparently ineluctable course of the world.

Tolkien resembles Tennyson in numerous more specific ways. First is his lexicon loaded with Tennysonian favorites—"bright," "dark," "fair," "foul," "dim," "pale," "fade(d) "faint," "clean," "sweet," "weary," "gleam," "flame," "gray," "thin," "shadow," "waste." Second is his habit of displacing psychological and moral analysis onto descriptions of landscape, weather, architecture, and ornament. It could be argued that this is a tendency Tolkien shares with several other writers—the *Beowulf*-poet, *Gawain*-poet and Spenser come to mind—yet, taken in combination with the close similarities in vocabulary, it often creates in his work a distinctly Tennysonian ambience. Direct borrowings are absent, but Tolkien's landscapes generally aspire to what J.S. Mill early identified in Tennyson: "the power of creating scenery, in keeping with some state of feeling; so fitted as to be the embodied symbol of it."[22] Examples abound: "to their right a grey river gleamed pale in the thin sunshine" (*LR* 1.12, 195); "The sun grew misty as the day grew old, until it gleamed in a pale sky like a high white pearl. Then it faded into the West, and dusk came early, followed by a grey and starless night" (*LR* 2.8, 370); "Only far away north-west there was a deeper darkness against the dying light: the Mountains of Mist and the forest at their feet" (*LR* 3.2, 419); "Over the last shelf of rotting stone the stream gurgled and fell down into a brown bog and was lost. Dry reeds hissed and rattled though they could feel no wind" (*LR* 4.2, 611). Tolkien's natural world is glossed with psychic and moral suggestions—"thin," "dying," "rotting," and "lost"—to the extent that what John D. Rosenberg writes of *Idylls of the King* applies equally well to *The Lord of the Rings*: it "uses landscape . . . not as a decorative adjunct to character but as the mythopoeic soil in which character is rooted and takes its being."[23] Further resemblances to Tennyson are seen in Tolkien's striving for aural imitation—"hissed and rattled"—, and in his creation of unease or apprehension by repeatedly giving colorless or imprecise features of description a precise location: a "grey" river viewed to the right," a "misty" sun fading "into the West," "darkness" to the "north-west." Tolkien's habitual glances to the sun and the horizon simultaneously orient his heroes on a realist map and surround them with an illimitable vista of psychic possibilities.

Tolkien also strongly resembles Tennyson in the broad political reliance he places on the central role of a true king, and particularly in his vision of good rule as environmental and moral cleansing, based on a prior inner cultivation of the self. Arthur praises the reformed Edyrn for "weeding all his heart / As I will weed this land before I go."[24] Arthur's role in "Gereint and Enid" is a political extension of the same theme:

> [A]nd [he] sent a thousand men
> To till the wastes, and moving everywhere
> Cleared the dark places and let in the law,
> And broke the bandit holds and cleansed the land.[25]

Tolkien's version of good kingship is a directly similar scouring and recultivation of the earth. In Aragorn's reign, Gandalf says, "The evil things will be driven out of the waste-lands. Indeed the waste in time will be waste no longer, and there will be people and fields where once there was wilderness" (*LR* 6.7, 971).

If the key to Tolkien's stylistic archaism is his nostalgic desire to reconnect with a heroic past, then the nostalgia is empowered by such links with a recent era of medievalist idealism. In particular, the comparison helps explain how Tolkien, who had, like Tennyson, a well-attested distaste for actual war, could nevertheless make it a "high" subject in the manner I have outlined. Within both writers' works, the description of war often tends more toward ideological symbol than toward direct description of military action: their war is a school of moral order, a preparation for future rule: "That is what you have been trained for," Gandalf tells Merry and Pippin before they "scour" the Shire, removing the "squint-eyed and sallow-faced" Orc-like enemy (*LR* 6.7, 974; 6.8, 981, 992) and restoring ethnic boundaries. As in Tennyson's Idylls, the enemy not only causes pollution but is moral pollution, "the beast," to be dispelled by force. War is relied on to restore the natural world: "Kill orc-folk!" says Ghân-buri-Ghân. "Drive away bad air and darkness with bright iron!" (*LR* 5.5, 816).

In dealing with war in his novel, Tolkien encountered a problem similar to Tennyson's in the Idylls. Like Tennyson he longs for a state beyond war—"the very last end of the War, I hope" (*LR* 6.8, 997) yet is committed to a story and an ethos in which martial heroism is a major currency. Both writers cope with the issue in a similar way, by moral allegory. Arthur's good wars are made a semisymbolic expression of moral superiority—"a voice / As dreadful as the shout of one who sees / To one who sins"[26]—and his early enemies are inhuman or alien: the "heathen," "beast," and "Roman." Evil war, when his knights have degenerated, in Mordred's civil rebellion, is physically gross:

> Oaths, insult, filth and monstrous blasphemies,
> Sweat, writhings, anguish, labouring of the lungs
> In that close mist, and cryings for the light,
> Moans of the dying, and voices of the dead.[27]

In *The Lord of the Rings*, battle alignments, as in Tennyson's self-styled "parabolic" wars, are also moral alignments. Tolkien mainly treats the nature of war according to the sides involved, which are identified by the rightness and wrongness of their overall causes. One side, led by Aragorn and advised by Gandalf, fights a "medieval" war of named volunteers and pledged faith, while the bad side is "modern," with its nameless conscripts, machines, slaves, and creatures of Sauron. The desolate Great War landscape of trenches, mud, shell holes, corpses, and total deforestation is associated with Isengard, the Paths of the Dead, or Frodo's and Sam's journey into Mordor, rather than with the book's actual battlefields: "Indeed the whole surface of the plains of Gorgoroth was pocked with great holes, as if, while it was still a waste of soft mud, it had been smitten with a shower of bolts and huge slingstones. The largest of these holes were rimmed with ridges of broken rock, and broad fissures ran out from them in all directions. It was a land in which it would be possible to creep from hiding to hiding, unseen by all but the most watchful eyes" (*LR* 6.3, 913). This wretched Mordor country, unlike the Somme where Tolkien fought in 1916, does not owe its destruction equally to both sides in the war. Rather, while it functions as an expression of Sauron's sterile, dispiriting power, it gives Frodo and Sam the chance to display selfless endurance as they struggle to get rid of the Ring. Where the war landscape does impinge on actual combat in *The Lord of the Rings*, as at Helm's Deep, it is only the Orcs who are associated with the horror of flares, shell bursts, and night raids from the enemy trenches: "For a staring moment, the watchers on the walls saw all the space between them and the dike lit with white light; it was boiling and crawling with black shapes, some squat and broad, some tall and grim, with high helms and sable shields. Hundreds and hundreds more were pouring over the dike and through the breach" (*LR* 3.7, 520). The Orcs must "pour" over a dike, while Aragorn, Legolas, and Gimli watch them from the walls of a medieval stronghold.

The mixture of realism and allegorical significance in such a war discourse is confusing. Tolkien argued that it was a "romance," and hence a nonrealist, quasi-allegorical narrative feature, derived from Christian psychomachia: "In real life they [the Orcs] are on both sides, of course. For 'romance' has grown out of allegory and its wars are still derived from the 'inner war' of allegory in which good is on one side and various modes of badness on the other. In real (exterior) life men are on both sides" (*Letters*, 82). Although the heroic-Germanic coloring may disguise it, in regard to war *The Lord of the Rings* is considerably more romance than epic or novel, because it gives an absolute aesthetic and moral privilege—aesthetics and morality becoming quite indistinguishable—to one side only. Tolkien re-creates, in effect, the "parabolic" war of Tennyson, in which the king's enemies are not merely political or military opponents but thoroughly evil forces who can be understood to represent evil itself. One sign of this is that weapons occasionally become spontaneous agents in battle: "The bow of Legolas was singing" (LR 2.4, 291); "Yet my axe is restless in my hand. Give me a row of orc-necks and room to swing . . . !" (LR 3.7, 520); "It has been knife-work up here" (LR 3.7, 524). Tolkien's use of the motif recalls medieval heroic poetry like The Battle of Maldon, but with the thoroughly Tennysonian difference that only the good characters have weapons privileged to act willingly.[28]

Gimli's Norse-like moments of battle-relish are fairly rare in Tolkien's narrative. Through the figure of Aragorn, especially, The Lord of the Rings more often displays what has been said about the medieval warriors of Victorian artists, that they are statuesque icons rather than action figures, with "a strong sense of arrested movement."[29] In Idylls of the King, Arthur's wars are "rendered mystically"[30] (allegorically) on the gates of Camelot, in a hierarchy rising from bestial savagery to angelic pureness, topped by the statue of Arthur himself.[31] As, over the course of Lord of the Rings, Strider turns into Aragorn, he often seems like a new version of the Victorian allegoric statuesque: "The grey figure of the Man, Aragorn son of Arathorn, was tall and stern as stone, his hand upon the hilt of his sword; he looked as if some king out of the mists of the sea had stepped upon the shores of lesser men" (LR 3.5, 489). The iconic quality of Aragorn emblematizes the simultaneously desired presence and absence of the past in Tolkien's heroic nostalgia. Is it that a statue has come to life, the heroic past returned, or that Aragorn's new status removes him from the contingent world of time, of "lesser men," into what is already a perfected retrospective understanding? The core of Aragorn's greatness is that it is already archaic. In such moments Tolkien, one might say, equally desires the return of the heroic age and the rememorializing of its loss—a renewal of the Tennysonian covenant with an idealized medievalist violence, but carefully removed from historical scrutiny, as the true idiom of national and personal heroic potential.

It could be argued that The Lord of the Rings maintains dialogue with Tennyson's Idylls to the very end. For Tolkien leaves us finally not with Frodo or Aragorn but with Sam Gamgee, just as the Idylls ends not with Arthur but with Bedivere, also staring westward, as his master's vessel passes beyond sight into a mysterious realm and a new age begins on earth. Both bereft companions grieve, but in comparison to Tennyson, Tolkien distances this world from the one to which his hero has departed. In Tennyson, Bedivere himself sees "the speck that bare the King, / . . . pass on and on . . . / . . . and vanish into light,"[32] and hears, though faintly, Arthur's reception in heaven:

> As from beyond the limit of the world,
> Like the last echo born of a great cry,
> Sounds, as if some fair city were one voice
> Around a king returning from his wars.[33]

In Tolkien, Frodo alone beholds the new day, "white shores and beyond them a far green country under a swift sunrise," and hears "the sound of singing that came over the water" as he nears his final home. With Frodo gone, a dejected Sam sees only "a shadow on the waters that was soon lost in the West," and hears "only the sigh and murmur of the waves on the shores of Middle-earth" (*LR* 6.9, 1007), much as Tennyson's Bedivere (following Malory) has done on his earlier, failed attempts to cast Excalibur away: "I heard the water lapping on the crag, / And the long ripple washing in the reeds."[34] Tennyson's triumphant "Return of the King" motif is absent in Tolkien at Frodo's parting, having been reserved appropriately for Aragorn's elaborate reception in Gondor: "And the shadow departed, and the Sun was unveiled, and light leaped forth; and the waters of Anduin shone like silver, and in all the houses of the City men sang for the joy that welled up in their hearts" (*LR* 6.5, 941–42), followed by "[A]nd amid the music of harp and viol and singing and clear voices the King passed through the flower-laden streets and came to the Citadel" (*LR* 6.5, 947).

It is here, too, that Tolkien most strongly foregrounds another Tennysonian theme "The old order changeth, yielding place to new"[35]—when Gandalf stresses that the king's triumph means "The Third Age of the world is ended, and the new age is begun" (*LR* 6.5, 949). Aragorn's warfaring and hold on power are, like Tennyson's Arthur's, finally subsumed within the broadest view of historical necessity. Already by the time Frodo and Sam are reunited with him in Ithilien, his sword has become ritual and symbolic, a sign of the right to rule: "On the throne sat a mail-clad man, a great sword was laid across his knees, but he wore no helm" (*LR* 5.4, 932). There can be no suggestion that superior military force alone has won the day in Gondor. This is the image of a "true king."

Tennyson is by no means the only Victorian medievalist who invites relation to Tolkien. Others such as William Morris could perhaps be considered as more direct influences on him. After all, *The Lord of the Rings* is an eclectic text with many possible points of reference. Yet the example of Tennyson best helps us understand the "high" style of war discourse and its symbolic tendencies that puzzle some Tolkien readers so much. It helps us to see how, against his personal experience of war and his political understanding, for reasons of moral allegory, Tolkien displaces the evils of modern war on to the bad side and reserves for the good the "bright swords" of medievalist idealism. The sword—medievalized war's archaic weapon—becomes for Tolkien both the real, which authenticates romantic nostalgia, and the sign of opposition to a debased modernity. As in Tennyson, the idea of war as an ennobling cultural and moral struggle is allowed precedence over the unpleasant history of war itself. Through Tolkien's continuing influence, so prevalent at the present time, we have not yet finished with the agenda of the nineteenth-century British Middle Ages.

Notes

1. Charlotte M. Yonge, *The Long Vacation* (London: Macmillan, 1895), chap. 13.

2. J.R.R. Tolkien, *The Lord of the Rings*, one-volume edn. (London: HarperCollins, 1994), foreword to the 2nd ed., 9 (hereafter cited in text and notes as *LR*).

3. See J.R.R. Tolkien, *The Letters of J. R. R. Tolkien: A Selection*, ed. Humphrey Carpenter with assistance from Christopher Tolkien (London: George Allen and Unwin, 1981), 303 (hereafter cited in text and notes as *Letters*): "Personally, I do not think that either war (and of course not the atomic bomb) had any influence upon either the plot or the manner of its unfolding. Perhaps in landscape. The Dead Marshes and the approaches to the Morannon owe something to Northern France after the Battle of the Somme. They owe more to William Morris and his Huns and Romans, as in *The House of the Wolfings* or *The Roots of the Mountains*."

4. J.R.R. Tolkien, "Beowulf: The Monsters and the Critics," in *"The Monsters and the Critics" and Other Essays*, ed. Christopher Tolkien (London: George Allen and Unwin, 1980), 5–34. See 31: "For *Beowulf* was not designed to tell the tale of Hygelac's fall, or for that matter to give the whole biography of Beowulf, still less to write the history of the Geatish kingdom and its downfall. But it used knowledge of these things for its own purpose to give that sense of perspective, of antiquity with a greater and yet darker antiquity behind. These things are mainly on the outer edges or in the background because they belong there, if they are to function in this way."

5. Hugh Brogan, "Tolkien's Great War," in *Children and Their Books: A Celebration of the Work of Iona and Peter Opie* (Oxford: Clarendon Press, 1989), 356.

6. Thomas A. Shippey, *J. R. R. Tolkien, Author of the Century* (London: HarperCollins, 2001), 151.

7. Brian Rosebury, *Tolkien: A Critical Assessment* (New York: St. Martin's Press, 1992), 126.

8. John Garth, *Tolkien and the Great War: The Threshold of Middle-Earth* (London: HarperCollins, 2003), 312.

9. Thomas A. Shippey, *The Road to Middle-Earth* (London: Allen and Unwin, 1982); Jane Chance, ed., *Tolkien the Medievalist* (London: Routledge, 2003).

10. *Beowulf*, ed. and trans. Michael Swanton (Manchester: Manchester University Press, 1978).

11. *The Battle of Maldon*, in *A Choice of Anglo-Saxon Verse*, ed. and trans. Richard Hamer (London: Faber, 1970).

12. Virginia Woolf, "How It Strikes a Contemporary," in *The Common Reader* (London: Hogarth Press, 1925), 302.

13. Geoffrey Chaucer, "Wife of Bath's Prologue," line 522, in *The Riverside Chaucer*, ed. L. D. Benson (Boston: Houghton Mifflin, 1987), 112.

14. Rosebury, *Tolkien*, 65, points out that "the basic style of narrative and description . . . is . . . largely free from archaic, let alone obsolete, forms."

15. Alfred Tennyson, "The Passing of Arthur," lines 179–80, in *The Poems of Tennyson*, ed. Christopher Ricks (London: Longman, 1969), 1747.

16. Rosebury, *Tolkien*, 82. Garth, *Tolkien and the Great War*, 35, 39–40, 59, 78–79.

17. Jay Winter, *Sites of Memory, Sites of Mourning: The Great War in European Cultural History* (Cambridge, UK: Cambridge University Press, 1995), 2–5, 54.

18. Tennyson's father had even held the living of Bag Enderby, in Lincolnshire, near the poet's birthplace. See Christopher Ricks, *Tennyson*, 2nd edn. (Basingstoke, UK: Macmillan, 1989), 3.

19. Susan Stewart, *On Longing* (Durham, NC: Duke University Press, 1993), 23.

20. J.R.R. Tolkien, "The Homecoming of Beorhtnoth Beorhthelm's Son," in *The Tolkien Reader* (New York: Ballantine, 1966), 124. The translation is Tolkien's own.

21. Alfred Tennyson, "The Epic [Morte d'Arthur]," lines 35–38, in *Poems of Tennyson*, 584.

22. J.S. Mill, review of *Tennyson, Poems, Chiefly Lyrical* [1830] and *Poems* [1833], *London Review* July, 1835, in *Tennyson: The Critical Heritage*, ed. John D. Jump (London: Routledge, 1967), 86.

23. John D. Rosenberg, *The Fall of Camelot: A Study of Tennyson's "Idylls of the King"* (Cambridge, MA: Harvard University Press, 1973), 67–68.

24. Alfred Tennyson, "Gereint and Enid," lines 905–06, in *Poems of Tennyson*, 1575.

25. Tennyson, "Gereint and Enid," lines 940–43.

26. Alfred Tennyson, "The Coming of Arthur," lines 115–17, in *Poems of Tennyson*, 1473.

27. Alfred Tennyson, "The Passing of Arthur," lines 114–17, in *Poems of Tennyson*, 1745.

28. See *The Battle of Maldon*, line 110: "Bogan waeron bysige, bord ord onfeng" ("bows were busy too, / Shield received spear"). See also Alfred Tennyson, "Fall battleaxe, and flash brand! Let the King reign," from "The Coming of Arthur," lines 485–86. See also "Coming of Arthur," lines 5–19, 94–120, 475–513.

29. Elizabeth Brewer and Beverly Taylor, *The Return of King Arthur* (Cambridge: D. S. Brewer, 1983), 131.

30. Alfred Tennyson, "The Holy Grail," lines 359, 235–45, in *Poems of Tennyson*, 1672, 1669.

31. Alfred Tennyson, "The Holy Grail," lines 235–45: "And in the lowest beasts are slaying men, / And in the second men are slaying beasts, / And on the third are warriors, perfect men, / And on the fourth are men with growing wings, / And overall one statue in the mould / Of Arthur, made by Merlin with a crown, / And peaked wings pointed to the Northern Star / And eastward fronts the statue and the crown / And both the wings are made of gold, and flame / At sunrise till the people in far fields, / Wasted so often by the heathen hordes, / Behold it, crying, 'We have still a King.'"

32. Alfred Tennyson, "The Passing of Arthur," lines 465–68, in *Poems of Tennyson*, 1754.

33. Tennyson, "The Passing of Arthur," lines 458–61.

34. Tennyson, "The Passing of Arthur," lines 284–85, in *Poems of Tennyson*, 1748.

35. Tennyson, "The Passing of Arthur," line 408, in *Poems of Tennyson*, 1752.

SUE ZLOSNIK

Gothic Echoes

The title of this collection invites some personal musings. I first read *The Lord of the Rings* as a post-war baby boomer in the psychedelic and politically charged 1960s; the years between then and my recent rereadings have witnessed a transformation in English Studies. I have not, I should add, been a serial reader of the text over this period; I remembered Tolkien's major work as a lengthy piece of entertaining whimsy, which I had enjoyed at the time but had no desire to revisit. However, the spectacle of the Peter Jackson films and the series of polls hailing *The Lord of the Rings* as 'the book of the century' (leading Tom Shippey to subtitle his new study of Tolkien's work 'author of the century') suggested that it was time to return to a text frequently dismissed even by those who had been busy firing the canon over the last quarter of a century. Given that I had thought Che Guevara more important than Frodo Baggins in an era when graffiti regularly claimed that both 'lived', I suspected that I would now read differently and perhaps more wisely. In returning to *The Lord of the Rings*, I have found a text more rooted in its recent history than I might have imagined. What I remembered as archetypal evil forces, I found represented through the discourses of late Victorian Gothic fiction. This perception has been enabled by the emergence of a wealth of scholarship in Gothic studies over the last 25 years. The work of Gothic scholars has established critical paradigms that enable us to

From *Reading* The Lord of The Rings: *New Writings on Tolkien's Classic*, pp. 47–58. © 2005 by Robert Eaglestone and contributors.

read *The Lord of the Rings* as a text that, although set in a mythical past, is preoccupied with the fears of a twentieth century still haunted by a legacy of late nineteenth-century anxieties.

While generally respecting Tolkien's dislike of allegory, a number of critics have embraced the 'freedom of the reader' to find 'applicability', which he endorsed in his foreword to the second edition of *The Lord of the Rings* (*FR*, xviii). Most have identified the traumas of twentieth-century history in the text. Some see Tolkien's own experiences in the trenches of the Great War as providing the powerful imagery for the hellish journey into Mordor and its outcome (see, e.g., Barton Friedman's 1982 essay 'Tolkien and David Jones: The Great War and the War of the Ring' which compares Tolkien's text with World War One writings). He himself acknowledged that the figure of Samwise Gamgee was inspired by his admiration for qualities of courage, endurance and loyalty that he saw in the enlisted soldiers who acted as officers' batmen in the battlefield (Carpenter 1977: 81). Most persuasively, the prospect of the 'Shadow' engulfing Middle-earth even into the sequestered rustic Shire mirrors the threats of a shrinking world in which there are no hiding places, not only from the ravages of war but also from the evil effects of corrupt power. The latter point is reinforced by the book's coda, 'The Scouring of the Shire', in which the returning Hobbits find their homeland despoiled by Gandalf's old adversary Saruman, now know as 'Sharkey'. Saruman is shown as behaving as a petty tyrant aided and abetted by 'ruffians' who are now 'on top, gathering, robbing and bullying, and running or ruining things as they like, in his name' (*RK*, VI, viii, 344). Tom Shippey sees Saruman as the most contemporary figure in *The Lord of the Rings*, 'both politically and linguistically', one who is 'on the road to "doublethink"' (Shippey 2000: 76). The despoliation is characterized by a creeping industrialization with its attendant pollution, the old mill having been replaced with one that is 'always a-hammering and a-letting out a smoke and a stench' (*RK*, VI, viii, 354), and environmental damage of fouled waters and lopped trees. Frodo asserts that 'this is Mordor ... just one of its works'. The influence of the great eye of Sauron manifests itself here in more mundane methods of surveillance and oppression: rules, enforcers, spies, and those who 'like minding other folk's business and talking big' (*RK*, VI, viii, 340).

In response to what he saw as his dark and debased century, Tolkien's acknowledged project was to create a mythology for England (Carpenter 1977: 89–90). His debt to the literature and languages of the first millennium has been well documented. The zeal with which he created his mythological world means that the appendices to the second edition of *The Lord of the Rings* constitute an extensive paratext that creates an elaborate, detailed and entirely fake history. Here the reader can find calendars, maps, family trees, linguistic guides and ancillary 'historical' material. In shoring up an illusion of reality created by his fantasy world in this way, Tolkien's work seems to indulge in a practice that has been characteristic of Gothic texts since Horace Walpole's 1764 novel *The Castle of Otranto*. The preface to the first edition of this text claimed that it had been found in 'the library of an ancient Catholic family in the North of England', and, relating events that had happened in 'the darkest ages of christianity', possibly dated from that era (Fairclough 1968: 39). In the preface to the second edition, following the success of his novel, Walpole confessed to the authorship of what he was now calling his 'gothick story'. Lest there be any confusion, it is in the sense of the tradition of 'gothick stories' following Walpole that I use the term 'Gothic' in this essay, rather than the language and lore of the ancient Goths that Tolkien drew on. Jerrold E. Hogle has suggested that the binary of 'fakery'/'authenticity' that helps structure the Gothic novel is indicative of a specifically modern and fractured subjectivity. For Hogle, the modern condition finds expression in the Gothic text through fakery and simulacra. He argues that:

> The Gothic refaking of fakery becomes a major repository of the newest contradictions and anxieties in western life that most need to be abjected by those who face them so that middle-class westerners can keep constructing a distinct sense of identity. The progress of abjection in the Gothic is inseparable from the progress of the ghost of the counterfeit, particularly as that symbolic mode and the ideologies at war within it keep employing each other— and acting out abjections—both to conceal and to confront some of the basic conflicts in western culture. (Punter 2000, 297)

Hogle thus suggests that the rise of modernity, from the Renaissance onwards, has resulted in a crisis of identity in the western world. Inflecting this perception with his reading of Jean Baudrillard's *Symbolic Exchange and Death*, Hogle goes on to argue that the stability of the feudal world has been replaced by the social mobility and geographical displacements/relocations characteristic of a post-Renaissance world. The resulting psychological instability has manifested itself in a breakdown between the sign and its referent: 'Educated Europeans felt that they were leaving behind the age of the "obligatory sign", the notion of signifiers as always referring to an ordained status in people and things where "assignation is absolute and there is no class mobility"' (Punter 2000: 297).

Tolkien's mythology for England is fake; his extended exercise in creating the language of Elvish, for example, constitutes the creation of a simulacrum, designed to look and feel like a retrieval of something ancient. Humphrey Carpenter's biography gives an account of his painstaking crafting of "'The Book of Mazarbul", a burnt and tattered volume that . . . is found in the Mines of Moria', and his disappointment that it had proved too expensive to include a facsimile of this in the first edition of *The Fellowship of the Ring* (Carpenter 1977: 217). The detail with which the fantasy world is constructed in Tolkien's work encourages a willing suspension of disbelief in its readers that appears to have been carried to extremes by some of its devotees, as a cursory glance at material on the Internet will confirm. This precarious boundary between the authentic and the fake makes reading *The Lord of the Rings* a Gothic experience in the sense that Hogle indicates. The dismissal of Tolkien's fiction by many in the literary world parallels the reception of Gothic in the academy until recent decades. *The Lord of the Rings* is, I suggest, best read like a Gothic novel: to expect the realism of psychological complexity in its characters is to be disappointed for, as in the Gothic novel, we find representative figures and no shortage of grotesques; to expect conformity to a critical paradigm of 'the marvellous' is to find the book 'weighed down by the mechanisms of the realistic novel' (Brooke-Rose 1980: 67). Gothic since its inception has been a hybrid and protean form, shifting its focus to adapt to the conditions of the time in which it is produced.

Since Walpole's location of supernatural and shocking events in a distant past that he inaccurately identified as 'gothick', Gothic writing has persisted as a form of discourse capable of giving shape to the unspeakables of post-enlightenment modernity. While (as critics broadly agree), the Gothic novel as a genre (however diverse its examples) can be located in the period from *The Castle of Otranto* (1764) to *Melmoth the Wanderer* (1820), Gothic as a mode of writing pervaded the fiction (and, indeed, other kinds of writing) of the nineteenth century as a kind of textual haunting. Similarly, the settings of Gothic became no longer confined to those of the earlier genre. As Julian Wolfreys suggests, 'Escaping from the tomb and the castle, the gothic in the Victorian period becomes arguably even more potentially terrifying because of its ability to manifest itself anywhere' (Robbins and Wolfreys 2000: xiv). In the last decades of the nineteenth century, Gothic writing gave expression to a range of contemporary anxieties in texts such as Stevenson's *The Strange Case of Dr Jekyll and Mr Hyde* (1864) and Bram Stoker's *Dracula* (1897) as well as a host of less-remembered works, which provoked horror or terror or both. Gothic elements are also apparent in the popular fictional form of the time known as 'Victorian quest romance', of which Stevenson, Haggard, Kipling and Conan Doyle were the major exponents. Several critics have drawn attention to Tolkien's debt to this form of fiction in the structuring of the narrative of *The Lord of the Rings* but less attention has been paid to the Gothic aspects of Victorian quest romance in Tolkien's text.

The quartet of Hobbits who set out from the Shire do so to defend a way of life readily identifiable as rooted in an English countryside already lost by the time the book was written. The portrait of an innocent rustic way of life under threat is not unfamiliar to the English reader. Thomas Hardy's early fiction paints a similar portrait of a passing world: Tolkien's Hobbits are not so different from Dick Dewey and the other villagers of Mellstock in *Under the Greenwood Tree* (1872), whose traditional customs are threatened by the appearance of a pert young schoolmistress who will play the organ that will supplant the old choir and its instruments in Mellstock Church. Hardy's symbolism is here more mundane than Tolkien's and his elegiac text remains firmly within the bounds of realism. Tolkien's Hobbits are the 'little people' of this world, literally miniaturized and with strong, hairy feet that make them close to the earth and also, like Frodo's Uncle Bilbo in *The Hobbit*, equipped for travelling when necessary. A mixture of Victorian gentlemen, with their liking for hearth, home and pipe (Shippey 2000: 5) and 'ordinary boys' (Carpenter 1977: 223), they make unlikely heroes. The journey undertaken by Frodo and his companions, however, is a journey of necessity rather than a search for adventure; for this is a quest narrative in which the aim is not to find something, an equivalent of the holy grail, but to be rid of something: the most powerful Ring of all with its destructive power to corrupt. As Gandalf tells Frodo, 'It would be a grievous blow to the world if the Dark Power overcame the Shire; if all your kind, jolly, stupid Bolgers, Hornblowers, Boffins, Bracegirdles and the rest, not to mention the ridiculous Bagginses, became enslaved' (*FR*, I, ii, 64).

The pervasive threat of the Ring's power is one that manifests itself not simply at the level of brute, or even monstrous, force but, more disturbingly, at the level of the individual psyche. It infects the bearer with the will to power in a manner that is destructive to him (always a him) as well as to others. Frodo's quest takes him into a world characterized by entropy and decay. This is a world in which creatures are fading or in decline: early in the story, Bilbo tells Gandalf that he feels 'thin, sort of *stretched* . . . like butter that has been scraped over too much bread' (*FR*, I, i, 42); the Elves are a remnant, most of their kindred having 'long departed' and 'only tarrying here a while, ere [they] return over the Great Sea' (*FR*, I, iii, 106); and Aragorn, revealed as heir to the decayed kingdom of Gondor, appears at first as 'Strider', an enigmatic figure reminiscent of the Gothic wanderer. Moreover, Middle-earth is a place in which the uncanny is ever present. Hardly out of the Shire, Frodo and his companions are imprisoned by a Barrow-wight, the undead inhabitant of a burial site, 'a tall dark figure like a shadow against the stars' with 'two eyes, very cold though lit with a pale light that seemed to come from a remote distance' (*FR*, I, viii, 184) until they are rescued by the benevolent forest-dweller Tom Bombadil. The Freudian sense of the uncanny is evoked by the description of Rivendell as 'The Last Homely House east of the Sea' (*FR*, II, i, 295). Indeed, the world of Middle-earth is one in which the last corners of civilization are threatened by the creeping Shadow from the East. In late Victorian Gothic fiction, the East is habitually represented as the locus of threat and often the source of demonic Gothic figures. Dracula comes out of the far reaches of Romania and Svengali, in George du Maurier's *Trilby* (1894), is described as originating from 'the poisonous East—birthplace and home of an ill wind that blows nobody good' (du Maurier 1992: 239).

Figures such as Dracula and Svengali exemplify the way in which late Victorian Gothic fiction is not only haunted by the uncanny but also pervaded by the anxieties of degenerationism. Daniel Pick identifies degenerationism as a complex phenomenon, the discursive descent of which cannot be tied to the roots of one ideology, but sees it as extending into many theories and fictions of the first 40 years of the twentieth century (Pick 1989: 234). Although slightly out of this time-frame, it is clear that Tolkien's epic is underpinned by the discourse of degenerationism and draws on those Gothic tropes of the popular fiction of the later Victorian period that expressed the multiplicity of anxieties to which it gave rise. Saruman's Orcs, for example, are 'foul folk', according to Treebeard, who suggests that he has 'been doing something to them' and that he has possibly 'blended the races of Orcs and Men', to produce, he implies, a degenerated creature that embodies the worst of both (*TT*, III, iv, 84). Kelly Hurley sees degenerationism as 'a "gothic" discourse, and as such … a crucial imaginative and narrative source for the *fin de siècle* Gothic' (Hurley, 65). This is, she claims:

> a genre thoroughly imbricated with biology and social medicine: sometimes borrowing conceptual remodellings of human physical identity, as it did from criminal anthropology; sometimes borrowing narrative remodellings of heredity and culture, as it did from the interrelated discourses of evolutionism, degeneration, and entropy; sometimes borrowing spatial remodellings of the human subject, as it did from the psychologies of the unconscious. (Hurley, 5)

The Victorian preoccupation with degenerationism often manifests itself in the fiction of the period in the form of the term 'abhuman' (a term that Hurley borrows from a popular Gothic writer of the time, William Hope Hodgson). Hurley recognizes that the concept of the abhuman resonates strongly with Julia Kristeva's concept of 'the abject', a concept that has proved useful in Gothic criticism (1982). Identifying 'the abject' as a psychic state deriving from our earliest experiences of being 'betwixt and between' in the process of birth, Kristeva applies the term to that which 'disturbs identity, system, order. What does not respect borders, positions, rules. The in-between, the ambiguous, the composite' (Kristeva 1982: 4). The abject has been seen as manifested in Gothic bodies and used as a way of understanding that which society itself has 'thrown down'. Culture is shored up by what it abjects; in the Gothic, in the words of Jerrold E. Hogle, 'struggles for cultural definition are what haunt the Gothic most in its anomalous monsters and spectres, as well as in the desires of its heroes and its heroines' (Hogle 1996: 826).

The Gothic fiction of the late nineteenth century abounds in monstrous figures, including the monstrous female. Studies such as those of Elaine Showalter (1987 and 1991) have built on the work of Foucault to point to the pathologization of women's bodies in that period; Eve Kosofsky Sedgwick's work (1985) identifies a prominent homosociality among men in response to a perception of the 'otherness' of women. The prevalence of anxiety about female corporeality finds expression in some memorable examples of female monstrosity in the fiction of the period: in the monstrous women of Rider Haggard, in the morphic beetle in Richard Marsh's story of the same name and in Arthur Machen's *The Great God Pan*, to take three examples. The polarity of nineteenth-century sexual ideology in the form of Madonna and whore figures so extensively uncovered by second-wave feminism is clearly demonstrated in *The Lord of the Rings*. Displaying the characteristic homosociality of the Victorian quest narrative in the bonding of its male characters, the story presents female figures who are representative of different forms of purity: the Elf, Arwen (eventually to become a fit queen to Aragorn's king), the powerful and demonstrably incorruptible Galadriel who resists the Ring and, to those inclined to read from a Catholic perspective, represents the Immaculate, the fierce and frosty shield maiden Éowyn, who is thawed by the love of Faramir, and the domestic ideal of Rosie Cotton to whom Sam eventually returns. There is, however, one memorably monstrous female figure in the form of Shelob, ancient spider of gigantic proportions and 'soft squelching body' which lives in the earth and feeds off men, 'the most loathly shape he [Sam] had ever beheld, horrible beyond the horror of an evil dream' (*TT*, IV, ix, 417). The episode in which Frodo is captured by Shelob and fought off by Sam using the phial of light given to the Hobbits by Galadriel has been persuasively examined from a feminist perspective by Brenda Partridge. Partridge concludes that 'the female linked with sexuality is seen as evil, paganism' (Giddings 1983: 191). Her analysis is best contextualized by seeing the abject figure of Shelob as representative of an anxiety that had become particularly acute in the late Victorian era.

Gollum is clearly an abject figure of a different kind, to all intents and purposes abhuman. Frodo and Sam's first sight of him presents him as a repulsive creature, behaving in a most un-Hobbitlike way:

> Down the face of a precipice, sheer and almost smooth it seemed in the pale moonlight, a small black shape was moving with its thin limbs splayed out. Maybe its soft clinging hands and toes

were finding crevices and holds that no Hobbit could ever have seen or used, but it looked as if it was just creeping down on sticky pads, like some large prowling thing of insect-kind. And it was coming down head first, as if it was smelling its way. Now and again it lifted its head slowly, turning it right back on its skinny neck, and the Hobbits caught a glimpse of two small pale gleaming lights, its eyes that blinked at the moon for a moment and then were quickly lidded again. (*TT*, IV, i, 268)

It is worth comparing this with Jonathan Harker's account of watching Count Dracula:

... my feelings changed to repulsion and terror when I saw the whole man slowly emerge from the window and begin to crawl down the castle wall over that dreadful abyss, *face down*, with his cloak spreading out about him like great wings. At first I could not believe my eyes. I thought it was some trick of the moonlight, some weird effect of shadow ... I saw the fingers and toes grasp the stones, worm clear of mortar by the stress of years, and by thus using every projection and inequality move downwards with considerable speed, just as a lizard moves along a wall. (Stoker 1996, 34)

There is a striking similarity of rhetoric here in the evocation of 'repulsion and terror' occasioned by these abhuman figures.

For Hurley, the abhuman subject is 'a not-quite-human subject, characterized by its morphic variability, continually in danger of becoming not-itself, becoming other' (Hurley 1996, 3–4). The transgression of boundaries characteristic of Gothic manifests itself most clearly in the late Victorian period as a preoccupation with the boundaries of the self. Gandalf tells Frodo the story of how Gollum had long ago been Sméagol, a member of a 'clever-handed and quiet-footed little people' (*FR*, I, ii, 69) who had killed his cousin Déagol for possession of the Ring that he had found. Under the influence of the Ring, he had degenerated into Gollum (so named because of 'the gurgling in his throat' [*FR*, I, ii, 71]) whom Bilbo had encountered deep inside the Misty Mountains, where he had been for an age having 'wormed his way [there] like a maggot' (*FR*, I, ii, 71). Frodo responds to the idea that Gollum had come from a people connected with Hobbits with the exclamation 'what an abominable notion' (*FR*, I, ii, 72). When he later encounters Gollum, his appeal to the Sméagol he once was causes that buried identity to surface and fight out a battle for consciousness with the monstrous and corrupted figure that he has become under the influence of the Ring. As Frodo observes, 'when

Gollum used *I* . . . that usually seemed to be a sign, on its rare appearances, that some remnants of old truth and sincerity were for the moment on top' (*TT*, IV, iii, 309). In many respects, Gollum resembles Stevenson's Dr Jekyll with Mr Hyde in the ascendancy (himself a descendant of other *doppelgänger* haunted selves such as Hogg's Robert Wringhim in the much earlier *Confessions of a Justified Sinner*). As Hurley points out, 'Freud's hint that a doubling relationship, which on the surface accomplishes a simple bifurcation of the self, gestures towards a more radical fissioning of the self—towards an amorphous version of the self which is a non-self, because it has forfeited all the boundaries that enabled it to distinguish itself from the world of things that surround it' (Hurley, 42). The Ring's power to disintegrate the subject and transform it into something abject is most powerfully demonstrated in Gollum but remains a constant threat to the identity of Frodo as long as he remains the Ring-bearer. At the moment of crisis when he must cast it into 'the very crack of Doom' he speaks with a voice 'clearer and more powerful than Sam had ever heard him use' and claims the Ring for his own (*RK*, VI, iii, 265). Now in the sights of the Eye of the Dark Lord, he is saved only by Gollum's bestiality in biting off the finger that bears the Ring. Infected by the Ring, Frodo's conscious will is not enough to complete the Quest.

There are vampiric resonances in *The Lord of the Rings*. The insidious evil that the Ring represents infects the artefacts that serve it and, by extension, those whose bodies who come into contact with them. The knife that pierces Frodo in an early struggle takes from him his strength in a way that is different from the trauma of a normal wound. It also infects him with a nameless poison that enhances the temptation of the Ring; like the bite of the vampire, it infects him with desire. The Ringwraiths, possessors of nine of the lesser rings, were once Mortal Men, but have long been reduced to 'shadows under his great Shadow, his most terrible servants' (*FR*, I, ii, 68). Éowyn's destruction of the Black Captain of the Ringwraiths on the Pelennor Fields is absolute: staked by her sword, he becomes nothing, leaving an empty mantle and hauberk, his destruction evoking echoes of the end of Dracula as described by Mina Harker: 'almost in the drawing of a breath, the whole body crumbled into dust and passed from our sight' (Stoker, 377). One critic, Gwenyth Hood, has offered a detailed comparison of Dracula and Sauron, using the image of the eye and vision as linking features between the two texts. Indeed, manifesting himself as a giant bestial eye, Sauron is an embodiment of another late Victorian Gothic preoccupation, the power of the eye. As Daniel Pick points out, long-standing theories about the forces projected from the seeing eye surfaced again in the late nineteenth century, to be subsumed into the speculations about mesmerism. The myth of the 'evil eye' is perhaps most dramatically represented in this period in the figure of Svengali but Pick also cites Conan Doyle's 'The Parasite', in which a 'rapacious and hypnotically dangerous' woman from the West Indies overpowers an eminent professor through the intensity of her gaze (Pick 2000: 169). Yet again it is possible to see the nineteenth-century anxiety about the integrity of the subject, as well as the twentieth-century fear of surveillance in the image of the eye of Sauron.

Tom Shippey identifies a contradiction between Boethian and Manichaean visions of evil as driving the plot of *The Lord of the Rings*. Hood's assertion that Sauron represents a twentieth-century vision of evil that is darker and more nihilistic than the evil of Dracula, 'which tempts with instinctual pleasure' (Hood 1987, 150), implies the Boethian vision of evil as absence, in the form of 'the Shadow'. Yet the Manichaean view of evil as a positive force, the 'Dark Power', seems to be demonstrated by the endowing of the Ring itself with evil powers. The Ring as symbol of evil may be seen as representing both of these apparently opposed visions: inscribed in Elvish letters but in the tongue of Mordor, it is, like Conrad's Kurtz, 'hollow at the core'. And what is at the core is the subject, human or humanoid.

Clearly, Tolkien was backward-looking in his choice of Gothic tropes from some 50 years earlier to represent deep fears of threats both external and internal. Yet in a twenty-first century that has already witnessed global politics increasingly framed in the Manichaean rhetoric of fundamentalism, the consolation of the happy ending or 'eucatastrophe' (to use Tolkien's own coinage [*Tree and Leaf*, 60]) of *The Lord of the Rings* seems to supply a deep-felt longing to some: perhaps to those who identify with the values of the Shire. Yet the destruction of Sauron cannot make Frodo what he once was—he is irreparably damaged—nor can it save the elves, who diminish further. For Ken Gelder, writing about Tolkien in the wake of 9/11, modern epic fantasy is a 'literary form of fundamentalism that troubles secular ideals', itself 'terroristic' in its attack on the modern world (Gelder 2003: 26). For those who find solace in Tolkien's fake mythology, there will be the hope of modest, reluctant heroes who offer themselves up to save their fellows from the worst that the modern world can do. So how should I have answered the bearded man with the folding bicycle who fixed me with an intense stare when I was rereading *The Lord of the Rings* on the train? Obviously believing he had spotted another devotee, he asked, 'So how many times have you read it?' The honest answer would have been, 'I read it every 35 years. I may not read it again.' In an uncanny, echoing coincidence we both left the train at Frodsham.

Works Cited

Brooke-Rose, C. (1980), 'The Evil Ring: Realism and the Marvellous'. *Poetics Today* 1 (4), 67–90.
Carpenter, H. (1977), *J. R. R. Tolkien: A Biography*. London: George Allen & Unwin.

Chance, J. (2001), *The Lord of the Rings: The Mythology of Power.* Lexington: University Press of Kentucky.

Clark, G. and D. Timmons (2000), *J. R. R. Tolkien and his Literary Resonances.* Westport CT: Greenwood Press.

Curry, P. (1997), *Defending Middle-earth.* London: HarperCollins.

Dickson, A. (ed.) (1985), *Sigmund Freud: The Penguin Freud Library.* Harmondsworth: Penguin Books, Vol. 14 'Art and Literature'.

Du Maurier, G. (1992), *Trilby* (1894), Leonee Ormond (ed.). London: Dent.

Ellison, J. (1991), 'Sublime Scenes and Horrid Novels: Milestones along the Road to Middle-earth'. *Mallorn* 28, 23–8.

Fairclough, P. (ed.) (1968), *Three Gothic Novels.* Harmondsworth: Penguin.

Friedman, B. (1982), 'Tolkien and David Jones: The Great War and the War of the Ring'. *Clio: A Journal of Literature, History and the Philosophy of History*, 11, (2), 115–35.

Gelder, K. (2003), 'Epic Fantasy and Global Terrorism'. *Overland* 173, 21–7.

Giddings, R. (ed.) (1983), *J. R. R. Tolkien: This Far Land.* London and Totowa, NJ: Vision.

Hogle, J. E. (1996), 'The Gothic and the "Otherings" of Ascendant Culture: The Original *Phantom of the Opera*'. *South Atlantic Quarterly*, 95, (3), 157–171.

Hogle, J. E. (ed.) (2002), *Gothic Fiction.* Cambridge: Cambridge University Press.

Hood, G. (1987), 'Sauron and Dracula', in *Mythlore: A Journal of J. R. R. Tolkien, C. S. Lewis, Charles Williams and The Genres of Myth and Fantasy Studies*, 14 (2(52)), 11–17.

Hurley, K. (1996), *The Gothic Body: Sexuality, Materialism and Degeneration at the Fin de Siècle.* Cambridge: Cambridge University Press.

Kocher, P. (1974), *Master of Middle-earth: The Achievement of J. R. R. Tolkien* (1972). Harmondsworth: Penguin Books.

Kristeva, J. (1982), *Powers of Horror: An Essay on Abjection*, trans. L. S. Roudiez. New York: Columbia University Press.

Nitzche, J. Chance (1979), *Tolkien's Art: A Mythology for England.* Basingstoke: Macmillan.

Partridge, B. (1983), 'No Sex Please—We're Hobbits: The Construction of Female Sexuality in *The Lord of the Rings*', in R. Giddings (ed.), *J. R. R. Tolkien: This Far Land.* London and Totowa, NJ: Vision.

Pearce, J. (1998), *Tolkien: Man and Myth.* London: HarperCollins.

Pick, D. (1993), *Faces of Degeneration: A European Disorder, c. 1848–c. 1918* (1989). Cambridge: Cambridge University Press.

Pick, D. (2000), *Svengali's Web: The Alien Enchanter in Modern Culture.* New Haven and London: Yale University Press.

Punter, D. (ed.) (2000), *A Companion to the Gothic.* Oxford: Blackwell.

Robbins R. and J. Wolfreys (eds) (2000), *Victorian Gothic: Literary and Cultural Manifestations in the Nineteenth Century.* Basingstoke: Palgrave.

Salisbury, J. D. (2001). 'Gothic and Romantic Wandering: The Epistemology of Oscillation'. *Gothic Studies* 3, (1), 45–59.

Sedgwick, E. Kosofsky (1985), *Between Men: English Literature and Male Homosocial Desire.* New York: Columbia University Press.

Shippey, T. (1992), *The Road to Middle-earth* (1982). London: HarperCollins.

Shippey, T (2000), *J. R. R. Tolkien: Author of the Century.* London: HarperCollins.

Showalter, E. (1987), *The Female Malady: Women, Madness, and English Culture, 1830–1980.* London: Virago.

Showalter, E. (1991), *Sexual Anarchy: Gender and Culture at the Fin de Siècle.* London: Bloomsbury.

Stoker, B. (1996), *Dracula* (1897), Maud Ellmann (ed.), Oxford: Oxford University Press World's Classics.

Tolkien, J. R. R. (1964), *Tree and Leaf*. London: George Allen & Unwin.

Tolkien, J. R. R. (2003), *The Lord of the Rings*. London: HarperCollins.

VERLYN FLIEGER

Tolkien and the Idea of the Book

Near the end of "The Council of Elrond," a chapter essential to *The Lord of the Rings* and one that presents a variety of oral narratives by different speakers, Bilbo Baggins unexpectedly (and, it might seem, irrelevantly) intrudes the divergent concept of a written record. Volunteering to take the Ring to Mount Doom, he remarks plaintively: "I was very comfortable here, and getting on with my book. If you want to know, I am just writing an ending for it. . . ." And he adds, "There will evidently have to be several more chapters." After finding that he is not to go on the quest, he once more brings up his book a few days before the Company sets out, assuring Frodo, "I'll do my best to finish my book before you return. I should like to write the second book (meaning the story of Frodo's adventures], if I am spared."[1]

When I first read *The Lord of the Rings* in 1957 and for many years thereafter, I took such passages to be nothing more than a gentle running joke at the old hobbit's expense. It seemed that besides finding ways to connect *The Lord of the Rings* to *The Hobbit*, Tolkien was also poking fun at his own book and its runaway length. I was aware, of course, of the Appendices at the end of volume 3, and took for granted that their Annals and Chronologies were there to convey to the reader that there was, however remotely, a story behind the story. Nevertheless, the possibility that there might also be a book behind

From The Lord of the Rings, *1954–2004: Scholarship in Honor of Richard E. Blackwelder*, edited by Wayne G. Hammond and Christina Scull, pp. 283–299. © 2006 by Marquette University Press.

the book—that Bilbo's "book" might have developed a life of its own—did not occur to me.

It did occur to Tolkien. He wanted to justify the fact that those oral narratives told at the Council of Elrond were now in print. One way to do that was to make somebody other than the "removed narrator" (Tolkien) responsible for writing them down—some character within the fiction. Since Bilbo was known to have literary inclinations (he recited poetry, and had already "written" (*The Hobbit*), since he was one of the few characters with the leisure and freedom from care to spend his time in writing, he was the obvious choice. Indeed, in this context, and quite aside from their necessary contributions to plot and theme, Bilbo, his heir Frodo, and Frodo's heir Sam,[2] are the sequentially obvious choices. Moreover, they can be seen collectively as the next-to-last in the long line of transmitters, translators, redactors, scribes, and copyists who have produced the varied history of Middle-earth.

These three are next-to-last because the last in the line is the primary author himself. Carrying the conceit about as far as it will go, Tolkien inserted his own name into the header and footer on the title-page of *The Lord of the Rings* (and thus into the history of the "book"), not as the author of the book but as its final transmitter/redactor. What appears to the first-time or untutored reader to be simply Tolkienian embellishment is in fact is a running inscription in Tolkien's invented scripts of Cirth and Tengwar. It can be put into English as follows: "*The Lord of the Rings* TRANSLATED FROM THE RED BOOK [in Cirth] OF WESTMARCH BY JOHN RONALD REUEL TOLKIEN HEREIN IS SET FORTH THE HISTORY OF THE WAR OF THE RINGS AND THE RETURN OF THE KING AS SEEN BY THE HOBBITS [in Tengwar]." He is not inventing this story, the running script announces, he is merely translating and recording.

With no other context in which to read it, this could easily be seen as mere playfulness, an author's tongue-in-cheek send-up of his own authorial role. To be sure, Tolkien had done something similar, though with considerably less mythological rationale, in the runes on the dust jacket of *The Hobbit*, where he was (and is) credited not as the author but as the "compiler" of Bilbo's memoirs. During the course of the development of *The Lord of the Rings*, however, this strategy became as much a part of Tolkien's overall scheme as Bilbo's repeated references to finishing his book. If we accept the fictionalized Tolkien identified by the scripts in the header, then we must see that his persona of translator, just as much as those of Bilbo or Frodo or Sam as authors, is in the service of the "book." This carries the "book" beyond an authorial conceit, or an imaginary artifact within the fictive world of Middle-earth, to make it an actual volume in the real world and in the reader's hand. The more widely I read in Tolkien's work, especially those parts of *The History of Middle-earth* that deal with oral story-telling and written transmission, the more clearly I began to see that this endeavor to account within the fiction for something intended to exist outside it was a conscious and deliberate strategy on Tolkien's part.

Now that I have at last caught up with him, I propose to examine what I see as his intentional, interconnected efforts to bridge the fictive world of the story and the outside, real world, to connect inside with outside and fantasy with actuality through the idea of the book. The place to start is with the inside world. Here, the "book" is a conceit, an entirely fictive construct whose reality exists solely within and depends entirely upon the sub-created world, where it is designed to be both the rationale for and integration of all Tolkien's major fiction. Within the Middle-earth of *The Lord of the Rings*, its precursor volume, *The Hobbit*, is presented as Bilbo's "memoirs," the beginning of the book he "will do [his] best to finish" at Rivendell so that he can go on to write "the second book."[3] This serial volume concept will eventually extend itself both forward and backward in time, and will culminate in a comprehensive, "real," imaginary construct—the Red Book of Westmarch.

Granted, the whole world of Middle-earth is an imaginary construct, a sub-creation. The Red Book takes the idea one step further to become a sub-sub-creation that is intended paradoxically to give rise to a real creation in the real world. In "The Interlace Structure of *The Lord of the Rings*," one of the all-time best articles on Tolkien, Richard West suggests that Tolkien's "use of the imaginary 'Red Book of Westmarch' is a medieval tradition adapted for a modern audience."[4] Richard was writing in 1975, before the publication of *The Silmarillion* and *The History of Middle-earth*, but he was certainly on the right track about *what* Tolkien was doing. I intend to explore *how* and *why* Tolkien was doing it.

As to *how*, it seems clear that Tolkien's Red Book was intended to echo the great medieval manuscript books whose names sound like an Andrew Lang color series for the Middle Ages—The White Book of Rhydderch, the Black Book of Carmarthen, the Yellow Book of Lecan, and most important as his immediate color model, the real Red Book of Hergest. These are unique, anonymously authored manuscripts, collections of stories from different periods by different narrators, and brought under one cover by a scribe or copyist. As artifacts, these books may well be centuries younger than the stories they preserve. They are almost certainly copies of copies of copies of much earlier manuscripts now lost.

The fictive Red Book of Westmarch is the same, but different. Like the real-world books, it is imagined as a manuscript collection of tales from many periods. Like them, it has been copied and re-copied. Christopher Tolkien has noted that "in the original edition of *The Lord of the Rings* Bilbo gave to Frodo at Rivendell as his parting gift 'some books of lore that he had made at various times, written in his spidery hand and labeled on their red backs: *Translations from the Elvish, by B.B.'"* But he adds that "in the second edition (1966) 'some books' was changed to 'three books.'" It is important to note that with this change, these three books had grown from "lore" to become "a work of great skill and learning in which . . . [Bilbo] had used all the sources available to him in Rivendell, both living and written."[5]

The Foreword to the first edition of *The Lord of the Rings* also mentions that a copy of the Red Book is kept with the Fairbairns of Westmarch who are "descended from . . . Master Samwise."[6] Expanding the range, the Prologue to the second edition lists copies in the Shire housed at Undertowers (home of the Fairbairns), at Great Smials (home of the Tooks), and at Brandy Hall (home of the Brandybucks), as well as a copy kept at Minas Tirith in Gondor.[7] In addition, and like the real Red Book, by the time of the second edition of *The Lord of the Rings*, Tolkien's Red Book is a compendium of different stories from sources both "living and written" stretching over many different periods and finally brought together in one place.

Unlike its medieval prototypes, Tolkien's Red Book has a traceable genealogy from earlier manuscripts, as well as a more coherent body of narrative than do many of the real-world books. Clearly, as Tolkien's concept grew, so grew the genealogy of the Red Book, from the first edition's ill-defined "lore" to the second edition's combination of orally-transmitted information (the "living" sources) with material copied from written records that clearly reached farther and farther back into Middle-earth's pre-history. At first, according to the Foreword in the first edition of *The Lord of the Rings*, that narrative was intended to be "drawn for the most part from the 'memoirs' of the renowned Hobbits, Bilbo and Frodo, as they are preserved in the Red Book of Westmarch . . . compiled, repeatedly copied, and enlarged and handed down in the family of the Fairbairns of Westmarch . . . supplemented . . . in places, with information derived from the surviving records of Gondor, notably the Book of the Kings . . ."[8] A few sentences later, *The Hobbit* is referred to as a "selection" from the Red Book.[9]

However, by the time of the second edition of *The Lord of the Rings*, the Red Book had reached back into the First and Second Ages for its sources, and was extended both backwards and forwards in terms of transmitters. It acquired a line of identifiable author-redactors. Among them Eriol/Ælfwine, Rúmil, Pengoloð, Gilfanon, and Findagil, as well as Bilbo and Frodo. From the "Note on the Shire Records" appended to the Prologue of the second edition we learn that the Red Book is now "*in origin* [compare with the first editions *drawn for the most part*] Bilbo's private diary [*The Hobbit*]" (emphasis mine), added to by Frodo and then by Sam (*The Lord of the Rings*); but also that "annexed to it and preserved with it . . . were the three large volumes, bound in red leather that Bilbo gave to [Frodo] as a parting gift."[10] The key word is *annexed*, making clear what before was implicit, that the volumes, whether lore or work of great skill and learning, were to be attached to the more recently-written private diary added to by Frodo and Sam.

Now as to *why* Tolkien was furthering this conceit. From the "Note on the Shire Records" I draw the fairly obvious conclusion that Tolkien's final scheme envisioned the combined set of these three volumes (Bilbo's "Translations") plus *The Hobbit* and *The Lord of the Rings* as comprising the "ideal" or archetypal Red Book of Westmarch. Moreover, I propose that this archetypal "book" was intended this to encompass the entirety of his major fiction. The "Note" makes the point that only the copy at Minas Tirith in Gondor "contains the whole of Bilbo's 'Translations from the Elvish'"[11] and thus includes all three author/translators—Bilbo, Frodo, and Sam. Thus the Red Book is written in what we might (with some license) call a Middle-earth equivalent of the "AB" language, since it shows traces of having originally been written by a scribe or scribes from a specific linguistic area and sharing a specific orthography.[12]

But what exactly are these "translations" of Bilbo's? We assume they are "The Silmarillion," but what does that really mean in practical terms? What particular, specific texts might Bilbo have been imagined as using, and how was he supposed to have found them? As to where he might have found them, both the passage from *The Book of Lost Tales* I quoted above and the 1966 "Note on the Shire Records" added in the second edition of *The Lord of the Rings* show that over time Tolkien settled on Rivendell as the final repository. This is supported by his 1966 statement in an interview with Richard Plotz that *The Silmarillion* might be published as Bilbo's "research in Rivendell."[13] Thus we have both written and oral confirmation of the content of those three annexed and preserved volumes.

That the actual texts of the stories were revised even more than the location of their eventual resting-place is less important in the present context than the scheme by which they were to be preserved. In answer to the question of what text Bilbo was using, the earliest candidate is likely to have been the Golden Book of Tavrobel, the record made by Eriol the Mariner of the tales he heard in what was to become Valinor.[14] The Golden Book as repository for the tales appears in Outline C of Tolkien's 1917 school notebook: "Eriol. . . . Goes to Tavrobel to see Gilfanon and sojourns in the house of a Hundred Chimneys. . . . Gilfanon bids him write down all he has heard. . . . The book lay [*sic*] untouched . . . during many ages of Men. The compiler of the Golden Book takes up the Tale: one of the children of the fathers of the fathers of Men. [*Against this is written:*] It may perhaps be much better to let Eriol himself see the last things and finish the book."[15] And in the prefatory note to an "exceedingly difficult text titled *Epilogue*" is written: "Eriol flees with the fading Elves from the Battle of the High Heath. . . . The last words of the book of Tales. Written by Eriol at

Tavrobel before he sealed the book" and left it in the House of the Hundred Chimneys, "where it lieth still for such to read as may."[16]

It had not "lain still" for very long before it picked up another author/scribe, a shadowy compiler called Heorrenda[17] (the son of Eriol who later became Ælfwine), and became the Golden Book of Heorrenda. This need not detain us, though it did lead Christopher Tolkien to caution future scholars that "in the early notes and outlines there are different conceptions of the Golden Book."[18] The confusion between a book either "finished" or "sealed" by Eriol and the notion of a later "compiler" who would add to it is due to its creator's continual re-visioning of the concept, leading to those "different conceptions" to which Christopher alludes, and culminating decades later in Tolkien's runic posture as the last compiler. If we could posit a straight shot from the Golden Book to the Red Book, we might suppose Tolkien to have been launching his own color series to rival the actual ones.

Of course, it is not that simple. Later redactions and "translations" intervened between the two books, as well as the not inconsiderable problem of having the earlier book escape the Downfall of Númenor and manage to survive the re-making of the world. Somehow, the 'book' had to get from the old world to the new one, and from the House of a Hundred Chimneys to Rivendell, the most likely place where it could be available to Bilbo. Moreover, several languages were involved, for while the stories of the First Age were presumed to have been written in the early Anglo-Saxon of Eriol/Ælfwine, the later versions of the great tales of Beren and Lúthien and Túrin Turambar were supposed to be in "Elvish" (most probably Sindarin).

In order to be read by any modern audience, both languages had to be "translated" into modern English or "Common Speech." Moreover, this had to be done by someone whom Tolkien could fictively authenticate as a translator. As his vision changed in the course of the re-visions of forty years, so did his concept of the "book," the redactor, and the putative translator, though not the strategy that lay behind the invention of all these. Over the years, "Golden" was dropped from the title, Eriol/Ælfwine as redactor was diminished, Heorrenda disappeared, and the book became just "the Book of Stories" or "the Book of Tales," arriving in Númenor in time for the Downfall, and barely making it to Beleriand ahead of the tidal wave.

To untangle all these complexities would demand not just special skill but Elvish craft, and is beyond the capacity of the present discussion. I simply want to establish the centrality of the idea of a physical book, by whomever written and however titled, as the source and archetype for a publishable volume. And that is where the inside conceit connects to the external reality of the world outside Middle-earth, where Tolkien's concept of the "book" was to be not just an imaginary construct, but also a hoped-for actuality. For publication in the real world was his ultimate goal. Like any author, he wanted his work to be read, and for that to happen it had to be between covers and on bookstore shelves.

Within the fiction, he might imagine the Golden Book "lying untouched" in the House of a Hundred Chimneys, but outside the fiction, he wanted somebody to discover and publish it. Among the problems inherent in writing a fictive mythology was how to get it published as fiction but authenticate it as a mythology. At the time Tolkien was writing, collections of folk- and fairy-tales from Ireland to India had been and were being collected, published, and eagerly read by those whose interests lay in this area. The Folklore movement was in full swing. Not just the Grimms in Germany, but Jeremiah Curtin and Lady Gregory in Ireland, Lady Charlotte Guest in Wales, Joseph Jacobs in England, Moe and Asbjørnsen in Norway, John Francis Campbell in the West Highlands of Scotland, and Elias Lönnrot in Finland had been and were providing a wealth of myth and folklore for their respective cultures. Tolkien's inside strategy had been to buttress his story by creating an imaginary artifact with the potential to be an actual outside volume publishable in the real world—the book behind the book, Bilbo's scholarly source.

In the curious way that life has of imitating art, just such a scholarly source was actually discovered at a crucial point in the arc of Tolkien's invention—when a version of "The Silmarillion" was near completion and before *The Lord of the Rings* was begun. This real-world analogue was the manuscript discovered in 1934 in the Fellows' Library of Winchester College, a major text in Arthurian mythology that predated and was the obvious source for William Caxton's 1485 printed edition of Sir Thomas Malory's *Morte D'Arthur*. In the context of Tolkien's vision, it was at once a serendipitous validation of the Golden Book, in that the Winchester too had been waiting undiscovered for "such to read as may," and a foreshadowing of his Red Book in that it brought a diversity of interrelated sources under one cover.

Like many fortunate discoveries, this one came about by accident. In June of 1934, while cataloguing and describing the early book-bindings of the Fellows' Library at Winchester College, the School Librarian, W.F. Oakeshott, obtained permission to open the safe in the bedroom of the College Warden. He needed to fill in gaps in his knowledge of the Library's holdings, and the safe contained the medieval manuscripts. Here is Oakeshott's account of what he found:

> I ... was dashed to see at a glance that on the twenty or thirty manuscripts not a single medieval binding remained. ... It was a disappointment. But ... I pulled them out one by one and ran through one after another. ... One was very fat, some 480 leaves, paper not vellum, the text prose not verse, clearly about King Arthur and his Knights, but lacking a beginning or an end.

Be it admitted to my shame that I had never read Malory, and
my knowledge of him was about as sketchy as my knowledge of
most things has alas had to remain. But I made a vague mental
note of this prose Arthurian manuscript, and passed on to the
next item.[19]

Oakeshott put the book back in the safe and went home to dinner. A few
weeks later, preparing for an exhibit of early printed books including some
by Caxton's successor Wynkyn de Worde, he consulted a reference work and
came across a sentence which, he said, "made my heart miss a beat": "The
compilation of the *Morte d'Arthur* was finished in 1469, but of the compiler
little is known save the name ... No manuscript of the work is known, and
though Caxton certainly revised it, exactly to what extent has never been
settled."[20]

The penny dropped. Oakeshott went straight to a bookshop, purchased
the Everyman edition of the Morte D'Arthur, and asked permission to re-
open the safe. Comparing the Everyman with the prose Arthurian manuscript,
he realized straight away that the latter was not just a version of Malory; it
was the manuscript of which Caxton's was the printed version. It was, as the
colophon[21] makes clear, the "hoole book" of King Arthur.

The news immediately hit the papers, appearing in the *Daily Telegraph*
on 24 June and with follow-up stories in the *Times* on 26 June and 25 August.
Writing in his diary on Monday, 27 August 1934, C.S. Lewis's brother Warnie
Lewis cited: "Saturday's *Times* which contains the very interesting news that
the only known MS of Malory's *Morte d'Arthur* has just been discovered in
the library of Winchester College."[22] The dean of Arthurian studies, Eugene
Vinaver, asked to see the manuscript, took on the job of editing it, and in
1947 published the three-volume *Works of Sir Thomas Malory* from Oxford
University Press.

Vinaver had been a lecturer in French language and literature at Lincoln
College, Oxford from 1924 to 1928, and university lecturer in French from
1928 to 1931.[23] At the time of the discovery, he had moved to the University
of Manchester, where he would later collaborate with Tolkien's friend E.V.
Gordon on a textual comparison of the Winchester and Caxton Malorys. In
1935, Vinaver gave a talk to the Arthurian Society at Oxford on "Malory's
Morte Darthur in the Light of a Recent Discovery," the recent discovery being
the Winchester manuscript. C.S. Lewis attended the lecture, as shown by
a letter he subsequently wrote Vinaver inquiring about the meaning of a
particular word and phrase.[24]

It seems more than probable that Tolkien would also have attended
Vinaver's talk. He would hardly have missed this opportunity to learn more at
first hand about so important a discovery—a new text in what was then, and

remains today (Tolkien notwithstanding), England's only native mythology. He would certainly have had a professional interest in the Winchester, first as a scholar (indeed, Lewis also consulted Tolkien on the textual problem[25]), second as the writer of a competitive work-in-progress, and third as an at-that-point unpublished author. Here was a discovery of a manuscript book of historical significance that, in circumstances uncannily like his fictive ones, had been lying untouched in plain sight for centuries. Furthermore it was going to be published.

The event affected Tolkien in at least two areas, one internal to the fiction, one external and related to his real-world problem as an author. First, the internal influence. I propose that the Winchester manuscript was the model for the book Sam Gamgee conjures in the conversation about stories on the Stairs of Cirith Ungol. In that passage so unnecessary to the plot but so appropriate in the context of Tolkien's myth-making strategy, Sam has been musing on the nature of stories, and on their serial transmission and continuance over many years. He tells Frodo he wants their story to be "put into words told by the fireside, or read out of a great big book with red and black letters, years and years afterwards."[26] Such specificity suggests reference to an actual book, a volume of stories from periods long years before.

Tolkien was familiar with medieval manuscripts, and knew that they come in all sizes. He knew the *Beowulf* codex, MS Cotton Vitellius A.xv, a modest, quarto-size book whose individual sections begin with large initial letters but which is otherwise devoid of calligraphic decoration. He knew the manuscript of *Sir Gawain and the Green Knight*, MS Cotton Nero A.x, for which he had edited the standard scholarly edition, and of which he made his own translation. Like the *Beowulf*, the *Gawain* codex is a modest quarto, though it does have ten full-page color illustrations, rare for a medieval manuscript. It also has ornamental colored capitals. However, neither book could properly be described as 'great big,' and neither makes a good match with Sam's description. Tolkien also knew (or knew of) the great medieval illuminated manuscripts such as the Book of Kells or the Book of Durrow, folio size and thus plausibly describable as 'great big,' with interlace borders and elaborate initial letters in many colors. These match somewhat better with Sam's imaginary book; nevertheless, they are a long way from a perfect fit.

There is one manuscript book that does fit Sam's description to a T, and that is the Winchester Malory. Like Sam's, it is a 'great big book,' a folio, not a quarto, of 480 leaves, copied out from an earlier, now lost manuscript by two different scribes. Like Sam's, it is a collection of stories. Most important for my argument is Sam's phrase "with red and black letters." This is the connecting link, for the Winchester manuscript is emphatically in red and black letters. While the narrative portions are in standard black ink, the proper names and all references to the Grail are carefully written in red ink. Thus, red and black letters appear on nearly every page. The introduction to the Early English Text Society facsimile edition of the Winchester manuscript cites this as a "remarkable feature,"[27] one that, so far as I know, is unique to this manuscript. In light of this, Tolkien's desire to have the "fiery letters" of the Ring inscription printed in red[28] deserves new consideration. In addition, his own calligraphic manuscript page of *The Tale of the Years*, a color plate of which appears as the frontispiece of *Morgoth's Ring*, is carefully written out in red and black: Christopher Tolkien has called this "among the most beautiful [manuscripts] that he made,"[29] and much of the effect comes from the use of the two colors. In both these instances, the specific red and black motif seems likely to have been inspired by the Winchester Malory.

Now for the external effect. It has to do with those three extra volumes annexed to the primary or nuclear Red Book. Quite unlike the medieval Red Book, the White Book, the Black Book, the Yellow Book, and all the other manuscript books of the Middle Ages, the Winchester manuscript could trace a clear line of descent from earlier texts. The author, Sir Thomas Malory, made no secret of the fact that he had drawn on previously existing sources, as his frequent references to the "Frenssh boke" make clear. Malory's "Frenssh boke" is in fact a number of texts in both French and English that were available to readers on both sides of the Channel in the years when he was writing his great work.

The stories of the Coming of Arthur, the romances of Tristan and Iseult and of Lancelot and Guinevere, the transcendent story of Galahad and the Grail Quest, and the final tragedy of the Death of Arthur, were to be found in various existing manuscripts. Among these were the cycle (from which only fragments survive) of Robert de Boron's *Joseph d'Arimathie*, *Merlin*, and *Perceval*; the *Queste del Saint Graal*; the prose *Tristan*; the French Vulgate Cycle, especially the *Morte Artu*; the anonymously authored *Suite du Merlin* that is the basis for the Post-Vulgate Cycle; and the Middle English Alliterative and Stanzaic *Morte* poems on the Death of Arthur. All were ready to hand. With due allowance for poetic license and his own genius, Malory "translated" them into his own Middle English.

Caxton's printed edition of Malory had fueled the speculation of scholars, but here was more immediate, primary manuscript evidence. Where Caxton had divided his printed edition into many chapters, the Winchester Malory is divided into a number of separate but interlaced "bokes,"[30] each given a separate title, and all but one, "The Tale of Sir Gareth of Orkney That Was Called Bewmaynes," having an identifiable outside source or sources. All the books are directly focused on the Matter of Britain, the interconnected sequence of myths and legends about Arthur and the Knights of the Round Table. This coherent content of myth and legend, stretching over a considerable span of time, fits remarkably with Tolkien's letter to Milton Waldman outlining his scheme for his own mythology:

I had a mind to make a body of more or less connected legend, ranging from the large and cosmogonic, to the level of romantic fairy-story.... It should ... be redolent of our "air" (the clime and soil of the North West, meaning Britain and the hither parts of Europe.... and while possessing (if I could achieve it) the fair elusive beauty that some call Celtic ... it should be "high", purged of the gross.... The cycles should be linked to a majestic whole, and yet leave scope for other minds and hands, wielding paint and music and drama.[31]

If we did not know better, and with the exception of the phrase "purged of the gross" (such as the adultery which is the plot pivot of the Arthurian story) we might easily imagine Tolkien to be describing the corpus of Arthurian myth and legend rather than his own mythology.

It is not unreasonable to conjecture that he was on a very private level comparing the two. It takes a special kind of confident imagination to make the leap from Malory's actual synthesis of earlier texts to the Red Book's fictive annexation of those three volumes with their separate but interconnected stories of the Singing of the Ainur, of Fëanor and the Silmarils, the romance of Beren and Lúthien, the tragedies of Thingol and Turin, and the apotheosis of Eärendil. I argue that Tolkien had that kind of imagination and that he made that leap. To position Bilbo as not just the narrator of *The Hobbit* and part of *The Lord of the Rings*, but also, through his "researches in Rivendell," as the translator and redactor of the earlier "book" (by whatever title it had acquired by then), is to place that unassuming hobbit on a fictive editorial footing with Malory, and equally, to put Tolkien's Red Book on a Middle-earth par with the Winchester manuscript.

My external argument extends beyond the discovery of the Winchester in 1934 to its publication in 1947.[32] I suggest that this publication offered Tolkien not just a conceptual model, but a possible precedent as well. I propose this as a conjectural rationale for what otherwise seemed then, as it does now, his impractical and unrealistic insistence on twofold publication—having "The Silmarillion" and *The Lord of the Rings* brought out together. With the advantage of over fifty years' hindsight, we can see that there could not have been an audience for "The Silmarillion" until *The Lord of the Rings* created one, a circumstance that effectively precluded dual publication in the mid-twentieth century. No such hindsight was available to Tolkien. In its absence, the successful publication of the Winchester might have suggested to him that there could be an audience for so large a mythological work if it were presented in such a way as to attract that audience. As was the Winchester.

Vinaver described his goal in editing that manuscript as "the endeavour to produce the text in a form similar to that of a modern work of fiction,"[33] and the motive was clearly to make it readable for a non-scholarly audience. If Vinaver could present a scholarly mythology in a form similar to that of modern fiction, why could not Tolkien publish his modern fiction in the form of a mythology? If despite post-war austerity, production costs, and paper shortages the Winchester manuscript could be brought out in a three-volume edition,[34] perhaps Tolkien's combined work could get similar treatment.

Although such twofold publication was impractical in terms not just of production expenses (letters between Tolkien and Sir Stanley Unwin during these years refer to paper shortages and mounting costs), but also of sales, he clung to that hope for three years, from 1949, when he first approached Milton Waldman at Collins publishers, to 1952, when he gave in and gave up. It was then that he wrote to Rayner Unwin, "I have rather modified my views. Better something than nothing!"[35] and settled for publishing *The Lord of the Rings* alone.

In addition to suggesting a possible rationale for an unrealistic hope, these circumstances may throw additional light on another and equally idiosyncratic aspect of Tolkien's stance as a British writer at that time. This was his dismissal of the story of King Arthur as the primary candidate for England's mythology. In his 1951 letter laying out the case for his own mythos to Milton Waldman, he had acknowledged the corpus of Arthurian material generally called the Matter of Britain, conceding that, "of course there was *and* is [my emphasis] all the Arthurian world." Nevertheless, he maintained that "powerful as it is," it did not meet his criteria. His grounds for its ineligibility were that its story was "imperfectly naturalized" (that is, native to the soil but not the language of England), that its Faery was "too lavish," and that it "explicitly contain[ed] the Christian religion."[36]

That it contained explicit Christianity is beyond question, for the Grail Quest had been an integral part of the story since the late twelfth century. That its Faery was too lavish is of course a matter of opinion. Imperfectly naturalized it might have been considered, though this again is a matter of opinion and open to question. However, this last judgment has a direct bearing on Tolkien's real reason for preferring his own myth, that in it he had created, as Christopher Tolkien has pointed out, "a specifically English [i.e. not British like Arthur] fairy lore."[37]

Nevertheless, and even though the explicit "Englishness" of his own mythos diminished over the years, at the time when Tolkien wrote his letter, the story of Arthur was newly in print while his mythology was not. Had his negotiations with Waldman and Collins succeeded, the hoped-for tandem publication of "The Silmarillion" and *The Lord of the Rings* would have put Tolkien's mythological "book," which he described to Milton Waldman as "one long Saga of the Jewels and the Rings"[38] on a competitive level with its Arthurian counterpart.[39] It would have brought to fruition his ambition of dedicating a mythology to England, one that would rival the Arthurian one in actuality as well as in his private vision.

It was not to be. Not in its author's lifetime, at any rate. However, though this was for him a deep disappointment—indeed, Christopher Tolkien describes it as "grief to him" and cites his "despair of publication"[40]— the delay may not in other respects have been the drawback that it at first appeared. Ultimately, the dream deferred only increased the resemblance between Tolkien's fictive "book" and his most recent real-world model, for both were forced by circumstances to lie for years in one or another repository, uncatalogued and unread, before being rescued from obscurity, edited, and published for modern readers. As circumstances turned out, it was neither Eriol/Ælfwine nor Heorrenda, not even Bilbo Baggins, but Christopher Tolkien who finally produced in its entirety his father's "hoole book," the multi-volume *History of Middle-earth*. Only the continuing popularity of *The Lord of the Rings* made possible the publication, three decades and more after that narrative's first appearance, of the vast and multi-voiced manuscript book that had lain unaccessed for so many years waiting for "such to read as may."

And that is we who come after, the generations following Tolkien who have found his "book" in all its aspects worthy not just of readerly enjoyment but also of scholarly study, of serious critical and textual examination through which we labor to enhance without dissecting his vision.

Notes

1. J.R.R. Tolkien, *The Lord of the Rings*, 2nd ed., 1 vol. (London: HarperCollins, 1991 [i.e. 1994]), 263, 271.

2. The participation of Frodo and Sam in the book project was set out in the Epilogue to *The Lord of the Rings*. Since that chapter was omitted from the published text, the account of their contributions to the book appears only in chapter 11 of *Sauron Defeated* (1992), "The Epilogue."

3. This "supplement" enhances the likeness to the Red Book of Hergest; whose second volume (the first contains the *Mabinogion*) is the *Bruts* or Stories of the Kings.

4. Richard C. West, "The Interlace Structure of *The Lord of the Rings*," in *A Tolkien Compass*, ed. Jared Lobdell (LaSalle, Ill.: Open Court, 1975), 91.

5. J.R.R. Tolkien, *The Book of Lost Tales, Part One*, ed. Christopher Tolkien, vol. 1 of *The History of Middle-earth* (Boston: Houghton Mifflin, 1984), 5.

6. J.R.R. Tolkien, *The Lord of the Rings*, 1st ed., 3 vols. (London: George Allen & Unwin, 1954–55), 1:8.

7. J.R.R. Tolkien, *The Lord of the Rings*, 2nd ed., 14.

8. Tolkien, *Lord of the Rings*, 1st ed., 1:7.

9. Ibid.

10. Tolkien, *Lord of the Rings*, 2nd ed., 14.

11. Ibid.

12. On p.108 of his essay "*Ancrene Wisse* and *Hali Meiðhad*," published in *Essays and Studies by Members of the English Association* 14 (1929), Tolkien had argued for "a closeness of

relationship between the language and the spelling of two distinct MSS. and hands that is astonishing, if not (as I believe) unique." He proposed that the scribes of these two manuscripts had used a language and orthography so nearly identical that the *Ancrene Wisse* (Language A) and *Hali Meiðhad* (Language B) were "in fact in one language and spelling (AB)."

13. Richard Plotz, "J.R.R. Tolkien Talks about the Discovery of Middle-earth," *Seventeen*, January 1967: 118.

14. The tales therein, "The Music of the Ainur" and the earliest accounts of Valinor, the Trees, and the Noldor, "The Fall of Gondolin," "The Tale of Tinúviel," "Turambar and the Foalókë," "The Nauglafring," and "The Tale of Eärendil," are in essence the Lost Tales, the earliest versions of the central stories of "The Silmarillion."

15. J.R.R. Tolkien, *The Book of Lost Tales, Part Two*, ed. Christopher Tolkien, vol. 2 of *The History of Middle-earth* (Boston: Houghton Mifflin, 1984), 283.

16. Ibid., 287.

17. *Heorrenda* was also Tolkien's choice for the name of the *Beowulf*-poet, one more indication of his early attempt to attach his mythology to English tradition.

18. Stated in J.R.R. Tolkien, *The Shaping of Middle-earth*, ed. Christopher Tolkien, vol. 4 of *The History of Middle-earth* (Boston: Houghton Mifflin, 1986), 274.

19. Walter F. Oakeshott, "The Finding of the Manuscript," in *Essays on Malory*, ed. J.A.W. Bennett (Oxford: Clarendon Press, 1963), 3.

20. Oakeshott, 4.

21. The colophon survives only in the Pierpont Morgan Library Caxton, and until the discovery of the Winchester manuscript, the word "hoole" was misread as "booke" and deleted on grounds of redundancy. Vinaver reads the correct colophon as making Malory's reference "crystal clear: the 'whole book' is the series which is here concluded" (*The Works of Sir Thomas Malory*, ed. Eugene Vinaver, 3rd ed. rev. P.J.C. Field [Oxford: Clarendon Press, 1990], 1:xlv).

22. *Brothers and Friends: The Diaries of Major Warren Hamilton Lewis*, ed. Clyde S. Kilby and Marjorie Lamp Mead (San Francisco: Harper & Row, 1982), 155.

23. Vinaver was founder in 1927 of the Arthurian Society in Oxford, and the first editor of its journal *Arthuriana*, which in 1931 expanded its scope and changed its name to *Medium Ævum*. Tolkien was one of the founding members of the Arthurian Society, and addressed the Society on *Beowulf* at a meeting in Hilary Term of 1932. He was also a member of the journal's editorial board. (I am indebted to Mr. Alan Reynolds for pointing me in this direction.)

24. C.S. Lewis, *The Collected Letters of C.S. Lewis*, vol. 2, ed. Walter Hooper (San Francisco: HarperSanFrancisco, 2004), 166.

25. The question was whether the word *hole* in the phrase "hole of the tree" meant "bole of the tree" or, as Tolkien suggested when Lewis consulted him, "fork of the tree," from Old English *healh'* Latin *angulus* "fork." Vinaver apparently preferred *bole*, which is what his edition uses (1:255). However, the phrase as it appears in the manuscript, "at the holy of the tre hongys a basyn [basin] of couper [copper] and latyne [brass]" (Sir Thomas Malory, *The Winchester Malory: A Facsimile* [London. Oxford University Press, 1976], f. 97) could mean either, since the initial letter in *holy* can be read as either *h* or *b*. Tolkien's conjecture, therefore, is plausible, and the whole incident is evidence for the high level of scholarly interest the discovery engendered in the academic community.

26. Tolkien, *Lord of the Rings*, 2nd ed., 697.

27. Malory, *The Winchester Malory*, xiv.

28. Humphrey Carpenter, *J.R.R. Tolkien: A Biography* (London: George Allen & Unwin, 1977), 217.

29. J.R.R. Tolkien, *Morgoth's Ring*, ed. Christopher Tolkien, Vol. 10 of *The History of Middle-earth* (Boston: Houghton Mifflin, 1993), 49.

30. Hence the necessary colophon at the end of the last book that established all of them as comprising the "hoole book."

31. J.R.R. Tolkien, to Milton Waldman, probably late 1951, in *The Letters of J.R.R. Tolkien*, selected and ed. Humphrey Carpenter with the assistance of Christopher Tolkien (Boston: Houghton Mifflin, 1981), 144–45. This volume is hereafter cited as *Letters*, by page.

32. Coincidentally, this lengthy period between discovery and publication is echoed in the equally lengthy stretch between Tolkien's December 1937 start on the "new Hobbit" that became *The Lord of the Rings* and his 1951 letter to Milton Waldman making the case for dual publication.

33. Malory, *Works*, vi.

34. It is one of the ironies of fate (or of the publishing business) that even without "The Silmarillion" and due entirely to the need to spread out production costs, *The Lord of the Rings*, like the Winchester, was first published in three volumes (though in the case of *The Lord of the Rings* this was also spread out over two years). Also like the Winchester, it had been written as a sequence of separate but interconnected books. Both were later published in one-volume editions.

35. J.R.R. Tolkien, to Rayner Unwin, 22 June 1952, in *Letters*, 163.

36. Tolkien, to Milton Waldman, probably late 1951, in *Letters*, 144.

37. Tolkien, *The Book of Lost Tales, Part Two*, 290.

38. Tolkien, to Milton Waldman, probably late 1951, in *Letters*, 139.

39. In this context, it is worth noting that Tolkien characterized the last departure of Bilbo and Frodo by ship into the West as "an Arthurian ending" (*Sauron Defeated*, ed. Christopher Tolkien, vol. 9 of *The History of Middle-earth* [London: HarperCollins, 1992], 132).

40. Tolkien, *Morgoth's Ring*, vii, viii.

MARY R. BOWMAN

The Story Was Already Written:
Narrative Theory in
The Lord of the Rings

Popularity, for a writer of fiction, can be a double-edged sword: Surely writers want their work to be read and appreciated, and royalty checks are always welcome; but some forms of enthusiastic reception may give other potential readers a misleading impression of what a work is like. Such may be the case with *The Lord of the Rings*. Its popularity with the opt-out culture in the '60s, the prevalence of buttons reading "Frodo Lives" in the '70s, and people in elf costume lining up for movies in this decade have, perhaps, led some to suppose that the work can appeal only to relatively naive readers, that it would not reward the kind of critical analysis that more sophisticated fiction receives. Or perhaps it is simply that many of us read the work as teenagers and have never returned to it. Whatever the reason, there has been a general neglect of *The Lord of the Rings* among scholars of fiction. Certainly, no articles on Tolkien have appeared in Narrative before, or in other journals with broad audiences such as ELH or PMLA. (Specialized scholarship on Tolkien, on the other hand, has proceeded quietly for many years and includes some work of very high quality; for an overview, see Drout and Wynne.) But this is beginning to change: *Modern Fiction Studies*, for example, recently ran a special issue on Tolkien (Hughes). With this article, I hope to contribute to that change by demonstrating some of the richness of Tolkien's fiction for inquiries into the structure and function of narrative. Specifically, I will explore

From *Narrative* 14, no. 3 (October 2006): pp. 272–293. © 2006 by Ohio State University Press.

the metanarrative aspects of *The Lord of the Rings*: These include characters' conversations about narrative (which are sometimes self-referential) and features of the novel's structure and narrative technique that illustrate some of the points made in the characters' conversations—and in ours.

One such conversation occurs between Frodo and Sam, the characters whose task it is to travel (alone but for the company of Gollum, their untrustworthy guide) into the stronghold of the Dark Lord Sauron to destroy the Ring that contains much of his power. On their last evening outside the borders of Mordor, they have what can only be described as a theoretical discussion of narrative and reader response. Sam muses on (among other things) what kinds of tales "stay in the mind," what kinds of adventures make for a good tale and which are "forgotten," and even what their own experiences will be like when made into a story, "put into words . . . told by the fireside, or read out of a big book" (IV.8, 696–7).[1] More surprisingly, perhaps, this conversation serves to lighten the mood of the two hobbits, in spite of the cheerless place in which they find themselves and the dangers that lie ahead of them. Though he observes that they are "still stuck in the worst places of the story," Frodo actually laughs—in a place where laughter is seldom heard—and tells Sam, "to hear you makes me as merry as if the story was already written" (IV.8, 697).

It is perhaps not surprising to find such a conversation, with its mood-altering impact, in a work written by a man who spent his professional career, as well as a good deal of his leisure time from boyhood, reading, teaching, editing, and writing about narratives of various sorts (not to mention creating them). Yet this attention to story as a topic of discussion is an aspect of *The Lord of the Rings* that Tolkien criticism has not yet fully explored. In addition to the characters' discussions—which run throughout the work, only becoming more extended and explicit in this example—there are a number of structural features of the work that give it a metafictional dimension. "This tale grew in the telling," as Tolkien famously begins his Foreword to the second edition (xiii), and its growth can be observed in the levels at which it operates as well as in its size and scope. What Frodo and Sam say in this remarkable conversation—along with other, less extended, comments by other characters—is illustrated by the very work in which their theorizing is contained. *The Lord of the Rings* goes beyond being an absorbing and moving story to constitute a meditation on the nature of story.

Beginning and Ending: "The Web of Story"

The Lord of the Rings's metanarrative concerns begin right at the beginning, not only of the text but of the process of its composition, and they include the much-discussed issue of closure and the problem of beginning anew after closure has apparently been achieved. Near the end of *The Hobbit*, readers are told that Bilbo "remained very happy to the end of his days, and those were extraordinarily long" (361). The emphatic closure of this sentence, as Douglas Anderson reminds us in his annotation to it, presented a problem for Tolkien as he began to comply with Stanley Unwin's suggestion to write another book about hobbits: It was "'an almost insuperable obstacle to a satisfactory link' between *The Hobbit* and its sequel" (364, quoting *Letters* 38). "Fortunately," Anderson comments, "Tolkien found his way around such an obstacle." We might say something stronger: that he turned the obstacle into an opportunity. For the "way around" it involved not merely introducing Frodo and making new discoveries about the Ring Bilbo found, but also constructing the flame of the Red Book of Westmarch, which becomes one of the major structural devices Tolkien uses to invite metafictional reflection. The Red Book, whose title echoes those of actual medieval manuscripts such as the White Book of Rhydderch, is a manuscript containing the texts of *The Hobbit* and *The Lord of the Rings*, among others—a manuscript Tolkien refers to a number of times in the Prologue and Appendices to *The Lord of the Rings*. Within the documentary history that Tolkien constructs for *The Lord of the Rings*, Tolkien himself is the editor/translator, not the author, of all the works published under his name. He claims, in essence, that the story was already written, and he is merely transmitting it.

The most immediate consequence of this construction is to disown the troublesome sentence at the end of *The Hobbit* and attribute it to Bilbo; the frame device effectively places the entire book inside quotation marks. Thus the "obstacle" of *The Hobbit*'s closure is overcome, and, more importantly, the implied author of *The Hobbit* (within the frame) becomes a character in its sequel, providing an opportunity for Tolkien to comment on the earlier work through the mouth of this character. Within *The Lord of the Rings*, Bilbo becomes both the author of his own story and a spokeshobbit for the type of narrative it embodies.

Not surprisingly, given the impetus for casting Bilbo in this dual role, Bilbo is very interested in discussing closure, a topic that has had no small interest for theorists of narrative: he is almost obsessive about both the authorial act of completing his book and the narratorial task of giving that book a decisive and satisfying ending. Unlike most modern theorists, however, he has a rather naive faith in the possibility and desirability of complete and watertight closure. He has a strong taste for the non-narratable, the "point where time lapses into benign repetition: where nature, along with 'naturalized' social probabilities, will resume a predictable run" (Miller 44). He is, indeed, somewhat reminiscent of the Austen heroines (as described by D. A. Miller), who "have practically to be abducted into narratable zones" (51). Almost the first thing we hear him say in *The Hobbit* is that "adventures" are "nasty disturbing uncomfortable things [that make] you late for dinner" (32). Though not abducted, he is prompted to enter into an adventure by a rather manipulative scheme of Gandalf's, and he repeatedly wishes that he "was at home ... by the fire, with the kettle just beginning to sing" (66). It's not surprising, then, that he is perturbed by the unfolding events of the first book of *The Lord of the Rings*, which threaten to explode the closure he thought he had achieved (in life) after his return home and that he hopes to achieve (in fiction) by turning his life into a book: "I wonder if it's any good trying to finish my book?" he laments to Frodo (II.1, 226), later observing that Frodo's experiences with the Ring have already created "whole chapters of stuff" (II.2, 243) before his arrival at Rivendell and predicting that "there will evidently have to be several more chapters" (263) before the whole tale is ended. All this new material is, to Bilbo, "a frightful nuisance," as he complains before the entire assembly at the Council of Elrond: "I was very comfortable here, and getting on with my book. If you want to know, I am just writing an ending for it. I had thought of putting: and he lived happily ever afterwards to the end of his days. It is a good ending, and none the worse for having been used before. But now I shall have to alter that" (263). As Peter Brooks might put it, Bilbo's "narrative desire is ultimately, inexorably, desire for the end" (52), and *The Lord of the Rings* insists on frustrating that desire. Not long after, talking with Frodo and Sam about what lies ahead of them, Bilbo repeats his belief that books "ought to have good endings" and suggests "and they all settled down and lived together happily ever after" (II.3, 266) as a possible ending for the longer book that the new adventures promise to require.

All this goes beyond a merely thematic discussion of closure; the frame of the Red Book of Westmarch renders these comments self-referential. Bilbo's unfinished book is, of course, the book we know as *The Hobbit*. The "whole chapters of stuff" Frodo has experienced are the first book of *The Lord of the Rings* (twelve chapters, as it turns out), and the new ending Bilbo proposes is, in effect, a possible ending for *The Lord of the Rings*, whose final length he has severely underestimated.

It is telling, then, that Bilbo's suggested ending is not in fact the way *The Lord of the Rings* does end, and with good reason. One message *The Lord of the Rings* conveys, in what becomes something of a debate with its predecessor, is that this kind of closure is always "artificial, arbitrary, ... casual and textual rather than cosmic and definitive" (Brooks 314). Bilbo himself recognizes this after a fashion: asking Frodo, "Don't adventures ever have an end?" he answers his own question, "I suppose not. Someone else always has to carry on the story" (II.1, 226). What for Bilbo is a distressing realization, to be resisted with mantra-like repetitions of the "happily ever after," is for Sam a wondrous discovery. In his narratological discourse, Sam stumbles unexpectedly on the realization that their story is in fact a continuation of stories they have heard of events in the distant past: "And why, sir, I never thought of that before! We've got—you've got some of the light of [the Silmaril of Eärendil] in that star-glass that the Lady gave you! Why, to think of it, we're in the same tale still! It's going on" (IV.8, 696–7). He asks Frodo, echoing Bilbo but with a notable difference of tone as well as grammar, "Don't the great tales never end?" This time it is Frodo who answers, acknowledging and accepting the truth of what Sam has breathlessly articulated: "No, they never end as tales. But the people in them come, and go when their part's ended" (697).

Sam and Frodo have, it seems, arrived at the same conclusion that Tolkien articulated in his essay "On Fairy-Stories," which was first written as a lecture in 1938, at about the time he was beginning to write *The Lord of the Rings*. Tolkien the scholar states that "there is no true end to any fairy-tale"; "[t]he verbal ending ... 'and they lived happily ever after' is an artificial device, ... no more to be thought of as the real end of any particular fragment of the seamless Web of Story than the frame is of the visionary scene, or the casement of the Outer World" (86, 98). By constructing an actual frame for his tale, Tolkien is able to incorporate this belief into his work as an explicit statement in the mouths of his characters, not merely as an abstract theory but as a meta-comment on his own work.[2] What Sam says of the events recounted in *The Lord of the Rings* in relation to tales of the Elder Days is equally true of the book that recounts them, *The Lord of the Rings* itself. The tales Sam refers to in fact existed, in some version, when Tolkien wrote this passage. Begun soon after World War I, they were substantially complete (though repeatedly revised throughout Tolkien's life), stories already written when he began *The Hobbit* around 1930, though they were not published until 1977, after Tolkien's death, as *The Silmarillion*.[3]

Despite the dangers of biographical criticism, it is tempting to add that there is an autobiographical element here as well as a theoretical one. Bilbo's reluctance to re-open his closed narrative and his habit of underestimating the length of the work ahead mirror Tolkien's own experience of writing *The Lord of the Rings*. In December of 1942 he thought it possible that he would "finish it off early next year" and estimated that he was six chapters from the end (*Letters* 58); "in the event," as his biographer points out, "there were to be not six but thirty-one more chapters" (Carpenter 198). Similarly, Sam's remarks reflect Tolkien's own sense of the continuity of the legendarium. As he told W. H. Auden in 1955, "*The Hobbit* was originally quite unconnected, though it inevitably got drawn in to the circumference of the greater construction" (*Letters* 215). When *The Lord of the Rings* was finally complete, he wanted to publish it together with "The Silmarillion," insisting to his publisher that the former "has become simply ["The Silmarillion"'s] continuation and completion, requiring *The Silmarillion* to be fully intelligible" (*Letters* 136–7). He continued to lament the unpublished state of the earlier material, the story of the "older world," when he wrote the Foreword to the second edition, describing *The Lord of the Rings* as "an account, as it were, of its end and passing away before its beginning and middle had been told" (xiii). With this remark he also suggests a less-frequently discussed aspect of narrative than closure: the problem of beginning, to which I shall return in a moment.

The idea that closure is never complete, endings never truly final, is also inscribed into the work in a number of less explicit ways. The conventional fairy-tale ending is pointedly revised, first by Saruman, who tells Frodo, "do not expect me to wish you health and long life. You will have neither" (VI.8, 996). Frodo, more kindly but still with qualification, predicts that Sam will be "as happy as anyone can be," not ever after but "as long as your part of the Story goes on" (VI.9, 1006). The actual ending of the book is denied strong closure by the presence of another structural feature, the appendices: appendices A and B literally continue the story, chronicling events (and even narrating them, as in the "Tale of Aragorn and Arwen," for example) up to Shire Reckoning 1541, some 120 years after the last chapter; the remaining appendices go beyond narrative to add a great deal more cultural and linguistic material.[4] There is also another chapter in manuscript ("The Epilogue"), set about fourteen years after "The Grey Havens," which has Sam reading out of the Red Book and talking with his children about where the characters are now (*Sauron Defeated* 114–135). This chapter, written but omitted from the published work, is marvelously self-referential, but its excision may do more to deny closure, for those who are aware of it, than its inclusion would have: there is, literally, another chapter beyond the ostensible end of the book.

In retrospect, the fact that *The Hobbit* does not quite end with the closural sentence to which Bilbo is so devoted, but continues on for seven more paragraphs, seems to do this same thing in embryo, a small prophecy of what Tolkien would do in *The Lord of the Rings*. The "happily ever after" is there, but in spite of the problems of beginning again that it appears to present, it is literally not the last word; *The Hobbit* already reveals, in spite of its (fictional) implied author's desire, that closure is always elusive and never absolute.[5]

And the same can be said for beginning: Sam's epiphany that the earlier stories don't really end but continue into this one, implies conversely that this story doesn't really begin where we thought, either. Sam realizes that the story he and Frodo are experiencing as it happens goes back at least as far as Beren, whose story comes about in the middle of "The Silmarillion" (and which, in turn, reaches back ultimately to the very beginning). This is another point about the nature of narrative and the messiness of experience that Bilbo does not at first understand. "Bilbo the silly hobbit started this affair," he comments when the Council comes to the point of choosing a Ringbearer, "and Bilbo had better finish it" (II.2, 263). He apparently believes, in spite of all he has learned in his years living in Rivendell as well as the specific story of the Ring that has been told that morning, that "this affair" began on the first page of *The Hobbit*. Gandalf, of course, corrects him immediately: "But you know well enough now that starting is too great a claim for any" (263). He is corrected again—still in the voice of Gandalf, though structurally rather than explicitly—by the tale included in Appendix A of Gandalf's meeting "Thorin Oakenshield one evening on the edge of spring in Bree" (1053), a conversation that led directly to the events narrated in *The Hobbit*. *The Hobbit* might just as easily have begun with this narrative—or at any of a number of other points in the Web of Story.[6] Theorist Gary Morson has argued that "a truly realist work must never have a point at which narrativeness ceases; there can be no denouement, no closure" (71). We might add, neither is there a point where narrativeness begins, and *The Lord of the Rings* (by this criterion, perhaps surprisingly, a truly realist work) metanarratively makes both points.

The idea that no one person can really claim to begin or end a tale is underscored by another effect of the frame: the multiple authorship of the work. Bilbo apparently finished writing *The Hobbit*; it bears the mark of his zeal for closure. However, he does not (as he assumes early on) write the "several more chapters" that constitute *The Lord of the Rings*. He hands the book off to Frodo, who works on it after his return to Bag End and "nearly finish[es] it" (VI.9, 1004) before leaving for the Grey Havens. But even Frodo doesn't complete the manuscript; he leaves "the last few pages" for Sam. This gives *The Lord of the Rings* three authors within the frame, and even they do not have full responsibility for the entire work, since they credit several other contributors.[7] As the title page of the Red Book describes it, these are "the memoirs of Bilbo and Frodo of the Shire, supplemented by the accounts of their friends and the learning of the Wise" (1004). This is essential to preserve the illusion of their authorship, since parts of the story are not and could not be narrated from their points of view (more on that later), but it also calls to mind what Walter Benjamin has said of storytellers: they "begin their story with presentation of the circumstances in which they themselves have learned what is to follow" (92). For Benjamin, these roots in "oral tradition" (87) distinguish storytelling from novels, forms also contrasting in their openness: "[T]here is no story for which the question as to how it continued would not be legitimate. The novelist, on the other hand, cannot hope to take the smallest step beyond that limit at which he invites the reader to a divinatory realization of the meaning of life by writing 'Finis'" (100). In these terms, *The Lord of the Rings* has declared itself, emphatically, a story.

STORY AND LIFE: BLURRING THE LINE

As Bilbo's experience and Sam's epiphany show, stories like the one recorded in *The Hobbit* have a status within the work, within the frame, somewhat different from what they have in, for want of a better word, reality: that is, for the twentieth- or twenty-first-century reader. The continuity of stories is due in part to the fact that most stories in Middle-earth are histories: tales of people and events which, within the fictional world, are historical rather than fictional. In the Foreword to *The Lord of the Rings*, Tolkien expresses a preference for "history, true or feigned" over allegory (xv), and indeed this provides an apt description for his own work: it is, as the frame emphasizes, feigned history. To put this in Peter Rabinowitz's terms, the implied narrator, like the narrator of War and Peace, is writing history, and the narrative audience should read it as such (127).

We are reminded of this even before the hobbits arrive at Rivendell to hear Bilbo talking about his book: They have a good laugh at themselves when they realize that the trolls they were alarmed to encounter are "the very three that were caught by Gandalf, quarrelling over the right way to cook thirteen dwarves and one hobbit" (I.12, 200). Frodo observes that they are "forgetting [their] family history" (i.e., *The Hobbit*—and indeed they are, since Bilbo had escaped from the trolls and was not in danger of being cooked). His remark suggests that they ought to have thought of Bilbo's tale as soon as they saw the trolls and used their knowledge of that story/history to more accurately interpret their present experience: drawing on art to read life.

Admittedly, this is a small moment and not much to hang a theory of reader response on. But the historicity of stories also leads many characters ("real" people, in the fictional world) to think of themselves as characters in songs and tales not yet written, even to imagine reader/hearer response to those tales. Sam and Frodo do this most notably and most at length in their extended conversation about narrative, and there are numerous other small examples. But what is most striking is the way in which this ever-present eye to what stories will say in the future influences not only how characters interpret experience but even how they choose to act. Merry, for example, longs to ride with the Rohirrim, motivated in part by the thought of how he will look in a tale if he does not: pleading with Théoden, he says, "I would not have it said of me in song only that I was always left behind! (V.3, 786). Éowyn, similarly frustrated at being told to stay in Dunharrow, laments that the Riders will "win renown" while she is left behind; Aragorn urges her to recognize the "need for valour without renown," unsuccessfully (V.2, 767). Both Merry and Éowyn defy orders and advice and find a way to the battlefield, and their story-motivated choices are crucial for the battle's outcome: It is they who defeat and kill the general of the opposing army, the Lord of the Nazgûl. In so doing they fulfill the prophecy that "no living man" can harm him: no man indeed, but a hobbit and a woman (V.6, 823).

A similar influence is at work when characters appropriate existing tales, remembering and applying them, history though they are, in ways that reflect their current situations. Christine Barkley has demonstrated how narrators such as Bilbo, Gandalf, and Aragorn "focus on different aspects of a tale due to their own personalities, interests, or concerns" as they retell stories such as Eärendil's or Beren and Lúthien's (257). In the "Tale of Aragorn and Arwen," Aragorn's backstory included in the Appendices, Aragorn sees Arwen for the first time while singing about Lúthien Tinúviel, and calls her by that name, as if the story had come to life before his eyes; she replies that though "her name is not" the same, perhaps her "doom will be not unlike hers" (App. A.v, 1033). Later, confronted by Elrond, Aragorn compares his situation to Beren's (as Barkley has noted, 260): "I have turned my eyes to a treasure no less dear than the treasure of Thingol that Beren once desired" (1034). The comparison is not merely figurative: Like her ancestor Lúthien, Arwen does choose to relinquish her immortality, and like the ancient king Thingol, Elrond sets a high bride-price for the mortal man who would marry his elven daughter (perhaps, though this is not made explicit, following Thingol's model): "She shall not be the bride of any Man less than the King of both Gondor and Arnor" (App. A.v, 1036). Aragorn's long quest to imitate Beren and fulfill that demand is what equips him and, to some degree, motivates him, to play the crucial role he does in the events of *The Lord of the Rings*.

The fact that this blurring of the line between history and story is rooted in a real continuity between the two, within the frame, makes the connection more prevalent and more explicit than it might be otherwise. Such connections, however, are not unprecedented in narratives or in the reading of narratives. Other purely literary examples exist, most famously Dante's Paolo and Francesca, who were moved to imitate the behavior of Lancelot and Guenivere only to wind up in the circle of the adulterers (Inferno 5.121–138). Crossing the line from fiction into life is the similarly famous example of the large numbers of suicides in imitation of Goethe's *Young Werther*. Contemporary debates about violence in the media frequently rest on the assumption that what one experiences as a consumer of fiction may, consciously or unconsciously, shape one's behavior and experience of the world.[8] The ways in which readers' interpretation of narratives is shaped by, and revelatory of, their psychology has also been of interest to reader response critics such as Norman Holland or David Bleich. As Holland put it early in his career, "all of us, as we read, use the literary work to symbolize and finally to replicate ourselves. We work out through the text our own characteristic patterns of desire and adaptation" (124).[9] *The Lord of the Rings* thematizes this, and adds, conversely, that we also use the literary work to read, and write, ourselves.

DRAWING THE LINE (AND BLURRING IT AGAIN)

In *The Lord of the Rings*, as we have seen, the continuity of story extends even across the line between reading/hearing and living, between story and life. But there is still a gap, not entirely bridgeable, between being a character in a story and reading a story, however closely a reader may identify with a character. This too is made explicit in the "narratological" conversation between Frodo and Sam.

Frodo makes what may be the most theoretically interesting point: "You may know, or guess, what kind of tale it is, happy-ending or sad-ending, but the people in it don't know. And you don't want them to" (IV.8, 696). Frodo is something of a genre theorist here, hinting at the impact that expectations about the kind of story one is reading have on a reader's experience. The truth of this argument can be felt by a reader of *The Lord of the Rings* at this point: we do have an idea that things are going to work out for the good in some sense; we also know that Gollum is up to something that Frodo doesn't yet suspect. Second- and subsequent-time readers know just what Gollum is planning (to lead Frodo and Sam into the lair of the giant spider Shelob) and can only wince at the irony. It's entirely reasonable to suppose that some auditors have at this point said, as Frodo predicts, "Shut the book now, dad; we don't want to read any more" (697).

However, it is Sam who offers the most voluminous and ultimately the most pointedly self-referential commentary. He makes a number of observations about the different experiences of "folk inside a story" and folk "outside it." For example, they have different ideas about what constitutes "a good end" (one thinks of Bilbo again here). Tales of "finding things all right" may be "the best tales to get landed into," but they aren't "the best tales to hear." Conversely, dangers and difficulties are much more welcome in a story than in life: "Things done and over and made into part of the great tales are different. Why, even Gollum might be good in a tale, better than he is to have by you, anyway" (696–7).

With this last comment, Sam's theoretical discussion has become a meta-commentary on *The Lord of the Rings*, the "great tale" made out of the story that he and Frodo have "fallen into." Indeed, Gollum has become one of the most memorable and interesting characters in the work for many readers. (I recently had a conversation with a colleague whose only knowledge of Tolkien was a long-ago reading of *The Hobbit*. Her only clear memory, but recalled with evident pleasure, was Gollum's signature phrase, "my precious"). The more general point is also certainly true of the tale that modern readers experience: few of us would want to face Shelob, or orcs or trolls or Nazgûl, but many of us enjoy reading about such encounters. Within the work, Bilbo concurs: "really I think it's much more comfortable to sit here and hear about it all" (VI.6, 965). As Robert Musil has put it, "lucky the man who can say 'when,' 'before,' and 'after'! Terrible things may have happened to him, he may have writhed in pain, but as soon as he can tell what happened in chronological order, he feels contented as if the sun were warming his belly. This is the trick the novel artificially turns to account" (qtd. in Abbott 81).

Or as Benjamin more famously put it, "The novel is significant, therefore, not because it presents someone else's fate to us, perhaps didactically, but because this stranger's fate by virtue of the flame which consumes it yields us the warmth which we never draw from our own fate" (101).

In constructing his own tale, Tolkien does much to exploit that distance between reader and character. At the same time, he often works against it, shaping a reader's experience so that it is as much as possible like that of the characters. While both strategies have received some attention from critics (the former more so), they have been looked at in isolation. But it is important to notice that he uses both, and to consider the purpose to which each is put.

Tolkien's most important tool for underscoring the distance between readers and characters is the interlace structure of the narration. This technique has received a good deal of critical attention, first by Richard West and most notably by Tom Shippey, and as Shippey's work in particular shows, the effect is often to create ironic distance between reader and character.[10] Contrasting the reader's ability to see a carefully planned structure with the "chaotic" and "bewilder[ing]" experiences of the characters (107), he remarks that "there is a constant irony, created by the frequent gaps between what the characters realize and what the reader realizes" (110). (Shippey goes on to add that "the reader is of course almost as often in the dark as the characters," but he does not explore this in the same depth.)

The most striking example of this effect (which Shippey has called the "ironies of interlace"), an important one to consider for its rhetorical function, occurs in Chapter 7 of Book V, when Denethor assumes that the ships with black sails he has seen in the palantír are filled with enemies. Brian Rosebury has described this well: "[W]hen Denethor, secluded within the Citadel while the battle rages, concludes his outburst of defeatism by saying to Gandalf, 'even now the wind of thy hope cheats thee and wafts up Anduin a fleet with black sails' [V.7, 835], the dramatic irony is highly effective, because the grounds of Denethor's error have been so carefully prepared that the text does not even need to spell them out" (59).[11] Shippey goes a step further to demonstrate how Denethor's "ironically misguided" suicide has the effect of killing Théoden by pulling Gandalf away from the battle and the Nazgûl (172–3). But the irony of this moment lies not only in its consequences. In this instance, the gap between what readers already know, because it has already been narrated for us, and what a character knows allows us to perceive clearly the cause of Denethor's error and to judge him for it: arrogance. Denethor believes he has knowledge superior to anyone else's and is supremely confident in his ability to interpret correctly what he has seen, but readers, with knowledge that is in fact superior to his, know how wrong he is. Refusing to listen to advice or criticism, he abandons his responsibility to his people, takes his own life, and attempts to take his son's as well—acts whose immorality Gandalf strenuously denounces: "'Authority is not given to you, Steward of Gondor, to order the hour of your death. . . . And only the heathen kings, under the domination of the Dark Lord, did thus, slaying themselves in pride and despair, murdering their kin to ease their own death'" (V.7, 835). Readers have been positioned to share in this judgment.[12]

Compare this to an earlier episode involving Aragorn, the King whose "return" gives the third volume its title and whom Denethor refers to as an "upstart" he is not willing to serve (V.7, 836). Following the trail of the Orcs who have captured Merry and Pippin, he must read the signs (or "riddle," as Legolas calls it) that the two hobbits left when they escaped (III.5, 478). Because those events have already been narrated, in the third chapter of Book III, readers know that Aragorn's interpretation is correct. The effect of superior knowledge here is to some extent simply one of pleasure: the fun of watching a careful thinker successfully work out a difficult problem. But more than that, the scene reveals an important aspect of Aragorn's character. Having offered his reading, Aragorn says simply, "There, that is my tale. Others might be devised" (III.5, 479). His interpretive humility contrasts with Denethor's arrogance; readers' knowledge that his reading is correct, and Denethor's wrong, makes that contrast all the more striking. While the effect here is not ironic, it works to the same end: pushing readers to evaluate characters as the author does.

A similar effect is achieved at a much more tense moment (V. 10, 871–2), when a minion of the Dark Lord displays Frodo's mailshirt and Sam's sword, threatening torture for their owner if the opposing army doesn't agree to his outrageous terms. Dismal as the situation appears, readers are equipped to see hope: Since we have already seen Sam take Frodo's sword and leave his own with what he thought was Frodo's dead body back in the tenth chapter of Book IV, we can suppose that Sam at least may still be at large. It would be much harder, though not impossible, for the Host of the West to see hope in the mismatch of Frodo's armor and Sam's sword (and the fact that there is only one sword and one cloak, rather than two): Pippin clearly sees none ("Pippin had bowed crushed with horror when he heard Gandalf reject the terms and doom Frodo to the torment of the Tower," V.10, 873). The fact that Gandalf rejects the terms, in context, may reflect his wisdom as much as his unwillingness to negotiate in a clear-cut battle between good and evil; at least, the reader's ability to see hope makes Gandalf's choice seem less heartless than it might otherwise.

One last example of the effects of interlace is worth considering. When Pippin breaks from his orc captors and drops his broach, he can merely hope that Aragorn is following and will see and read the sign. In fact, he has little even of hope: "There I suppose it will lie until the end of time," he laments. "I don't know why I did it. If the others have escaped, they've probably all gone with Frodo" (III.3, 439–440). Since readers have already seen Aragorn find and accurately read the signs in the previous chapter, we have not only hope, but certainty. As with the later scene, when Aragorn interprets signs after their placement is narrated, this scene is devoid of irony. The reader's superior knowledge creates no sense of moral or ethical superiority; if anything, it adds admiration for Pippin's quick thinking and risk-taking in spite of his inability to see hope. Indeed, the interlace structure never creates irony at the expense of any of the hobbits. While readers are invited to judge characters like Denethor (negatively) and even Aragorn and Gandalf (positively), hobbits are largely immune. This is significant because, as Shippey has demonstrated, the hobbits are our intermediaries in the fictional world (6–11), and it is fair to say that they best embody the values of the work. While there is irony in the work, there is never satire, nothing that undermines the "good" characters or the goals they are trying to achieve, the fictional world, or the old-fashioned genre of heroic quest romance that the work participates in. As Rosebury puts it, the work lacks the "two kinds of irony" associated with modernism: "irony about value, and irony about the literary text itself" (141); instead, irony supports the text's values by distancing readers from those characters who do not support those values.

Empathy with the characters that readers are meant to admire, particularly hobbits, is a chief effect of the structural features that narrow the distance between readers and characters, that put us very much in the same boat with the characters as far as knowledge and understanding of what is going on are concerned. Our sense of being in the dark along with the characters is created in part by point of view: for the most part, any given bit of the story is narrated with a third-person limited perspective; our experience of events is filtered through, "focalized" to use Genette's term, one character at a time, almost always a hobbit.[13] As Christine Barkley has observed, "[t]his third-person/limited viewpoint narrows our focus to what that character is aware of or interested in. The choice of this character determines what details we will have, and how those details will be weighted or interpreted for us" (257).[14] Notably, point of view is often used to leave readers profoundly ignorant of what is going on.

This effect is reinforced by the use of another important structural device, inset narration: events narrated by one character to others out of chronological sequence. The best example of this technique is the story of Gandalf's capture by Saruman, which is narrated in great detail (as Gandalf himself recognizes, asking "Elrond and the others [to] forgive the length of it" [II.2, 258]), only after the hobbits, and readers with them, have traveled many weeks through many dangers and many pages wondering why he "broke tryst and did not come when he promised." If readers knew this part of the story before Frodo, our position relative to Frodo would be dramatically altered. We would know that Gandalf wasn't coming and that the danger facing Frodo was far greater and closer than he knows; impatience for him to leave on his own, and perhaps frustration at how long he waits for Gandalf's arrival, would be likely reactions. While any competent reader can guess that things will not go as Frodo expects, the structure of the narrative prevents readers from knowing better than Frodo just what the problem is and what he ought to do about it—keeping us from imitating Denethor's kind of arrogance.

Another notable example is the narration of Aragorn's travels through southern Gondor, the capture of the Corsairs' fleet, and the journey up Anduin, which we do not get until after the battle, in chapter 9 of Book V. Though readers have seen him through the Paths of the Dead as far as the Stone of Erech, we are not much better prepared than Éomer to know who is in the black ships when they appear during the battle; we may share in his despair ("hope died in his heart") and certainly in his "wonder . . . and great joy" when Aragorn's standard is unfurled (V.6, 828; 829). Readers may, in fact, be slower on the uptake in this instance than Pippin, who guessed rightly (or at least claims to have afterwards: "I guessed it was you in the black ships. But they were all shouting corsairs and wouldn't listen to me" [V.8, 845]).

Brian Rosebury objects aesthetically to this example, finding neither moment—the surprise and the later inset narrative—up to the standard of other parts of the work: "Despite a surge of triumphant rhetoric . . . the episode fails to be the emotional climax of the battle, just because it comes out of the blue and not out of a developed situation. . . . The subsequent retrospective account of the capture of the ships—narrated by Legolas and Gimli to Pippin—has an inevitably dutiful and 'staged' quality, as Tolkien was aware" (59). But though Tolkien "was aware" that the passage of inset narration "hold[s] up the action," in his own words, the letter Rosebury cites for this point also includes a clear statement of why he chose to go ahead with what he calls an "imperfect" solution: "Told in full in its proper place [III.2], . . . it would have destroyed Chapter 6" (*Letters* 258). The effect of surprising readers along with the armies during the battle was clearly intentional. One major effect of changing the structure (of "destroy[ing] Chapter 6"), one damaging to Tolkien's larger purpose, would be to distance readers emotionally from Éomer, a "good" character who has briefly taken over as focalizer.

This carefully-structured reader ignorance is another notable instance of the author's experience written into the finished work: Tolkien frequently describes the bewilderment he felt during the composing process. In the "Introductory Note" to Tree and Leaf he describes the period when "*The Lord of the Rings* was beginning to unroll itself and to unfold prospects of labour and exploration in yet unknown country as daunting to me as to the hobbits. At about that time we had reached Bree, and I had then no more notion than they had of what had become of Gandalf or who Strider was; and I had begun to despair of surviving to find out" (31). In a letter to W. H. Auden, he lists a number of "things along the way that astonished" him, including Gandalf's absence: "Most disquieting of all, Saruman had never been revealed to me, and I was as mystified as Frodo at Gandalf's failure to appear on September 22" (*Letters* 217). Upon learning the answers to these questions, Tolkien chose not to backtrack and fill readers in (though he refers to having "largely rewritten [the work] backwards" in the Foreword, xiv), instead letting the first-time reader experience the same curiosity and astonishment.

What is interesting, then, is that both of these effects are part of the same work: At times readers have superior knowledge distancing us from the characters, even in some cases permitting us to judge their errors severely; at other times we wallow in precisely the same ignorance and experience events very much as the characters do. Some techniques work primarily to call attention to and ironize our distance from the characters; others connect us to them and create to the extent possible the illusion of living the tale.[15] Tolkien's use of the former strategy allows him to play with the line between reader and character in a meta-fictional way; his selective use of both preserves the integrity of the moral values of his project.

"Inside a Very Great Story"

To appreciate the importance of this last point, one needs to consider Tolkien's expressed views about the goals of story-telling and the hallmarks of its success. In "On Fairy-Stories," he discusses the nature of "literary belief" or, as he coins the term, "Secondary Belief." Bouncing off the Coleridgean formula "willing suspension of disbelief," he argues that instead, "the story-maker proves a successful 'subcreator.' He makes a Secondary World which your mind can enter. Inside it, what he relates is 'true': it accords with the laws of that world. You therefore believe it, while you are, as it were, inside. The moment disbelief arises, the spell is broken; the magic, or rather art, has failed. You are then out in the Primary World again, looking at the little abortive Secondary World from outside" (60). Suspension of disbelief may be necessary "to find what virtue we can in the work of art that has for us failed," but for readers who truly "like the tale," this is unnecessary: "they would not have to suspend disbelief: they would believe—in this sense" (61).

Here we may see Tolkien anticipating ideas worked out with greater care by Peter J. Rabinowitz in his distinction between authorial audience and narrative audience. Rabinowitz's authorial audience exists in Tolkien's Primary World; the narrative audience, which actual readers must join imaginatively, exists in Tolkien's Secondary World. Both Tolkien and Rabinowitz stress the necessity for readers to enter into the narrative audience if the work is to be successful: Rabinowitz argues that "[t]he act of joining the narrative audience

... is an essential step ..., and many novels fail to make an impact because they are unable to make their readers join the narrative audience" (133)—the spell is broken, or never cast in the first place.

Rabinowitz goes beyond Tolkien's thinking in understanding the dual presence of readers in both worlds, both audiences, at once. What Tolkien says is "true" within the Secondary World is, for Rabinowitz, "both 'true' and 'untrue' at the same time": "We can treat the work neither as what it is nor as what it appears to be; we must be aware simultaneously of both aspects" (125). His own reformulation of Coleridge is to "argue not that disbelief is suspended but rather that it is both suspended and not suspended at the same time" (128, n.5). As theory, Tolkien's essay falls short of the complexity and nuance of Rabinowitz's. However, while Tolkien the theorist talks as if readers enter entirely into the narrative audience and no longer stand in the Primary World (except when art has failed), his fiction exploits the simultaneity Rabinowitz describes, addressing readers' presence in both audiences—at times playfully, at times with serious intent.

We have seen the text fostering an awareness (both structurally and thematically) of the line that always exists between readers who have temporarily entered the Secondary World and fictional characters who exist only there. While there is some blurring of the distinction between story and life, nothing in the work ever crashes through that line. Tolkien is intent on creating a Secondary World that readers can "simply ... get inside ... and take it (in a sense) as actual history," but by reminding readers that we are not inside it in the same way that the characters are, he can, without "breaking the spell," communicate with the reader at a level outside the Secondary World, inviting us to perceive the frame: to stand in the Primary World, watch the subcreator at work, and notice our own reactions as readers, creating what Rabinowitz calls a "double-leveled aesthetic experience" (130).[16]

Considering the work with this in mind, we can see moments of playful self-referentiality. Some are fairly obvious. Not long after Sam wishes he could "hear" the tale that he and Frodo "have been in," which he imagines will be called "the story of Nine-fingered Frodo and the Ring of Doom" (VI.4, 929), he gets his wish at the field of Cormallen when the minstrel offers to "sing ... of Frodo of the Nine Fingers and the Ring of Doom" (933). With this performance, an oral tradition of the story is inscribed within the written version (not unlike the song of Beowulf that Hrothgar's scop sings on the way back from Grendel's mere). Other, subtler moments play with the reader's awareness of being a reader. When Treebeard tells Merry and Pippin that they "speak of Master Gandalf, as if he was in a story that had come to an end" (II.4, 455), there is a level at which the description is accurate: though Gandalf is not dead, as the hobbits believe, he is in fact in a story that has come to an end, been written and revised and published: *The Lord of the Rings*.[17] Later,

Gandalf points out that Treebeard speaks of Saruman in the past tense: "'I observe, my good Fangorn,' said Gandalf, 'that with great care you say dwelt, was, grew. What about is? Is he dead?'" (VI.6, 958). He is not, of course, any more than Gandalf was (less so, in fact), but it is tempting to say that this time it is Treebeard who speaks of Master Saruman "as if he was in a tale that had come to an end"—and with the same self-referential truth available only to the reader of the finished work, which always uses the past tense.

These examples suggest a point of similarity with the otherwise very different works of metafiction studied by Robert Scholes. Iris Murdoch's *The Unicorn*, for example, "presents Marian seeing herself as entering a 'tale' which has materialized around her," just as Tolkien's characters repeatedly do. As Scholes points out, Marian's perception is "of course, strictly true in an ironic way. Marian is a character in a tale by Iris Murdoch" (65–6).[18] Like metafiction, *The Lord of the Rings* repeatedly reminds readers of its status as artifact and of their own existence in the world outside the fiction. But there is a crucial difference: Tolkien never violates verisimilitude. John Barth's *Giles Goat-Boy* provides a telling contrast: Barth's work contains a scene in which a character is discovered to be reading that very scene in *Giles Goat-Boy* itself (as Scholes points out, 99). This Escher-esque moment, impossible in reality but entirely possible within the art form, is delightful and fascinating, but it renders readers unable to "believe." This is not a fault in Barth, of course; he is up to something very different. Rather, the contrast serves to put into relief what Tolkien is doing. His work is not metaleptic in the way Barth's so often is; his characters would never be shown reading a chapter of *The Lord of the Rings* during the chapter itself. But they are frequently shown writing it. He manages to operate at a meta-fictional level while preserving the illusion of historicity and the integrity of a very traditional kind of narrative.

At its heart, what he is up to with this "double awareness" (as Rosebury has called it, 57) is less about literary form than about literature's capacity to change readers. Once we have been made aware of the crucial difference between reader experience and character experience—as we are, within the work, by Sam—it can provide perspective: knowing that the view from inside one's own partial experience of the story is different from the view outside can qualify one's interpretation of that experience. We see characters do this: Aragorn, for example, knows that the events of Books III and V are "but a small matter in the great deeds of this time" and that the "true Quest" lies with Frodo and Sam (III.2, 416). Sam himself is comforted by the perspective his bit of theorizing has given him, reading his experience *sub specie aeternitatis*: "the thought pierced him that in the end the Shadow was only a small and passing thing: there was light and high beauty forever beyond its reach" (VI.2, 901).

It is just this perspective—notably, phrased as an understanding of story—that Tolkien in propria persona offers his son Christopher during

World War II (and the writing of *The Lord of the Rings*): "Your service is, of course, as anybody with any intelligence and ears and eyes knows, a very bad one, living on the repute of a few gallant men, and you are probably in a particularly bad corner of it. But all Big Things planned in a big way feel like that to the toad under the harrow, though on a general view they do function and do their job. [...] Keep up your hobbitry in heart, and think that all stories feel like that when you are in them. You are inside a very great story!" (*Letters* 78). This is a perspective, also, that takes on an ethical dimension. More than once characters in *The Lord of the Rings* are exhorted to take a long view. According to Gandalf, the Council of Elrond has an obligation to think of future generations: not "to take thought only for a season, or for a few lives of Men, or for a passing age of the world. We should seek a final end of this menace, even if we do not hope to make one" (II.2, 260).

With this, Gandalf connects the work to readers in another way, reminding us that the conditions of our own existence are shaped in part by the choices made by those who have gone before, and that, conversely, our choices shape the world for those who follow us. During the Last Debate, Gandalf again reminds his listeners—within and without the work—that even victory over Sauron will not be final: "Other evils there are that may come; for Sauron is himself but a servant or emissary. Yet it is not our part to master all the tides of the world, but to do what is in us for the succour of those years wherein we are set, uprooting the evil in the fields that we know, so that those who live after may have clean earth to till. What weather they shall have is not ours to rule" (V.9, 861). We have come a long way from Bilbo's obsession with concluding his own story, and arrived at something like Susan Winnett's argument about *Frankenstein*. As she reads it, *Frankenstein*'s "indulgence in the retrospective mode" is irresponsible in that it is blind to "the consequences of an act of creation that he regards as a triumph in and of itself" (510). Gandalf, clearly, would concur: Like "*Frankenstein*'s completed feat," and like the end of *The Hobbit*, the apparently decisive, victorious climax of *The Lord of the Rings* "represents a beginning instead of an end" (Winnett 510).[19]

CONCLUSION

For whatever reason, *The Lord of the Rings* is among the twentieth-century works most beset by misperception on the part of literary scholars. This applies to a number of features of the text. Michael Drout and Hilary Wynne have claimed (rightly, I think), that "a major reason that modernist and post-modernist critics reject *LoTR* is that they see Tolkien's sentence-level writing as being inferior to that of many of his contemporaries" (Drout and Wynne 123). In proposing an agenda for future work on Tolkien, they suggest that "until the issue of style ... is fully addressed ... , Tolkien's work and criticism of it ... will probably remain less influential in elite literary criticism than it should be" (124). Drout himself has contributed to that project in a more recent article ("Tolkien's Prose Style"), and the books of Shippey and Rosebury, and an essay by Ursula Le Guin, have also done important work in that direction.

Drout and Wynne also observe that "much of the animosity directed toward Tolkien's work is due to its presumed political content or its subject matter" (123), which are often seen as reactionary. Countering this perception has been another significant concern in recent Tolkien criticism. Patrick Curry, for example, has argued that the values—social, ecological, and spiritual— embodied in *The Lord of the Rings* "speak to precisely [the] conditions" created by the "horrendous" costs of modernity (23; 22); "they are just the values whose jeopardy we most now feel" (23). Thus the oft-maligned nostalgia of the work is, for Curry, best understood as "radical nostalgia": "an emotionally empowering nostalgia, not a crippling one" (25).

But there is a third area of misperception of *The Lord of the Rings*, somewhat analogous to the two Drout and Wynne highlight, and that is its mode of narration. Rosemary Jackson's work on fantasy provides a stunning example. She has little to say about Tolkien in her book (legitimately so, given the definition she adopts for 'fantasy'), but what she does say about his work is surprisingly dismissive in such an otherwise intelligent book. Jackson defines the fantastic very precisely: fantasy incorporates experiences that cannot be decisively categorized as real or unreal. Drawing on the work of Tzvetan Todorov, she insists that "the purely fantastic text establishes absolute hesitation in protagonist and reader: they can neither come to terms with the unfamiliar events described, nor dismiss them as supernatural phenomena. Anxiety, then, is not merely a thematic feature, but is incorporated into the structure of the work to become its defining element" (27–8). In her taxonomy, Tolkien's work—which, of course, creates no such anxiety, instead vying for "secondary belief"—falls rather into the category of the marvelous.

Jackson's description of the marvelous merits quoting at length:

> The narrator is impersonal and has become an authoritative, knowing voice. There is a minimum of emotional involvement in the tale—that voice is positioned with absolute confidence and certainty towards events. It has complete knowledge of completed events, its version of history is not questioned and the tale seems to deny the process of its own telling—it is merely reproducing established 'true' versions of what happened. The marvellous is characterized by a minimal functional narrative,

whose narrator is omniscient and has absolute authority. It is a form which discourages reader participation, representing events which are in the long past, contained and fixed by a long temporal perspective and carrying the implication that their effects have long since ceased to disturb. Hence the formulaic ending too, 'and they lived happily ever after', or a variant upon this. The effect of such a narrative is one of a passive relation to history. The reader, like the protagonist, is merely a receiver of events which enact a preconceived pattern. (33)

Though she explicitly includes Tolkien in this description ("Tales by the Grimm brothers, Hans Andersen, Andrew Lang and Tolkien all belong to this mode"), one can only wonder if she stopped reading at *The Hobbit*. The earlier work does have many of these traits,[20] but *The Lord of the Rings* does not, and, if my analysis has been at all persuasive, this laundry list includes precisely those narrative features that Tolkien makes a subject of meta-fictional reflection. Many a modern work of fiction does less to call attention to "the process of its own telling"; and the critique of "happily ever after" could not be more explicit. Tolkien manages the delicate balance of having both "complete knowledge of completed events" and multiple authorship; focalized narration and authoritative history; an immeasurably ancient setting and a sense of continuity between story and history that leads all the way to the present. That Jackson does not like one side of this balancing act is legitimate as a personal preference. To imply, as I think this passage does, that *The Lord of the Rings* is unsophisticated because it asks for secondary belief is, I hope I have demonstrated sufficiently, emphatically wrong.

I submit rather that Tolkien has succeeded in having his narrative cake and theorizing it too: he has given us a work of "feigned history," but he has also invited us to reflect on the nature of the tale and our experience of reading it in much the way that narrative and reader-response theories do. Just as Curry sees the values of *The Lord of the Rings* as not simply old-fashioned but responding to contemporary needs, I see the form as at once old-fashioned (a heroic quest romance in which good defeats evil) and contemporary (self-referential, self-critical). *The Lord of the Rings* encourages readers both to embrace the power of story and to think critically about the nature of that power and how it operates.[21]

NOTES

1. To accommodate the many different printings of *The Lord of the Rings* in circulation, quotations from *The Lord of the Rings* are cited by book and chapter number; page numbers are added for the convenience of any readers who have access to the same edition.

2. Dominic Manganiello has anticipated a number of my observations in this section, though he stops short of pointing out the way that the frame device and the attribution of *The Hobbit* to Bilbo render these self-referential. I do not think we disagree here, but regard my reading as building on his.

3. A convention has emerged in Tolkien criticism to refer to this body of constantly evolving material as "The Silmarillion," the quotation marks distinguishing it from the specific version published in 1977. *The Silmarillion* is actually a composite version, a remarkably successful effort by Tolkien's son Christopher to create as coherent and consistent a version as possible out of the tangled mass of drafts in varying states of (sometimes incompatible) revision. Christopher Tolkien has since undertaken to edit all of this material, published as the 13-volume *History of Middle-earth*.

4. This point has also been made by Manganiello (12). Brian Rosebury has said of the appendices that "one feels that they could go on for ever, and that an essential feature of the invented world (as of the real one) is this exhilarating illimitableness" (29).

5. Tolkien also made similarly good use of another problem that emerged from producing a "sequel" (and from some unclear communication between him and Stanley Unwin): the original version of the chapter "Riddles in the Dark" and, later, the existence of two versions of the chapter. Two possibilities suggested themselves: "either the first must be regarded as washed out, a mere miswriting that ought never to have seen the light; or the story as a whole must take into account the existence of two versions and use it" (*Letters* 142). Characteristically, he took the latter option. The first version, which became incompatible with what Tolkien came to discover about the Ring, is rehabilitated as a false version concocted by Bilbo to strengthen his claim to the Ring—a lie that renders the "wrong" story not merely compatible with but symptomatic of the evil influence of the Ring as Tolkien came to know it. The "Prologue" to *The Lord of the Rings* calmly explains that Bilbo's false account "still appeared in the original Red Book, as it did in several of the copies and abstracts" (12), copies that now explain the story's presence in the first edition of *The Hobbit*.

6. Richard West has argued that the interlace structure of the narrative contributes to this quality of "openendness": "We feel that we have interrupted the chaotic activity of the world at a certain point and followed a selection from it for a time, and that after we leave, it continues on its own random path. The author, or someone else, may perhaps take up the threads of the story again later and add to it at beginning, middle, or end" (78–9). Connecting this point to Sam's recognition of being "in the same story," West adds, "the reader has the impression that the story has an existence outside the confines of the book and that the author could have begun earlier or ended later, if he chose" (90).

7. The multiple authorship of tales, along with their continuity with one another, is also mirrored structurally in the Council of Elrond, where what is essentially one story—of the Ring and Sauron's current search for it—is told by multiple narrators, no one of whom is possessed of the whole story; the interconnection of the several pieces each brought with him is discovered in the course of the Council. Shippey observes that the story of the Ring is told with "a great deal of art . . . through a series of interjections, as one character or another manages to turn the conversation to their immediate concerns" (80). He compares this to the structure of a committee meeting.

8. In a recent essay on the violence question, Dwight Garner directly compares these concerns to the Goethe example.

9. This suggests an interesting point of comparison between *The Lord of the Rings* and *Beowulf*, a work Tolkien himself did much to put on literary scholars' maps at a time when it was regarded as primarily of linguistic or anthropological interest. Laurence N. de

Looze has argued that *Beowulf* also uses narrative to interpret experience and make choices, particularly in his monologue before going to face the dragon, in which he recalls Hrethel's tragic loss of one son to another and invents the example of the father of a hanged man. De Looze concludes, "In an effort to find a satisfactory solution, *Beowulf* reviews historical precedents, and when they fail he fictionalizes events in an attempt to resolve his own crisis, this fiction forming the structural center of a series of frame narratives" (250).

10. Shippey also provides a useful chart of the structure of Books III through VI (104). Stephen Yandell also supplies a chart of the structure (386) and a useful list of passages where one strand of the narrative refers to another, allowing us to orient ourselves chronologically (390–91).

11. Yandell has also pointed out the irony of "the death of Denethor," which "gains poignancy because it is described after the arrival [of the fleet], and the victory at Minas Tirith has been assured" (389).

12. The irony of interlace is something else Tolkien might have borrowed, consciously or unconsciously, from *Beowulf*, at least if one accepts such readings of the use of interlace in the Anglo-Saxon poem as John Leyerle's, who argues, for example, that "[i]n this way the poet undercuts *Beowulf*'s single-minded preoccupation with the dragon by interlacing a stream of more and more pointed episodes about the human threats to his people, a far more serious danger than the dragon poses. Beowulf wins glory by his heroic exploit in killing the dragon, but brings dire affliction on his people, as Wiglaf quite explicitly states" (153).

13. The exceptions are the chapters in which no hobbit is present, which are mostly narrated without access to any character's perceptions, though there are brief forays into other characters' minds; there is also one extended use of the dwarf Gimli as focalizer (the second half of V.2, "The Passing of the Grey Company"). There is a clear pattern to the use of hobbits as focalizers, Frodo playing that role exclusively for most of *The Fellowship of the Ring*, Sam taking over permanently from Frodo during the last chapter of that volume, and Pippin assuming the role in the sections where he and Merry are together. This careful orchestration of perspectives deserves more thorough discussion than it has yet received, though that project lies beyond the scope of this article.

14. Theorist Nicholas Royle has called this the "telepathy effect." The care with which point of view is controlled is evident from comparing drafts with the final version: David Bratman points out that an early outline of the chapter that becomes "Mount Doom" (VI.3) takes readers into Frodo's mind, whereas the published version is focalized through Sam, as all of Book IV and the first two chapters of VI have been (33).

15. The mixed effects of at times superiority and at times shared ignorance with characters is also a feature of *Beowulf* as read by Richard Ringler. "The audience's superior knowledge—both of Beowulf's presence and his destined victory—combines with Grendel's erroneous assumptions to produce a typical situation of dramatic irony" (131); but when Grendel's mother comes, "[i]f there is any irony, it is that the Danes themselves have not exercised sufficient *andgit* [perception] and *forepanc* [forethought]—hence to them in their turn comes ironic *edhwyrft* [reversal]. . . . Wisely, this time, the poet lets us share the ignorance and worry of his characters" (145).

16. Cf. the observation of Stratford Caldecott that "[i]t is part of the author's mastery that he can make the characters become conscious of playing a part in the tale without losing their credibility as characters" (44).

17. This is also, of course, another mistaken belief that closure has been achieved, a point Manganiello notes (12).

18. Scholes also discusses a work that plays games with beginnings and endings reminiscent of what Tolkien does in *The Lord of the Rings*. While Tolkien's work must begin

by breaking open what was closed by Bilbo's "happily ever after," the traditional opening "once upon a time" provides "the last words, or almost the last words, of Lawrence Durrell's *Alexandria Quartet*" (29).

19. This is why I believe Gunnar Urang is profoundly wrong when he says that *The Lord of the Rings* "is the history of the end; it is eschatology" (115); to think so is to miss the point Gandalf takes such care to make.

20. An analysis of *The Hobbit* along these lines is beyond the scope of this article, but Lois R. Kuznets's piece on the rhetoric of the narrator provides a useful starting point.

21. I would like to thank the colleagues who read earlier drafts of this article for their helpful feedback and suggestions: Mark Balhorn, Sarah Pogell, Michael Steffes, Rebecca Stephens, and especially Lorri Nandrea.

WORKS CITED

Abbott, H. Porter. *The Cambridge Introduction to Narrative*. Cambridge: Cambridge Univ. Press, 2002.

Anderson, Douglas A., ed. *The Annotated Hobbit*. By J. R. R. Tolkien. Revised and expanded ed. Boston: Houghton Mifflin Company, 2002.

Barkley, Christine. "Point of View in Tolkien." In *Proceedings of the J. R. R. Tolkien Centenary Conference 1992*, edited by Patricia Reynolds and Glen H. Goodnight, 256–262. Mythlore 80 [vol. 21, no. 2] (Winter 1996). Altadena: Mythopoeic Press, 1995.

Benjamin, Walter. "The Storyteller: Reflections on the Works of Nikolai Leskov." In *Illuminations*, 83–109. New York: Harcourt, Brace & World, 1955.

Bratman, David. "Top Ten Rejected Plot Twists from *The Lord of the Rings*: A Textual Excursion in to the 'History of *The Lord of the Rings*.'" *Mythlore* 86 [vol. 22, no. 4] (Spring 2000): 13–37.

Brooks, Peter. *Reading for the Plot: Design and Intention in Narrative*. New York: Knopf, 1984.

Caldecott, Stratford. "The Horns of Hope: J. R. R. Tolkien and the Heroism of Hobbits." *Chesterton Review: The Journal of the G. K. Chesterton Institute* 28 (2002): 29–55.

Carpenter, Humphrey. *J. R. R. Tolkien: A Biography*. Boston: Houghton Mifflin Company, 2000. First published London: Allen & Unwin, 1977.

Curry, Patrick. *Defending Middle-Earth: Tolkien, Myth and Modernity*. Edinburgh: Floris Books, 1997.

Dante. *Inferno*. Vol. 1 of *The Divine Comedy*. 3 vols. Edited and translated by John D. Sinclair. New York: Oxford Univ. Press, 1961.

de Looze, Laurence N. "Frame Narratives and Fictionalization: Beowulf as Narrator." In *Interpretations of Beowulf: A Critical Anthology*, edited by R. D. Fulk, 242–250. Bloomington and Indianapolis: Indiana Univ. Press, 1991. First published in Texas Studies in Language and Literature 26 (1984): 145–56.

Drout, Michael D. C. "Tolkien's Prose Style and its Literary and Rhetorical Effects." *Tolkien Studies* 1 (2004): 137–62.

Drout, Michael D. C. and Hilary Wynne. "Tom Shippey's J. R. R. Tolkien: Author of the Century and a Look Back at Tolkien Criticism since 1982." *Envoi* 9, no. 2 (Fall 2000): 101–167. http://members.aol.com/JamesIMcNelis/9_2/Drout_9_2.pdf.

Garner, Dwight. "Violence or Entertainment?" *Salon*, May 21, 1998. http://archive.salon.com/mwt/feature/1998/05/21feature2.html.

Holland, Norman. "Unity Identity Text Self." In *Reader-Response Criticism: From Formalism to Post-Structuralism*, edited by Jane P. Tompkins, 118–133. Baltimore: Johns Hopkins Univ. Press, 1980. First published in *PMLA* 90 (1975): 813–22.

Hughes, Shaun F. D., ed. "J. R. R. Tolkien." Special Issue, *Modern Fiction Studies* 50.4 (2004).

Jackson, Rosemary. *Fantasy: The Literature of Subversion. New Accents.* London and New York: Methuen, 1981.

Kuznets, Lois R. "Tolkien and the Rhetoric of Childhood." In *Tolkien: New Critical Perspectives*, edited by Neil D. Isaacs and Rose A. Zimbardo, 150–162. Lexington: Univ. Press of Kentucky, 1981.

LeGuin, Ursula K. "Rhythmic Pattern in *The Lord of the Rings.*" In *The Wave in the Mind: Talks and Essays on the Writer, the Reader, and the Imagination*, 95–107. Boston: Shambhala, 2004.

Leyerle, John. "The Interlace Structure of *Beowulf.*" In *Interpretations of Beowulf: A Critical Anthology*, edited by R. D. Fulk, 146–167. Bloomington and Indianapolis: Indiana Univ. Press, 1991. First published in *University of Toronto Quarterly* 37 (1967): 1–17.

Manganiello, Dominic. "The Neverending Story: Textual Happiness in *The Lord of the Rings.*" *Mythlore* 69 [vol. 18, no. 3] (Summer 1992): 5–14.

Miller, D. A. *Narrative and Its Discontents: Problems of Closure in the Traditional Novel.* Princeton: Princeton Univ. Press, 1981.

Morson, Gary Saul. "Narrativeness." *New Literary History* 34 (2003): 59–73.

Rabinowitz, Peter J. "Truth in Fiction: A Reexamination of Audiences." *Critical Inquiry* 4 (1977): 121–41.

Ringlet, Richard N. "Him seo wen geleah: The Design for Irony in Grendel's Last Visit to Heorot." In *Interpretations of Beowulf: A Critical Anthology*, edited by R. D. Fulk, 127–145. Bloomington and Indianapolis: Indiana Univ. Press, 1991. First published in *Speculum* 41 (1966): 49–67.

Rosebury, Brian. *Tolkien: A Critical Assessment.* Basingstoke: MacMillan; New York: St. Martin's Press, 1992.

Royle, Nicholas. "The 'Telepathy Effect': Notes toward a Reconsideration of Narrative Fiction." In *Acts of Narrative*, edited by Carol Jacobs and Henry Sussman, 93–109. Stanford: Stanford Univ. Press, 2003.

Scholes, Robert. *Fabulation and Metafiction.* Urbana: Univ. of Illinois Press, 1979.

Shippey, T. A. *J. R. R. Tolkien: Author of the Century.* Boston: Houghton Mifflin Company, 2001.

Tolkien, J. R. R. *The Annotated Hobbit.* Edited by Douglas A. Anderson. Revised and expanded ed. Boston: Houghton Mifflin Company, 2002.

———. *The Letters of J. R. R. Tolkien.* Edited by Humphrey Carpenter. Boston: Houghton Mifflin Company, 1981.

———. *The Lord of the Rings.* 3 vols. Boston: Houghton Mifflin Company, 1994. First published London: Allen & Unwin, 1954–55.

———. "On Fairy-stories." In *The Tolkien Reader*, 33–99. New York: Ballantine Books, 1966. First published in *Tree and Leaf.* London: Allen & Unwin, 1964.

———. *Sauron Defeated.* Edited by Christopher Tolkien. *The History of Middle-earth* 9. Boston: Houghton Mifflin Company, 2002.

Urang, Gunnar. *Shadows of Heaven: Religion and Fantasy in the Writing of C. S. Lewis, Charles Williams, and J. R. R. Tolkien.* Philadelphia: Pilgrim Press, 1971.

West, Richard C. "The Interlace Structure of *The Lord of the Rings.*" *A Tolkien Compass*, edited by Jared Lobdell, 77–94. LaSalle, IL: Open Court Press, 1975.

Winnett, Susan. "Coming Unstrung: Women, Men, Narrative, and Principles of Pleasure." *PMLA* 105 (1990): 505–18.

Yandell, Stephen. "'A Pattern Which Our Nature Cries Out For': The Medieval Tradition of the Ordered Four in the Fiction of J. R. R. Tolkien." In *Proceedings of the J. R. R. Tolkien Centenary Conference 1992*, edited by Patricia Reynolds and Glen H. Goodnight, 375–392. *Mythlore* 80 [vol. 21, no. 2] (Winter 1996). Altadena: Mythopoeic Press, 1995.

NANCY ENRIGHT

Tolkien's Females and the Defining of Power

In *The Lord of the Rings*, J. R. R. Tolkien's female characters, though few in number, are very important in the defining of power, a central thematic concern of the text. In fact, in *The Lord of the Rings*, power, when presented in the traditional male-oriented way, is undercut as often as it is asserted. Even typically "heroic" characters like Aragorn and Faramir use traditional masculine power in a manner tempered with an awareness of its limitations and a respect for another, deeper kind of power. Aragorn shows this recognition of an alternative kind of power in his reverence for the Elves, who though brave fighters, are not known for their physical prowess. The stereotypical and purely masculine kind of power, as represented by Boromir for instance, is shown to be weaker morally and spiritually than its non-traditional counterparts, thus allowing Boromir to fall, while less typically heroic characters, including all the major female characters, stand. In the context of these depictions of power, both asserted and subverted, the female characters interact with the males in a much more complex world than might at first be assumed when reading *The Lord of the Rings*. The general lack of a female presence in battle scenes (with the important exception of Éowyn's contest with the Nazgûl) or even among the members of the Fellowship does not imply that female power and presence are unimportant. On the contrary, Tolkien's female characters epitomize his critique of traditional, masculine and worldly power, offering an

From *Renascence* 59, no. 2 (Winter 2007): pp. 93–108. © 2007 by *Renascence*.

alternative that can be summed up as the choice of love over pride, reflective of the Christ-like inversion of power rooted in Scripture, and ultimately more powerful than any domination by use of force.

Jane Chance, in her insightful study, *The Lord of the Rings: the Mythology of Power*, explores the development of the theme of power throughout *The Hobbit* and *The Lord of the Rings*, coming to the very accurate conclusion that "the ability to understand the necessity for locating a 'paradise' within" turns out to be "the greatest power of all" (138). She explores how Tolkien, whom she links with philosopher Michel Foucault and C. S. Lewis in this regard, "questioned the validity of the human sciences to represent the rationality of the age" (20), arguing that, for Tolkien, "true power emerges from wise and healing service to the community" (24). In another study concerned with the issue of power, Anne C. Petty argues that power, as depicted in *The Lord of the Rings*, can be divided into two varieties—internal (as in power, such as magic, intrinsic to someone, as in the case of the Elves) and external (power contained in a thing, such as the Ring)—but goes on to argue that this distinction is far less important than how power is used—or abused (138–39, and elsewhere). In light of these insights into Tolkien's depiction of power, it is important to consider how this thematic concern connects with Tolkien's Christian beliefs *and* his depiction of gender, linking them in a meaningful way.

J. R. R. Tolkien has been criticized for creating too few female characters in *The Lord of the Rings* and, of those few, having them fill supposedly traditionally feminine and, therefore, stereotypical roles. As a member of the Inklings, the famous group of writers and thinkers including C. S. Lewis and Charles Williams, Tolkien was included in an all-male community, and, according to Candice Fredrick and Sam McBride, this community was blatantly sexist. Specifically referring to Tolkien's works, they argue that the "males operate within a system that is overtly patriarchal. Men are the doers, workers, thinkers, and leaders. Women are homemakers, nurses, and distant love interests"(109). Fredrick's and McBride's book, *Women Among the Inklings: Gender, C. S. Lewis, J. R. R. Tolkien, and Charles Williams*, offers a chapter including a summary of other feminist critiques of the works of the Inklings with regard to lack of female characters and / or the way they are depicted (Chapter 5, "Mere Feminism: Gender, Reading, and the Inklings" 163–70). The range of these critical responses goes from some who feel there is no problem with gender in the Inklings' writings to Fredrick's and McBride's own suggestion that gender bias is a very serious failing in these works. In a collection of essays on Tolkien written by other writers of fantasy, Terri Windling, while crediting Tolkien for inspiring her own works of fantasy, remembers feeling as a child that "there was no place for me, a girl, on Frodo's quest" (226). And, though his article basically challenges the negative criticism of Tolkien for lack of female characters, William H.

Green says that "there is certainly a bias here, an emotional charge pushing the women to margins of stories or deep into their symbolic cores" (190), referring not only to *The Hobbit* (though his article focuses on that text), but on what he calls "the marginalization" of women characters in Tolkien's other writings.[1] Along these same lines, Jes Battis claims, ". . . women are not given easy identities to inhabit within *The Lord of the Rings*, and many are stereotyped to the point of excess" (913).[2]

Other critics have attempted to justify the small number of females in *The Lord of the Rings* by pointing out the powerful roles they play or the fact that these roles are important as archetypes or as mythologically resonant images. Jessica Yates argues that Tolkien's style of epic fantasy necessitates the placing of all major characters into archetypal roles, "[a]nd so we have Aragorn the Hero, Arwen the Princess, Éowyn the Amazon, Galadriel the Enchantress, and Gandalf the Wizard;" Yates claims that it renders them less "developed" than characters in a more typical twentieth-century novel. Another critic connecting Tolkien's female characters with myth is Leslie A. Donovan, who points out many symbolic associations from Norse legend apparently attached to Galadriel, Arwen, and Éowyn, as well as the evil spider Shelob (106–107 and elsewhere). However, I would disagree with Donovan when she argues that "applications of Christian typology [with the exception of the connection between Galadriel and the Virgin Mary] hold little promise for explaining the authority of other women in Tolkien's trilogy" (107). Furthermore, the view of Tolkien's depiction of females as being a mere reflection of traditional or archetypal gender roles does not account for the religious depth of these characters, nor does their scarcity in number lead to an explanation such as the overly simplified argument that Tolkien is, in fact, "sexist." On the contrary, I would argue that it is only through a careful examination of Tolkien's depiction of power that the role of his female characters can be fully understood. In *The Lord of the Rings*, the female characters, in their inversion of power, exhibit a virtue that, in Tolkien's view, is crucial to salvation—the choice of love over pride—a message central to the novel and one that transcends all gender roles.

The prototype for other, more significant female characters in *The Lord of the Rings* (such as Arwen, Éowyn, and Galadriel) is Goldberry, the wife of Tom Bombadil, in *The Fellowship of the Ring*. This character offers an interesting introduction to the kinds of female power important in the story. Prior to the forming of the "Fellowship of the Ring" at the Council of Elrond, the four hobbits travel through the Old Forest on their way to Bree, where they hope to meet Gandalf. In this chapter, the four previously sheltered hobbits, along with the reader, are being introduced to the world of danger and beauty outside the Shire. The Old Forest, evocatively linked with hobbits' lore but, for the most part, left unexplored by them, is a place of ancient beauty and grave dangers. One of these dangers is Old Man Willow, a humanized and wicked tree, who captures Merry and Pippin in its roots. As Frodo runs off, calling for help, he comes across an odd character, a personification of nature, called Tom Bombadil. Tom knows the proper song to calm Old Man Willow, causing him to release the two hobbits. At Tom's home, the hobbits are introduced to Bombadil's wife, Goldberry, the "River daughter." Physically resembling Galadriel, who appears later, Goldberry is golden-haired, slender, and exquisitely beautiful, but she is more "natural," less ethereal than her Elven counterpart. Goldberry is, in fact, mythologically similar to a water nymph or a dryad. Her clothing, like her husband's, suggests a link with nature, as Jane Chance points out (41); for instance, in one scene, Goldberry "was clothed all in silver with a white girdle, and her shoes were like fishes' mail" (*FR*, I, vii, 183). Seeing Goldberry, the hobbits experience a kind of awe, abashed at her beauty and appreciative of her kindness (188 and elsewhere). While Tom Bombadil is called "Master," it is clear that both husband and wife are equally in command of their little household, though their roles differ from each other. The hobbits watch the dance-like movements of Tom and Goldberry as they set the table, hers defined by grace and beauty, his both merry and whimsical. They respect each other most deeply, and, together, offer the hobbits what they need on this resting place of their journey. As the hobbits look at Goldberry upon their leaving, she stands "small and slender like a sunlit flower against the sky" (189). Despite her lack of overt physical strength, she represents the power of nature, ancient and renewing. However, more significant female representations of power follow, the first of these being Arwen, daughter of Elrond.

When the hobbits first meet Arwen, she has already met, fallen in love with, and pledged her troth to Aragorn, a love story told in the Appendix to *The Return of the King*. Arwen is descended from Lúthien, another Elven princess[3] who falls in love with a mortal man (*Silmarillion*, XIX). In fact, when Aragorn meets Arwen in Lothlórien, where she is visiting her grandparents, Galadriel and Celeborn, he is "singing a part of the Lay of Lúthien, which tells of the meeting of Lúthien and Beren in the forest of Neldoreth. And behold! there Lúthien walked before his eyes in Rivendell . . ." (Appendix A, v, 421). Lúthien was, according to the legend told by Aragorn to the hobbits on Weathertop, "the fairest maiden that has ever been among all the children of this world. As the stars above the Northern lands was her loveliness, and in her face was a shining light" (*FR*, II, i, 260). When Aragorn himself first sees Arwen, he is enchanted by her beauty just as Beren was by Lúthien's, as Arwen appears to him "clad in a mantle of silver and blue, fair as the twilight in Elven-home; her dark hair strayed in a sudden wind, and her brows were bound with gems like stars" (Appendix A, v, 421). Her beauty is of a kind so high that the one viewing it is abashed, as Frodo feels when he first sees

Arwen at the dinner preceding the Council of Elrond. A key component of Arwen's beauty, like Lúthien's, is the fact that it is not simply physical; her intellectual and spiritual essence is conveyed through it: "Young she was and yet not so. The braids of her dark hair were touched by no frost; her white arms and clear face were flawless and smooth, and the light of stars was in her bright eyes, grey as a cloudless night; yet queenly she looked, and thought and knowledge were in her glance, as of one who has known many things that the years bring ... Such loveliness in living thing Frodo had never seen nor imagined in his mind" (298).

The inner power of Arwen is subtly conveyed, but present throughout *The Lord of the Rings*. Arwen does not ride out "on errantry," as do her brothers; instead, like her father, she remains at Rivendell, inspiring events through her relationship with Aragorn from afar. It is the thought of Arwen that comes to Aragorn at moments offering him a release from the burdens he must carry and allowing him to seem to the eyes of Frodo "clothed in white, a young lord tall and fair," speaking words in Elvish to Arwen, though she is not physically present (*FR*, II, vi, 343). Lynnette R. Porter calls Arwen a "hero" for offering this kind of inspiration (118–25), and truly there is a heroic quality to the length and depth of her devotion to Aragorn. At a crucial moment, she sends him the banner she has woven for him, with the words, "The days now are short. Either our hope cometh, or all hopes end. Therefore I send thee what I have made for thee. Fare well, Elfstone" (*RK* I, ii, 56). But what is most crucial about Arwen is her renunciation of Elven immortality for love. Like Lúthien, she must become mortal if she marries a mortal, a choice she willingly makes when she and Aragorn plight their troth on Cerin Amroth (Appendix A, v 425). As Elrond sadly says to Aragorn, "Maybe it has been appointed so, that by my loss [i.e. of Arwen] the kingship of Men may be restored" (Appendix A, v 425).

Even more so than Elrond's, Arwen's loss is personal and profound. She herself must suffer separation from all her kindred and experience personal mortality. Of all the characters in *The Lord of the Rings*, Arwen is the one who makes the Christ-like choice of taking on mortality out of love. And her decision, though rooted in her love of Aragorn, becomes part of the "*eucatastrophe*,"[4] as Tolkien calls it, the "good catastrophe" that saves Middle-earth. This paradoxical *power through the abdication of power* echoes the *kenosis* of Jesus, as described by St. Paul:

> Have this attitude in yourselves which was also in Christ Jesus, who, although He existed in the form of God, did not regard equality with God a thing to be grasped, but emptied Himself, taking the form of a bond-servant, and being made in the likeness of men. And being found in appearance as a man, He humbled

Himself by becoming obedient to the point of death, even death
on a cross. (Phil. 2: 5–8)

Arwen, while certainly never "in the form of God," does exist in a form higher
than human, and her renunciation of her Elven immortality suggests the
humility of Christ in laying aside the privileges of divinity (while retaining
His divine nature), enjoined by St. Paul on all believers. Tolkien is not writing
an allegory, so Arwen cannot be looked at as an allegorical representation of
Jesus; no character in *The Lord of the Rings* has that role. However, Arwen's
Christ-like renunciation of power leads to her role in the healing of Frodo
from the results of his bearing of the Ring. Referring to the end of *The Return
of the King*, where Arwen offers her jewel and her passage to the West to Frodo,
Tolkien wrote in a letter: "Arwen was the first to observe the disquiet growing
in him, and gave him her jewel for comfort, and thought of a way of healing
him" (*Letters*, #246, 327). Therefore, her loss—freely chosen out of love for
Aragorn—becomes yet another means of salvation for someone else, in fact,
the very person (i.e. Frodo) who has helped to bring about the *eucatastrophe*
which has saved Middle-earth and in which Arwen's and Aragorn's love has
become entwined.

The Appendix of *The Return of the King* tells the end of her story. Though
experiencing years of happiness with Aragorn, Arwen eventually has to face
both the loss of her beloved husband, first, and then her own death. Dying,
Aragorn acknowledges to Arwen the pain of death: "I speak no comfort to
you, for there is no comfort for such pain within the circles of the world"
(App. A, v, 427). Linda Greenwood argues that this story "involves an element
of sacrifice, a sacrifice that does not belong solely to the lives of Aragorn and
Arwen, but also to those who give their lives as a gift for the salvation of others"
(187), her phrasing certainly connecting this story implicitly to the sacrificial
death of Jesus. Greenwood approaches the entire text in terms of what she
calls the "deconstruction" allowed by love, which literally turns evil into good,
death into life (171); she uses the term "deconstruction" apparently to mean
an overturning of a usual evil result, a kind of *eucatastrophe*. However, this
transformation of evil into good does not take away the reality of suffering for
those willing to undergo it for the sake of others. Greenwood says, "Instead
of giving up mortality for immortality, Arwen does the exact opposite. As
with Lúthien, Arwen surrenders immortality and takes on mortality as a gift
to Aragorn" (188). Watching Aragorn die, "[Arwen] tasted the bitterness of
the mortality that she had taken upon her" (App. A, v, 427). After Aragorn's
death, Arwen leaves Minas Tirith and faces her own death in the fading
woods of Lothlórien, where her Elven relatives no longer live. Her story ends
thus: "with the passing of Evenstar no more is said in this book of the days
of old" (App. A, v, 428). As an Elf-Human, Arwen provides a bridge between

the Third Age and the Fourth, and in renouncing her Elven heritage, she embodies in her loss the sacrifice the Elves, in general, willingly endure in accepting with the destruction of the Ring, the end not only of Sauron's evil, but of all that belongs to "the days of old," the world of Elves and Dwarves, as well as Orcs and Nazgûl, a world that is being turned over to human beings.

No Elf sees more clearly the nature of this loss than Galadriel, Lady of the Galadrim and of Lothlórien, and Arwen's grandmother. Galadriel is the most powerful female figure in *The Lord of the Rings* and, in fact, one of the most important characters of either gender in the story. One of the three Elven ring-bearers, Galadriel uses her power for healing, not domination. As Elrond explains to Gloin at the Council:

> The Three [rings] were not made by Sauron, nor did he ever touch them ... They are not idle. But they were not made as weapons of war or conquest: that is not their power. Those who made them did not desire strength or domination or hoarded wealth, but understanding, making, and healing, to preserve all things unstained. (*FR*, II, vii, 352).

The kind of power described here is the alternative to traditional, male-oriented power. Galadriel is a stronger embodiment of this power than her husband, Celeborn. It is she who is the wiser and more powerful, though both rule together, and he clearly has both wisdom and power. When the Fellowship enters Lothlórien, Haldir, the Elf, tells Frodo and Sam, "You feel the power of the Lady [not the Lord] of the Galadrim" (*FR*, II, vi, 342). It is Galadriel, not Celeborn, who realizes that Gandalf did, indeed, set out with the company, as planned, but did not come to Lórien with them (*FR*, II, vi, 346), and it is she who corrects Celeborn for his harsh words to Gimli (*FR*, II, vi, 347), exemplifying "forgiveness, hospitality, understanding" that "serve as a model for toleration of difference" (Chance 54). Galadriel also is the one who mentally tests each member of the Fellowship, offering him a choice between the danger that lies ahead and something else that he greatly desires (*FR*, II, vi, 348–49). And she tells the Fellowship that she is the one who first summoned the White Council and, "if my designs had not gone amiss, it would have been governed by Gandalf the Grey, and then mayhap things would have gone otherwise" (*FR*, II, vi, 348). Clearly, Galadriel is important, not only as a queen among Elves, but as a mover and planner of the great things in Middle-earth, affecting all its peoples.

Yet, despite her own power, or perhaps because of it, Galadriel knows the dangers of power used wrongly. She even knows the temptation toward the other kind of power, that of domination and pride. When Frodo offers her the Ring, she admits her desire for it:

I do not deny that my heart has greatly desired to ask what you offer. For many long years I had pondered what I might do, should the Great Ring come into my hands, and behold! it was brought within my grasp ... And now at last it comes. You will give me the Ring freely! In place of the Dark Lord you will set up a Queen. And I shall not be dark, but beautiful and terrible as the Morning and the Night! Fair as the Sea and the Sun and the Snow upon the Mountain! Dreadful as the Storm and the Lightning! Stronger than the foundations of the earth. All shall love me and despair! (*FR*, II, vii, 356)

The characteristic Elven links with nature, in its beauty and healing, become in Galadriel's momentary fantasy and temptation part of the seductive quality of the Ring and potentially forces of domination, both powerful and destructive. Had she succumbed to this temptation, Galadriel herself would have become dominated by the pride linked to this kind of power, normally most tempting to males, but here, luring this most powerful female. However, Galadriel resists the temptation and rejects the Ring. After her temptation, successfully resisted, "she let her hand fall, and the light faded, and suddenly she laughed again, and lo! She was shrunken, a slender Elf-woman, clad in simple white, whose voice was soft and sad. 'I pass the test,' she said. 'I will diminish, and go into the West, and remain Galadriel'" (*FR*, II, vii, 357). Like her granddaughter, Arwen, Galadriel is willing to endure personal abdication of power out of love, and it is this renunciation that reveals her spiritual and moral strength.

Prior to the scene of temptation where Frodo offers her the Ring, Galadriel explains the nature of her struggle with the Dark Lord: "... [D]o not think that only by singing amid the trees, nor even by the slender arrows of Elven-bows, is this land of Lothlórien maintained and defended against its Enemy. I say to you, Frodo, that even as I speak to you, I perceive the Dark Lord and know his mind, or all of his mind that concerns the Elves. And he gropes ever to see me and my thought. But the door is closed!" (*FR*, II, vii, 355). As if symbolic of her strength of will, Galadriel's Elven ring is of Adamant (356). Her gifts to the Fellowship reflect the nature of her strength, rooted in wisdom; each gift is perfectly suited to its recipient's character, from Aragorn's kingly scabbard, reflecting his lineage and destiny, to Sam's gardening soil and seed. As Aragorn says to Boromir, who has expressed skepticism about Galadriel's intentions: "Speak no evil of the Lady Galadriel! There is in her and in this land no evil, unless a man bring it hither himself. Then let him beware! ..." (*FR*, II, vi, 349). In fact, Tolkien has suggested that his depiction of Galadriel is linked to a Catholic image of Mary, the mother of Jesus. In a letter, written in 1958, Tolkien wrote: "... I am a Christian (which can be deduced from my stories), and in fact a Roman Catholic. The latter 'fact' perhaps cannot be deduced; though one critic (by letter) asserted that the invocations of Elbereth, and the character of Galadriel as directly described (or through the words of Gimli and Sam) were clearly related to Catholic devotion to Mary" (*Letters*, #213, 288). And, more specifically, in another letter, written in 1971, he says: "I was particularly interested in your remarks about Galadriel . . . I think it is true that I owe much of this character to Christian and Catholic teaching and imagination about Mary, but actually Galadriel was a penitent . . ." (#320, 407). Tolkien is referring to Galadriel's participation in the rebellion under Fëanor of the Noldor against the Valar, as told in *The Silmarillion*, where Galadriel, "the only woman of the Noldor to stand that day tall and valiant among the contending princes, was eager to be gone" (83–4). However, in the same letter, Tolkien says that Galadriel "was pardoned because of her resistance to the final and overwhelming temptation to take the Ring for herself" (#320, 407). And, in a letter written very close to his death in 1973, to Lord Halsbury, Tolkien offers what may be a revised view of Galadriel:

> Galadriel was "unstained": she had committed no evil deeds. She was an enemy of Fëanor. She did not reach Middle-earth with the other Noldor, but independently. Her reasons for wanting to go to Middle-earth were legitimate, and she would have been permitted to depart, but for the misfortune that before she set out the revolt of Fëanor broke out, and she became involved in the desperate measures of Manwë, and the ban on all emigration. (#353, 431).

This view of Galadriel would certainly seem to contradict her own words in *The Silmarillion*: ". . . we were not driven forth, but came of our own will, and against that of the Valar . . ." (127). Stratford Caldecott,[5] in an essay exploring the Catholic influence on *The Lord of the Rings*, suggests that "the pressure of the Marian archetype in Tolkien's imagination on the development of the character of Galadriel" specifically caused his later revision of her as having ever been involved in a prior rebellion (6); certainly, his view of Galadriel, as revealed by these letters, developed over time. However, even if Galadriel remains a redeemed sinner, by grace a penitent *can* reflect the beauty of Mary and even of Christ, and Galadriel does this certainly.

As mentioned earlier, Tolkien was not creating allegorically exact parallels to any religious figure, but instead conveying an overall sense of "evangelium," as he refers to the gospel in his famous essay "On Fairy Stories" (see note 4). In this context, Galadriel suggests some of the power and beauty of Mary, the mother of Jesus. To Father Robert Murray, S.J., who had written that *The Lord of the Rings* had "a strong sense of the order of Grace" and noted a connection between the depiction of Galadriel and the image of Mary, Tolkien wrote:

> I think I know what you mean by the Order of Grace; and of course by your references to Our Lady, upon which all my own small perception of beauty both in majesty and simplicity is founded. *The Lord of the Rings* is of course a fundamentally religious and Catholic work; unconsciously so at first, but consciously in the revision. That is why I have not put in, or have cut out, practically all references to anything like "religion," to cults or practices, in the imaginary world. For the religious element is absorbed into the story and the symbolism. (#142, 172)

Stratford Caldecott expounds on the reference to Mary in this letter by pointing out that "as Tolkien's Catholic faith was profound and instinctive, it would have been as hard for him to separate the Virgin Mary's presence from Christ's as to separate Our Lord from Scripture or the Church" (6). Since as a Catholic Tolkien would see Mary as a reflection of Christ, symbolism linked to her would be an important part of the religious resonance permeating *The Lord of the Rings*. Other symbolic associations connected with Mary, pointed out by Caldecott, include the phial of light given to Frodo, the overthrow of Sauron on March 25 (the Feast of the Annunciation to Mary of her conception of Jesus), and the overall theme of humility triumphing over power and evil pervading the entire story, specifically expressed in Mary's beautiful prayer, the Magnificat, in Luke 1 (Caldecott 6–8). In addition, closely analyzing the Loreto Litany, Fr. Michael W. Maher, S.J. links Galadriel and the land of Lórien with a large number of symbolic images of Mary, taken from this famous prayer, "Seat of Wisdom" and "Mother of Good Counsel" being two examples (230). All the Marian references serve to undergird the link between Tolkien's depiction of his female characters and power, since, as Caldecott observes, the humility of Mary is a central component of her character and, paradoxically, the one attribute that enables her, through her submission to God's will, to be instrumental in bringing about the most powerful overthrow of evil through the Incarnation. Mary's willingness to say "yes" to the Lord's request of her, through the Angel, her surrender of her own will to God, is the act that leads to her ultimate empowerment as a vehicle of grace (6).

Tolkien's reference to the "Order of Grace" in his letter to Fr. Murray is important with regard to the two kinds of power polarized in the story. While the conflict is, indeed, between good and evil on the largest scale, there exists even among those on the "good side" two kinds of power, with the spiritually based but physically "weaker" type of power invariably shown to be the stronger in the long run. Frodo, in his victory over Sauron, is a prime example of the power of moral and spiritual strength and courage overcoming physical strength. It is fitting that Arwen and Galadriel, being female and therefore (like the hobbits) outside the Man-dominated world of physical prowess, understand Frodo better than do many other characters. They empathize with his suffering and his sacrifice, offering help and consolation through the wisdom and power they possess.

The Christian roots of the victory of apparent weakness over physical strength are clearly outlined in Scripture. In John's gospel, Jesus graphically illustrates this concept when He takes a towel, ties it around His waist, and does the task of a slave, washing the disciples' feet (John 13: 5–11). Jesus' teaching about love of one's enemies and turning the other cheek (Luke 6:27–38 and Matt. 5:38–48) inverts traditional uses of power in a way that is truly radical. And, of course, Jesus' Passion and Death present the ultimate example of the laying down of power and of life itself, leading to triumph over evil and death.

The key thing to remember with regard to Jesus' renunciation of traditional power is that it is not equivalent to weakness or passivity; rather, it is a conquering of evil through spiritual rather than physical force, ultimately through love. The resurrection proved the validity of Jesus' non-traditional use of power. In the letter to the Hebrews, the early believers are reminded: "Since then the children share in flesh and blood, He Himself likewise also partook of the same, that through death He might render powerless him who had the power of death, that is, the devil: and might deliver those who through fear of death were subject to slavery all their lives" (Heb. 2:14–15). As Tolkien says, "The Birth of Christ is the *eucatastrophe* of Man's history. The Resurrection is the *eucatastrophe* of the story of the Incarnation. This story begins and ends in joy" ("On Fairy Stories" 89). Tolkien acknowledges in the same essay that his work is rooted in this ultimate *eucatastrophe* of Christ's birth, death, and resurrection: "if by grace what I say has in any respect any validity, it is, of course, only a facet of a truth incalculably rich, finite only because the capacity of man for whom this was done is finite" (88).

A key concept involved in *eucatastrophe*, in a fairy story or its gospel prototype, is the transformation of death. Linda Greenwood argues, "In Tolkien's work, love motivates faith to reach beyond the boundaries of the known, to rekindle hope in the midst of the uncertain. Love turns death into a gift and transforms defeat into victory" (171). In other words, characters who are ultimately most powerful are those, whether male or female, who willingly lay down their own power and even, in some cases, their lives for others. As mentioned with regard to Arwen, though no character in *The Lord of the Rings* perfectly represents Jesus, nor does any action perfectly convey the unequalled importance of His death and resurrection, some of the characters (including Galadriel and Arwen) do suggest aspects of His renunciation of physical power for the spiritual power of love.

This renunciation, experienced by both characters, involves giving up unending life in this world. Arwen, as we have seen, literally becomes mortal, but Galadriel also accepts the "fading" of the Elves and their quickened departure from Middle Earth. As Charles Huttar, in his discussion of Tolkien's story as an heir to the Golden Age myths of classical writers, says, Elves were "especially susceptible" to the temptation toward "the prevention or slowing of *decay*" (*Letters* 152, quoted by Huttar, emphasis in original). Both Arwen and Galadriel willingly choose to let go of the illusion of changelessness that the nearly (but not completely) immortal nature of the Elves enables them to enjoy. Huttar points out that all "Elves who remain in Middle-earth at the end of the Third Age have proved victorious over their natural 'clinging to Time' (*Letters* 267)" (Huttar 102). However, Tolkien uses two female characters to emphasize the refusal of the power of endless time in this world, as it moves toward a new age dominated by mortal human beings.

The female character depicted most complexly with regard to issues of power is the human woman Éowyn, niece of King Théoden of Rohan. As a part of a culture that highly values physical prowess and strength in arms, Éowyn has grown up feeling cramped and devalued. As Gandalf explains to her brother Éomer; during Aragorn's healing of Éowyn after her heroic victory over the leader of the Nazgûl: "My friend . . . you had horses, and deeds of arms, and the free fields; but she, born in the body of a maid, had a spirit and courage at least the match of yours. Yet she was doomed to wait upon an old man, whom she loved as a father, and watch him falling into a mean dishonoured dotage; and her part seemed to her more ignoble than that of the staff that he leaned on" (174). Through Gandalf, Tolkien is expressing a perspective on gender which, while it may not be called explicitly feminist, is certainly sensitive to the pain felt by a woman such as Éowyn living in a male-dominated world; as a woman, Éowyn has been patronizingly kept from activities that she proves herself to have been more than capable of performing. Her encounter with the Nazgûl shows the strength of her spirit and her skill in battle. She will, as Jane Chance points out, "serve Rohan in battle better than any other Rider from the Mark" (72). The perfect irony of her reply, "No living man am I!" to the Nazgûl's boast, "No living man may hinder me!" turns gender expectations on their head, as she drives her spear into the invisible skull (*RK*, 141–42).

However, Éowyn's victory is not complete with this triumph over the Nazgûl, for her understanding of power remains the male-dominated, physically oriented kind. Though her action is truly heroic and self-sacrificial, as pointed out by Lynnette Porter (99), her experience of power must deepen through renunciation of it. One of the most touching chapters in *The Lord of the Rings*, entitled "The Steward and the King," tells of the beginning of the love relationship between Éowyn and Faramir. Both wounded in the battle with the Nazgûl, they have also been wounded by a culture that has devalued them, Éowyn (as we have seen) because she is a woman and Faramir because he is not the "typical" warrior his brother Boromir was. Both need to understand that skill in battle, though they have it to a high degree, is not enough for peace and wholeness. Together, they must find healing, which at first seems particularly far from Éowyn. Éowyn tells Faramir early in their friendship: "Look not to me for healing! I am a shieldmaiden and my hand is ungentle . . ." (294). As Faramir discerns, part of Éowyn's hurt involves a mistaken "love" for Aragorn: "You desired to have the love of the Lord Aragorn. Because he was high and puissant, and you wished to have renown and glory and to be lifted far above the mean things that crawl on the earth. And as a great captain may to a young soldier he seemed to you admirable" (297). However, Aragorn, who is in love with Arwen, has not returned Éowyn's love, a rejection that is most painful to her and part of what has led her into battle, as well as part of what still needs to be healed after the battle is over. When Faramir declares his love for her, "the heart of Éowyn changed, or else at least she understood it. And suddenly her winter passed, and the sun shone on her" (299).

What exactly has happened to Éowyn? A superficial reading might render her transformation no more than a return to a traditional female role; she is marrying the man she loves and giving up her attempts to be a fighter; as she says, "I will be a shieldmaiden no longer, nor vie with the great Riders, nor take joy only in the songs of slaying" (300). Fredrick and McBride sum up her transformation as a triumph of patriarchy: "an unruly impulse to transcend prescribed gender roles has been successfully thwarted" (113). However, her healing is not so easily defined. Her love relationship with Faramir is intimately linked with the healing of Middle-earth because of the destruction of the Ring. Though news of the overthrow of Sauron has not yet reached Minas Tirith, Faramir and others in the city somehow sense it. In a passage that evokes a sense of the joy of "*eucatastrophe*," Tolkien describes the commingling of these two lives with the great event of their time:

> And so they stood on the walls of the City of Gondor, and a great wind rose and blew, and their hair, raven and golden, streamed out mingling in the air. And the Shadow departed, and the Sun was unveiled, and the light leaped forth; and the waters of Anduin shone like silver, and in all the houses of the City men sang for the joy that welled up in their hearts from what source they could not tell. (297)

Her personal healing involves, not only being open to love, but a movement from a desire for power and domination (i.e. as a queen) to the desire to heal and to help things grow. She says, "I will be a healer and will love all things that grow and are not barren ... No longer do I desire to be a queen" (300). Now like Faramir, who always valued the other, gentler sort of power to the dismay of his father, Éowyn seeks only the power of healing and of peace, the power enjoyed for many years by the Elves, and now being brought into the Age of Men, through the conquering of Sauron and through Aragorn's and Arwen's incipient reign. As she and Faramir come down from the high walls, people see "the light that shone about them" (300). Éowyn has begun to enjoy the kind of high beauty linked to the spiritual powers of love and forgiveness.

Éowyn and the other female characters in *The Lord of the Rings* are crucial to the meaning of the tale. *The Lord of the Rings* is far more than a story of battle and adventure in the external sense, where those with the greatest physical prowess prove to be the victors. It is also more than a tale of the spiritual battle between Good and Evil, though, of course, it *is at least that*. *The Lord of the Rings* is an illustration of various choices regarding the use of power, but with only one of them shown to be the best, the ultimately good choice. Arwen, Galadriel, and Éowyn (by the end of the tale) all make this good choice by opting for the Christ-like power of love, healing, and gentleness. The fact that they are female (and thus among the less valued members of the society Tolkien is depicting) emphasizes a larger theme, as clarified by Jane Chance: "Humility in Tolkien is always ultimately successful," as we see in case after case of the triumph of a "marginalized protagonist," whether Hobbit, or female, or other member of a less dominant group (Chance 79). Is this kind of power *only* for females (and others perceived as weaker), somehow *relegated* to them? Definitely not. In fact; if *The Lord of the Rings* shows anything about power, it makes clear the fact that true power for *anyone* comes from renouncing earthly dominance and from giving of oneself for the healing and love of others. Aragorn, Gandalf, Faramir—to name just a few key male characters—all exhibit this renunciation and enjoy a greater power because of it (as contrasted with Denethor, Saruman, and Boromir, for instance). However, the fact that Tolkien shows female characters exhibiting this kind of power better and more significantly than many of the males undercuts much of the supposed male dominance perceived by some readers of the novel, a perception largely based on the low number of female characters (which is less significant than the roles they play) and the supposed stereotypes these female characters fulfill (stereotypes undercut by an accurate analysis of gender in connection with the definition of power in the text). In *The Lord of the Rings* the kind of power associated with masculine strength and physical prowess is subverted through female characters who lay down their own power in Christ-like renunciation, part of the *eucatastrophe* that overturns the strongest evils in the world.

Notes

1. Green qualifies his remarks, saying that he is not going so far as Catherine Stimpson, whom he quotes as referring to Tolkien's "subtle contempt and hostility toward women" (Stimpson 19; quoted by Green 190).

2. Green and Battis go on to argue that Tolkien's *apparent* limitation with regard to female characters is at least somewhat redeemed through a certain "feminization" (in Battis' article, the homosexual resonance) attached to key male characters. Green attributes the absence of women characters to Tolkien's supposed "fear of sex."

3. Arwen lives the life of an Elf, and I refer to her as "Elven" here, but strictly speaking she is one of the Half-Elven. Her father, Elrond, child of a mortal and an Elf and given the choice of Elven immortality or human mortality, chose the former. His brother, Elros, chose the latter.

4. See Tolkien's essay "On Fairy Stories" in *A Tolkien Reader* for a detailed definition of this term.

5. Stratford Caldecott's article gives a detailed analysis of the Marian symbolism attached not only to Galadriel, but also to Elbereth.

Works Cited

Battis, Jes. "Gazing upon Sauron: Hobbits, Elves, and the Queering of Post-Colonial Optic." *MFS Modern Fiction Studies* 50.4 (2004) 908–26.

Chance, Jane. *The Lord of the Rings: The Mythology of Power*. Lexington, KY: UP of Kentucky, 2001.

Donovan, Leslie A. "The valkyrie reflex in J. R. R. Tolkien's *The Lord of the Rings*: Galadriel, Shelob, Éowyn, and Arwen." *Tolkien the Medievalist*. Ed. Jane Chance. London and New York: Routledge, 2003 (106–32).

Fredrick, Candice and Sam McBride. *Women Among the Inklings Gender, C. S. Lewis, J. R. R. Tolkien, and Charles Williams*. Contributions in Women's Studies, Number 191. Westport, Ct. and London: Greenwood Press, 2001.

Green, William H. "Where's Mama? The Construction of the Feminine in *The Hobbit*." *The Lion and the Unicorn* 22.2 (1998) 188–95.

Greenwood, Linda. "Love: the Gift of Death." *Tolkien Studies* 2.1 (2005) 171–95.

Huttar, Charles A. "Tolkien: Epic Traditions and Golden Age Myths." *Twentieth Century Fantasists: Essays on Culture, Society and Belief in Twentieth-Century Methopoeic Literature*. Ed. Kath Filmer. NY: St. Martin's Press, 1992.

Maher, Michael W., S.J. "'A land without stain': medieval images of Mary and their use in the characterization of Galadriel." *Tolkien the Medievalist*. Ed. Jane Chance. London and New York: Routledge, 2003 (225–36).

New American Standard Bible. Lockman Foundation.

Petty, Anne C. *Tolkien in the Land of Heroes, Discovering the Human Spirit*. Cold Spring Harbor, NY: Cold Spring Press, 2003.

Porter, Lynnette R. *Unsung Heroes of The Lord of the Rings From the Page to the Screen*. Westport, Ct. and London: Praeger, 2005.

Stimpson, Catherine. *J. R. Tolkien*. New York: Columbia UP, 1969.

Tolkien, J. R. R. *The Letters of J.R.R. Tolkien*. Humphrey Carpenter, ed. with the assistance of Christopher Tolkien. London: George Allen & Unwin; Boston: Houghton Mifflin, 1981.

————. *The Lord of the Rings, The Fellowship of the Ring.* 1954. Boston and New York: Houghton Mifflin, 1994.

————. *The Lord of the Rings, The Return of the King.* 1955. New York: Ballantine, 1989.

————. *The Lord of the Rings. The Two Towers.* 1954. Boston and New York: Houghton Mifflin, 1994.

————. *The Silmarillion.* Christopher Tolkien, ed. London: George Allen & Unwin; Boston: Houghton Mifflin, 1977.

————. *The Tolkien Reader.* New York: Ballantine, 1966.

Windling, Terri. "On Tolkien and Fairy-Stories." *Meditations on Middle-Earth.* Ed. Karen Haber. New York: St. Martin's Press, 2001.

Chronology

1892	John Ronald Reuel Tolkien, called Ronald, is born in Bloemfontein, Orange Free State (now South Africa) on January 3. He is the first son of Mabel Suffield Tolkien and Arthur Tolkien.
1894	Brother, Hilary Arthur Reuel, is born.
1895	Goes with mother and brother to England, where parents had lived earlier, to visit family.
1896	Father dies of rheumatic fever in Africa.
1900	Ronald enters King Edward's School.
1904	Mother dies in November. Father Francis Morgan is designated the boys' guardian.
1910	Awarded a scholarship to study classics at Exeter College, Oxford.
1913	Transfers from classics to English and formally studies Old Norse.
1914	Engaged to Edith Bratt.
1915	Receives degree in English from Oxford. Enters the army.
1916	Marries Edith Bratt. Participates in the Battle of the Somme. Sick with trench fever, returns home in November.
1917	First son, John, is born.
1918	Joins staff of the *Oxford English Dictionary*.
1920	Becomes reader in English language at Leeds University.

	Second son, Michael, is born.
1924	Promoted to professor of English language at Leeds. Third son, Christopher, is born.
1925	Along with E. V. Gordon, edits *Sir Gawain and the Green Knight,* which is published. Leaves Leeds for Oxford, where he becomes Rawlinson and Bosworth Professor of Anglo-Saxon.
1929	Daughter, Priscilla, is born.
1932	Continues to publish poems and articles.
1937	*The Hobbit* is published.
1945	Named Merton Professor of English Language and Literature at Oxford University.
1949	*Farmer Giles of Ham* is published.
1954	First two volumes of *The Lord of the Rings* (*The Fellowship of the Ring* and *The Two Towers*) are published.
1955	Last volume of *The Lord of the Rings* (*The Return of the King*) is published.
1959	Retires from Oxford University.
1962	Publishes *The Adventures of Tom Bombadil.*
1964	*Tree and Leaf* is published.
1967	*Smith of Wootton Major* is published.
1971	Wife dies.
1972	Becomes resident honorary fellow at Merton College, Oxford. Receives honorary doctorate from Oxford and is honored by the queen.
1973	Dies on September 2.
1976	*The Father Christmas Letters* is published.
1977	*The Silmarillion* is published.
1983–1996	Twelve volumes of *The History of Middle-earth* are published.

Contributors

HAROLD BLOOM is Sterling Professor of the Humanities at Yale University. He is the author of 30 books, including *Shelley's Mythmaking, The Visionary Company, Blake's Apocalypse, Yeats, A Map of Misreading, Kabbalah and Criticism, Agon: Toward a Theory of Revisionism, The American Religion, The Western Canon,* and *Omens of Millennium: The Gnosis of Angels, Dreams, and Resurrection. The Anxiety of Influence* sets forth Professor Bloom's provocative theory of the literary relationships between the great writers and their predecessors. His most recent books include *Shakespeare: The Invention of the Human,* a 1998 National Book Award finalist, *How to Read and Why, Genius: A Mosaic of One Hundred Exemplary Creative Minds, Hamlet: Poem Unlimited, Where Shall Wisdom Be Found?,* and *Jesus and Yahweh: The Names Divine.* In 1999, Professor Bloom received the prestigious American Academy of Arts and Letters Gold Medal for Criticism. He has also received the International Prize of Catalonia, the Alfonso Reyes Prize of Mexico, and the Hans Christian Andersen Bicentennial Prize of Denmark.

MICHAEL MOORCOCK is a British writer of numerous novels, who has also been the editor of the science fiction magazine *New Worlds.* Most of his work is science fiction and fantasy, the most popular being his *Elric* books. He has won many awards for his books and also has won lifetime achievement awards.

JANE CHANCE is a professor at Rice University. She is the author of several titles, including *Tolkien's Art: A Mythology for England*, and has edited *Tolkien and the Invention of Myth: A Reader*.

MICHAEL N. STANTON retired from teaching English at the University of Vermont. He has written on science fiction and fantasy literature as well as on Dickens and Melville.

MARK T. HOOKER is a specialist in comparative translation associated with Indiana University's Russian and East European Institute. He is the author of *A Tolkienian Mathomium* and *Tolkien Through Russian Eyes*.

JARED LOBDELL has taught at Millersville University. He is the author of *The Rise of Tolkienian Fantasy* and has edited *A Tolkien Compass*.

MARJORIE BURNS is a professor at Portland State University. She is the author of *Perilous Realms: Celtic and Norse in Tolkien's Middle-earth*.

ANDREW LYNCH is an associate professor at the University of Western Australia. He is the author of *Malory's Book of Arms* and coeditor of *Venus and Mars: Engendering Love and War in Medieval and Early Modern Europe*.

SUE ZLOSNIK is a professor and head of the English department at Manchester Metropolitan University in the United Kingdom. She is coauthor of *Daphne du Maurier: Writing, Identity and the Gothic Imagination* and *Gothic and the Comic Turn*.

VERLYN FLIEGER is a professor at the University of Maryland. She has done much work on Tolkien and is the author of, among other works, *Interrupted Music: Tolkien's Making of a Mythology* and *Splintered Light: Logos and Language in Tolkien's World*.

MARY R. BOWMAN teaches English at the University of Wisconsin–Stevens Point. She is working on a book on modern revisions of medieval heroes.

NANCY ENRIGHT teaches at Seton Hall University. She has published essays on Tolkien, Dante, and Hazlitt.

Bibliography

Amendt-Raduege, Amy M. "Dream Visions in J.R.R. Tolkien's *The Lord of the Rings.*" *Tolkien Studies: An Annual Scholarly Review* 3 (2006): 45–55.

Ankeny, Rebecca. "Poem as Sign in *The Lord of the Rings.*" *Journal of the Fantastic in the Arts* 16, no. 2 (Summer 2005): 86–95.

Auden, W. H. "The Quest Hero." *Texas Quarterly* 4 (1962): 81–93.

Bassham, Gregory, and Eric Bronson, ed. The Lord of the Rings *and Philosophy: One Book to Rule Them All.* Chicago: Open Court, 2003.

Bibire, Paul. "J. R. R. Tolkien's *The Lord of the Rings.*" In *British Writers: Classics, Volume II,* edited by Jay Parini, 155–175. New York, NY: Scribner's, 2004.

Bramlett, Perry C. *I Am in Fact a Hobbit: An Introduction to the Life and Works of J.R.R. Tolkien; with a Reflective Chapter by Joe R. Christopher.* Macon, Ga.: Mercer University Press, 2002.

Brisbois, Michael J. "Tolkien's Imaginary Nature: An Analysis of the Structure of Middle-Earth." *Tolkien Studies: An Annual Scholarly Review* 2, no. 1 (2005): 197–216.

Chance, Jane. *Tolkien's Art: A Mythology for England.* Lexington: University Press of Kentucky, 2001.

Chance, Jane, ed. *Tolkien and the Invention of Myth: A Reader.* Lexington: University Press of Kentucky, 2004.

———. *Tolkien the Medievalist.* London; New York: Routledge, 2003.

Chance, Jane, and Alfred K. Siewers, ed. *Tolkien's Modern Middle Ages*. New York: Palgrave Macmillan, 2005.

Curry, Patrick. *Defending Middle-earth: Tolkien, Myth and Modernity*. New York: St. Martin's Press, 1997.

Dickerson, Matthew T. *Following Gandalf: Epic Battles and Moral Victory in* The Lord of the Rings. Grand Rapids, Mich.: Brazos Press, 2003.

Eaglestone, Robert, ed. *Reading* The Lord of the Rings: *New Writings on Tolkien's Classic*. London; New York: Continuum, 2006.

Ellwood, Gracia Fay. *Good News from Tolkien's Middle Earth, Two Essays on the "Applicability" of* The Lord of the Rings. Grand Rapids, Mich.: W. B. Eerdmans, 1970.

Flieger, Verlyn. "Fantasy and Reality: J. R. R. Tolkien's World and the Fairy-Story Essay." *Mythlore: A Journal of J. R. R. Tolkien, C. S. Lewis, Charles Williams, and Mythopoeic Literature* 22, no. 3 (Winter 1999): 4–13.

Ford, Judy Ann. "The White City: *The Lord of the Rings* as an Early Medieval Myth of the Restoration of the Roman Empire." *Tolkien Studies: An Annual Scholarly Review* 2, no. 1 (2005): 53–73.

Fredrick, Candice, and Same McBride. *Women Among the Inklings: Gender, C.S. Lewis, J.R.R. Tolkien, and Charles Williams*. Westport, Conn.: Greenwood Press, 2001.

Greenwood, Linda. "Love: The Gift of Death." *Tolkien Studies* 2, no. 1 (2005): 171–195.

Haber, Karen, ed. *Meditations on Middle Earth*. New York: St. Martin's Press, 2001.

Hammond, Wayne. *J. R. R. Tolkien: A Descriptive Bibliography*. New Castle, Del.: Oak Knoll Books, 1993.

Hammond, Wayne G. and Christina Scull. The Lord of the Rings: *A Reader's Companion*. Boston: Houghton Mifflin, 2005.

Hart, Trevor, and Ivan Khovacs. *Tree of Tales: Tolkien, Literature, and Theology*. Waco, Tex.: Baylor University Press, 2007.

Honegger, Thomas, ed. *Reconsidering Tolkien*. Zollikofen, Switzerland: Walking Tree, 2005.

Hopkins, Lisa. *Screening the Gothic*. Austin, Tex.: University of Texas Press, 2005.

Huttar, Charles A. "Tolkien: Epic Traditions and Golden Age Myths." In *Twentieth Century Fantasists: Essays on Culture, Society and Belief in Twentieth-Century Methopoeic Literature*, edited by Kath Filmer. New York: St. Martin's Press, 1992.

Isaacs, Neil D., and Rose A. Zimbardo, ed. *Tolkien and the Critics, Essays on J.R.R. Tolkien's* The Lord of the Rings. Notre Dame, Ind.: University of Notre Dame Press, 1968.

Keefer, Sarah Larratt. "'Work-Writing' to Create the Fictional Portrait: Tolkien's Inclusion of Lewis in *The Lord of the Rings.*" *English Studies in Canada* 18, no. 2 (June 1992): 181–198.

Kreeft, Peter. *The Philosophy of Tolkien: The Worldview Behind* The Lord of the Rings. San Francisco: Ignatius Press, 2005.

Lobdell, Jared. *England and Always: Tolkien's World of the Rings.* Grand Rapids, Mich.: W.B. Eerdmans, 1981.

———. *The World of the Rings: Language, Religion, and Adventure in Tolkien.* Chicago: Open Court, 2004.

Loy, David R., and Linda Goodhew. *The Dharma of Dragons and Daemons: Buddhist Themes in Modern Fantasy.* Boston: Wisdom Publications, 2004.

Miesel, Sandra. *Myth, Symbol & Religion in* The Lord of the Rings. Baltimore: T-K Graphics, 1973.

Nagy, Gergely. "The 'Lost' Subject of Middle-Earth: The Constitution of the Subject in the Figure of Gollum in *The Lord of the Rings.*" *Tolkien Studies: An Annual Scholarly Review* 3 (2006): 57–79.

Nelson, Charles W. "But Who Is Rose Cotton?: Love and Romance in *The Lord of the Rings.*" *Journal of the Fantastic in the Arts* 3, no. 3 (1994): 6–20.

Petty, Anne C. *One Ring to Bind Them All: Tolkien's Mythology.* Tuscaloosa: University of Alabama Press, 1979.

———. *Tolkien in the Land of Heroes, Discovering the Human Spirit.* Cold Spring Harbor, NY: Cold Spring Press, 2003.

Ready, William. *Understanding Tolkien and* The Lord of the Rings. New York: Warner, 1969, 1968.

Rearick, Anderson, III. "Why Is the Only Good Orc a Dead Orc? The Dark Face of Racism Examined in Tolkien's World." *MFS: Modern Fiction Studies* 50, no. 4 (Winter 2004): 861–874.

Rockow, Karen. *Funeral Customs in Tolkien's Trilogy.* Baltimore: TK Graphics, 1973.

Rosebury, Brian. *Tolkien: A Critical Assessment.* New York: St. Martin's Press, 1992.

Rutledge, Fleming. *The Battle for Middle-earth: Tolkien's Divine Design in* The Lord of the Rings. Grand Rapids, Mich.; Cambridge, U.K.: William B. Eerdmans, 2004.

Shippey, T. A. *The Road to Middle-earth*. London; Boston: Allen & Unwin, 1982.

Treschow, Michael, and Duckworth, Mark. "Bombadil's Role in *The Lord of the Rings*." *Mythlore: A Journal of J. R. R. Tolkien, C. S. Lewis, Charles Williams, and Mythopoeic Literature* 25, nos. 1–2 (Fall–Winter 2006): 175–196.

West, Richard C. *Tolkien Criticism: An Annotated Checklist*. Kent, Ohio: Kent State University Press, 1981.

Wilson, Edmund. "Oo! Those Awful Orcs." *The Nation* 182 (April 14, 1956): 312–314.

Acknowledgments

Michael Moorcock, "Epic Pooh," from *Wizardry and Wild Romance: A Study of Epic Fantasy*, pp. 121–139. © 1987 by Michael Moorcock.

Jane Chance, "'Queer' Hobbits: The Problem of Difference in the Shire," from *The Lord of the Rings: The Mythology of Power*, pp. 26–37. © 2001 by the University Press of Kentucky.

Michael N. Stanton, "Mind, Spirit, and Dream in *The Lord of the Rings*," from *Hobbits, Elves, and Wizards: Exploring the Wonders and Worlds of J. R. R. Tolkien's* The Lord of the Rings, pp. 159–170. © 2001 by Michael N. Stanton. Reproduced by permission of Palgrave Macmillan.

Mark T. Hooker, "Frodo's Batman," from *Tolkien Studies*, vol. 1, pp. 125–136. © 2004 by West Virginia University Press.

Jared Lobdell, "In the Far Northwest of the Old World," from *The World of the Rings: Language, Religion, and Adventure in Tolkien*, pp. 71–93. © 2004 by Carus Publishing.

Marjorie Burns, "Spiders and Evil Red Eyes: The Shadow Sides of Gandalf and Galadriel," from *Perilous Realms: Celtic and Norse in Tolkien's Middle-earth*, pp. 93–127. © 2005 by Marjorie Burns.

Andrew Lynch, "Archaism, Nostalgia, and Tennysonian War in *The Lord of the*

Rings," from *Tolkien's Modern Middle Ages,* pp. 77–92. © 2005 by Jane Chance and Alfred K. Siewers. Reproduced by permission of Palgrave Macmillan.

Sue Zlosnik, "Gothic Echoes," from *Reading* The Lord of the Rings: *New Writings on Tolkien's Classic,* pp. 47–58. © 2005 by Robert Eaglestone and the contributors.

Verlyn Flieger, "Tolkien and the Idea of the Book," from The Lord of the Rings, *1954–2004: Scholarship in Honor of Richard E. Blackwelder,* pp. 283–299. © 2006 by Marquette University Press. Reproduced by permission of the author.

Mary R. Bowman, "The Story Was Already Written: Narrative Theory in *The Lord of the Rings,"* from *Narrative* 14, no. 3, October 2006, pp. 272–293. © 2006 by the Ohio State University Press.

Nancy Enright, "Tolkien's Females and the Defining of Power," from *Renascence* 59, no. 2, Winter 2007, pp. 93–108. © 2007 by *Renascence.*

Every effort has been made to contact the owners of copyrighted material and secure copyright permission. Articles appearing in this volume generally appear much as they did in their original publication with few or no editorial changes. In some cases, foreign language text has been removed from the original essay. Those interested in locating the original source will find the information cited above.

Index